a guide to earthTrips

nature travel on a fragile planet

by Dwight Holing

Conservation International

LIVING PLANET PRESS

LOS ANGELES

Published in the United States by Living Planet Press
558 Rose Avenue, Venice, California 90291

**Note: Although no standard now exists for certifying a
company as environmentally responsible, all the tour
operators and travel agencies listed in this book claim to
be so. It is up to each traveler to determine if the
company being considered lives up to its claims.**

Living Planet Press is registered in the U.S. Patent and
Trademark Office.

Cover design and interior design: Patricia Moritz
Typesetting: R. Bruce McFadden, Jr.

Printing and binding: Delta Lithograph

Cover photo: courtesy Animals Animals/Stefan Meyers
Earth photo: courtesy NASA

**Discounts for bulk orders are available
from the publisher.
Call (213) 396-0188.**

ISBN 1-879326-05-1

 Printed on recycled paper

Manufactured in the United States of America

Library of Congress catalog card number 90-064448

10 9 8 7 6 5 4 3 2 1

author's acknowledgments

To the many people and organizations who contributed their time, resources, insights, expertise, and logistical help during the research and writing of this book, my heartfelt gratitude. Special thanks to the staff of Conservation International, especially Brent Bailey, Lee Hannah, Chuck Hutchinson, Lindsey Lambert, Kreg Lindberg, Cynthia Mackie, Jim Nations, Sharon Pitcairn, Karen Ross, Wendy Tan, Melida Tzabakhsh, and Karen Ziffer; to Dinah Berland of Living Planet Press; to Mary Pearl and Amy Vedder of Wildlife Conservation International; to Shelley Attix, Bridget Bean, Liz Boo, Victor Emanuel, Megan Eppler-Wood, Dave Heckman, Leslie Jarvie, Kurt Kutay, and Ken Margolis of EcoTrust; and to Garuda Indonesia and Sobek.

contents

preface

Recent years have brought a meteoric rise in public awareness of and interest in our planet's endangered ecosystems. But amidst all the talk and work on behalf of saving the Earth, most of us experience our planet's most exotic environments at arm's length. We view the lives of lions, pandas, and gorillas via television documentaries. We read magazine articles about endangered species of the tropics. Newspapers print features on the destruction of fragile rainforest ecosystems in the Amazon. But however dramatic the visual images and verbal descriptions may be, nothing can compare to experiencing these places yourself.

earthTrips: A Guide to Nature Travel on a Fragile Planet is your invitation to encounter the Earth's natural wonders firsthand. As the first comprehensive guide to ecotourism, *earthTrips* charts a new chapter in world travel coupled with planetary conservation. Moving beyond traditional notions of tourism, today's ecotravelers can have a direct, positive impact on the ecosystems and communities they visit—in part, simply by choosing their destinations with the environment in mind.

The rapid growth of ecotourism is fueled in part by the growing awareness of the destruction of the world's most biologically diverse natural areas. Although our planet faces many environmental threats, I firmly believe that the single greatest danger is loss of biological diversity—the wealth of species, ecosystems, and ecological processes that makes our living planet unique in the universe. Loss of biological diversity is so very critical because we depend on other life for our own survival and because this loss is an irreversible process. Once a species of plant or animal becomes extinct, it is gone forever.

In the quest to conserve our planet's natural wealth, we must seek innovative ways to demonstrate the economic benefits that accrue from wise use of these resources. Conservation-based development, such as ecotourism, seeks to meet human needs while preserving ecosystems. Properly planned ecotourism programs can provide an incentive for governments and local residents to preserve their rainforests and other important ecosystems, especially in developing countries where economic need is often the first concern. Revenues generated by the rapidly growing ecotourism industry are the most persuasive arguments to local people, decision makers, and the global community at large that good conservation is also good economics. In East Africa, the oft-quoted phrase "wildlife pays, so wildlife stays" sums it up.

It is also my hope that increased yet carefully planned travel to the "hot spots" of the Earth's biodiversity will create a new generation of committed environmentalists. Only when we explore our planet firsthand can we truly appreciate its variety and fragility—not to mention its natural splendor. No one who spends a week traveling down the Amazon can ever feel indifferent to the fate of the rainforests and the people who call them home. It is impossible to glimpse Rwanda's imperiled mountain gorillas without becoming committed to their survival. Anyone who has ever seen and heard thousands of Canada geese settle in unison on a midwestern marsh will never doubt the importance of preserving our nation's wetlands. After traveling with a knowledgeable guide through the forests of Costa Rica, the mountains of Thailand, or the Spiney Desert of Madagascar, the concept of biodiversity in all its richness takes on new meaning.

Achieving the goals of ecotourism is no small feat, but every small action in the right direction helps. *earthTrips* will give you a host of ways in which you can make a contribution. You can participate in valuable scientific research. You can volunteer your special skills to reconstruction efforts. And your travel dollars can help create economic incentives for protecting and preserving these endangered habitats for generations to come.

I hope *earthTrips* will inspire you to pack your bags and experience for yourself the beauty, variety, and fragility of our planet's most spectacular wild places, and the urgent need to assure their survival.

— Russell A. Mittermeier
President, Conservation International

introduction

travel with a cause

Welcome to a new way of exploring our fragile planet. Travel where you discover the wonders of Earth and help protect them at the same time. Embark on unforgettable journeys that will enrapture your soul, enlighten your mind, and enkindle your spirit.

This new way of travel shares many of the same destinations, itineraries, and physical rewards as nature and adventure travel but with the added twist of being a tool for conservation and development of local economies. Think of it as an environmental adventure to the wild places on Earth. You visit beautiful and uncommon landscapes, see rare and endangered species of wildlife, and encounter traditional cultures. Most of all, you make a difference in the world you treasure and celebrate.

Picture it. First light on Rwanda's Virunga Mountains, and as you focus your camera on a tangle of bamboo and hagenia, a family of mountain gorillas suddenly lumbers into view. *Click*. You just photographed some of the rarest animals in the world. More importantly, you also helped save them from extinction. Part of the fee you paid to view these magnificent creatures goes toward protecting their habitat and preventing poaching.

Feel it. The sun shines on your face as it arcs above the Himalayas. You trek along a narrow footpath above the clouds. A sense of beauty, wonder, and awe fills you, but even greater is your feeling of accomplishment. Not only did you meet the challenge of the trail, but you also helped repair an ancient monastery that lies along a sacred route in Ladakh.

Hear it. Within earshot of the turbid Amazon, a Brazilian ecologist tells you how the rainforest is being destroyed and what can be done to protect it. He leads you upriver for a firsthand look into the problems and a few of the solutions. First he shows you a cattle ranch. An empty silence hangs over the scorched and barren landscape. Then he takes you to a village that practices sustainable agriculture. In the surrounding trees, parrots chatter and monkeys howl. The rainforest here is still alive.

ecotourism

Many conservationists see ecologically sensitive and carefully planned tourism as a pragmatic way to preserve the planet's most delicate and biologically rich regions. This exciting new venture is called "ecotourism"—ecologically sensitive travel that combines the pleasures of discovering and understanding spectacular flora and fauna with an opportunity to contribute to their protection. The idea behind ecotourism is simple. Protected natural areas attract tourists. That brings money to the region, which translates into jobs for local people. This gives government and local residents the economic incentive to stop uncontrolled logging, poaching, and slash-and-burn farming. Leaders and residents soon realize that if the natural areas go, so go the tourists and their dollars. In fact, Conservation International considers ecotourism to be one of the best ways of demonstrating quickly to local people and government decision-makers that good conservation is also good economics.

Ecotourism wields enormous potential financial clout because travel has become one of the largest industries in the world. According to the World Tourism Organization, people spend more than $2 trillion a year on tourism; tourism to the developing world generates $55 billion alone. Nearly 400 million people travel each year, supporting 65 million jobs and accounting for 25 percent of world trade. Though nature-oriented travel accounts for less than 10 percent of the total tourism figures, it is the fastest-growing segment of the industry, expanding at nearly 30 percent a year.

Many countries designate significant portions of land as nature reserves in order to attract tourist revenues. Take Kenya, for example. The country established and manages an extensive national park system populated by a Noah's Ark of animals. The parks bring in $250 million annually in tourism income, according to a report conducted by the International Union for the Conservation of Nature. That translates into earning power of about $27,000 a year per lion or about $610,000 per elephant herd. Another study determined that net returns on Kenya's parklands amount to $40 per 2.5 acres a year compared to 80 cents earned from agriculture. Hence the East African saying, "Wildlife pays, so wildlife stays."

Costa Rica launched its ambitious ecotourism program in the belief that making money by not cutting the rainforest is easier than making money by cutting it. Twelve percent of this tiny Central American republic's territory has been set aside as national parks and privately funded reserves. Together these lands provide shelter for almost all of the country's 1,500 distinct species of trees, 205 species of mammals, 850 species of birds, and more than 6,000 kinds of flowering plants, including 1,500 varieties of orchids.

Replacing industrial and agricultural exploitation with ecotourism is paying off handsomely for Costa Rica. Tourism now ranks as the country's third largest source of income. The creation of locally owned and operated tours and lodges has created new employment opportunities. Visitor rates have leaped dramatically—70 percent in just eight years. A survey conducted by the World Wildlife Fund cited ecotourism as a main reason given by one out of three tourists for visiting Costa Rica. One-third of the approximately thirty travel agencies in Costa Rica specialize in ecotours. More importantly, the trend may help slow the rate of deforestation, which has been proceeding at a rate of 150,000 acres a year. Conservation International believes that ecotourism could become a major foreign exchange earner for a dozen or more tropical countries within a few years' time.

At its best, ecotourism promotes environmental education among international visitors and local people as well. Visiting protected areas increases everyone's sensitivity to protection needs. It also stimulates appreciation of wildlands back home. And by seeing so many people traveling great distances to learn about the natural heritage in their backyards, residents of the host country become encouraged to explore them, too. Learning to appreciate their own natural heritage can convert local residents into faithful guardians, admirers, and promoters of wildlands.

The desire to increase environmental awareness and promote conservation worldwide has prompted the nation's top nonprofit environmental organizations to sponsor ecotours of their own. These trips typically combine fundraising with education and membership benefits. A percentage of the tour's cost goes toward funding conservation programs at home and abroad. Visiting foreign destinations and learning about their precious natural resources and the pressures they face encourage many travelers to donate directly to local conservation efforts in the host countries.

trekking lightly

Successful ecotourism strongly depends on careful management and proper implementation. Large numbers of people visiting sensitive areas can create rather than remedy environmental problems if safeguards aren't in place. Many natural areas have already been compromised by too many visitors, poorly planned facilities, and improper waste disposal. It's a case of nature lovers loving nature to death.

In Nepal, for instance, more than 50,000 tourists now trek along the well-trod routes to Mount Everest and its sister peaks each year. The demand for wood and fuel by the fifty lodges that have been built in the Annapurna Range in recent years to accommodate the flood of visitors has lowered the tree line by several hundred feet and left an adjoining wildlife preserve, Annapurna Sanctuary, completely deforested. The increased need for yaks to portage trekking gear has also degraded the environment. More yaks means turning more land into grazing areas, which results in soil erosion. Litter is an additional problem. The steady stream of climbing expeditions and trekkers over the years has left a mountain of garbage and discarded gear behind.

The fragile ecosystems of Antarctica have also suffered from uncontrolled tourism, coupled with the growing human presence brought about by scientific research. Visits to "The Ice" have jumped from 800 to more than 7,000 people a year in less than a decade. In 1989, two ships carrying tourists went aground, despoiling the once pristine polar world. One of these, an Argentine ship that was carrying 300 passengers on an eleven-day cruise, spilled approximately 250,000 gallons of fuel oil. The slick washed ashore near one of Antarctica's premier rookeries. No one knows what the long-term effects of oil pollution will have on the 20,000 Adélie and chinstrap penguins that nest there. Part of the rusting hulk still sticks out of the bay where it foundered, a grim reminder of the hazards posed by the growing human presence in what has always been Earth's final frontier.

Irresponsible tourism often claims plants and animals as its first casualties. An overabundance of visitors can alter animal behavior, disrupt migration patterns, and decrease population levels. For instance, the recent decline in the cheetah population in Kenya's Amboseli National Park has been blamed on the rapid rise in the number of tourists.

Indigenous people, especially the native inhabitants of remote regions of the world, fall victim to indiscriminate tourism, too. The seizure of land by centralized governments to create national parks and preserves in order to serve foreign tourists can displace tribal peoples who have little voice in decision-making. An even greater problem can arise from sustained contact between indigenous people and affluent Western tourists: the loss of cultural identity. The list of traditional cultures that have disappeared under the new colonialism of athletic foot gear, portable tape players, and day-glow activewear is shocking.

For these reasons, it's imperative that strategic planning go into the selection of natural areas before they are promoted as tourist destinations. Buffer zones must be designated, facilities properly sited, tour operators and guides trained, and expeditions limited. Most importantly, the local population has to be closely involved in the process from the start. The more local people benefit from nature tourism, the more they will help in preserving natural areas and wildlife.

You'll have a more enriching experience, too, if the natural areas you visit include indigenous people in management positions. Local people often make the best preserve managers, guides, and interpreters because of their intimate knowledge of the environment and its people. Residents and regional specialists are often best equipped to answer your questions about the natural resources of an area—such as which plants are used for food, medicine, textiles, and tools. In turn, you can help them perpetuate their traditional cultural values by supporting their knowledge, skills, and life-styles.

You, too, play a vital role in making ecotourism work. Because you're traveling to uncommon places, to distinctive cultures, to exceptional yet fragile environments, acting responsibly is critical. Follow the code of conduct formulated by the National Audubon Society:

- Biotas (flora and fauna of a region) shall not be disturbed.
- Tourism to natural areas shall be resource-sustainable (only taking what can be replaced).
- Sensibilities of other cultures shall be respected.
- Waste disposal shall have neither environmental nor aesthetic impacts.

- The experience you gain shall enrich your appreciation of nature, conservation, and the environment.
- Tours shall strengthen the conservation effort and enhance the natural integrity of places visited.
- Traffic in products that threaten wildlife and plant populations shall not occur.

Decide on the kind of trip you want to have, and prepare well for it. Read as much as you can about the area you plan to visit. Find out what you'll need to bring to make your visit as pleasurable as you'd like it to be. Choose your tour operator carefully. Then, go visit the wild places. Look for lemurs in Madagascar. Hike through a Malaysian rainforest. Watch the Huli perform a ritual "singsing" dance in Papua New Guinea. And always remember: as a visitor on another's soil, you must tread carefully.

The rewards of environmental adventure provide more than just Kodachrome memories of colorful and unusual places. An "Earthtrip" will increase your appreciation of nature, knowledge of science, and understanding of environmental issues. Even more, it will heighten your own sense of self-awareness. By seeing for yourself how nature works when it is undisturbed, you will better understand your own role on this planet and what you must do to help protect our fragile home.

earthTrips

The opportunities for exploring Earth's natural areas are vast and grow larger every day. You can join a litter patrol on the Inca Trail to Machu Picchu, visit a biosphere in Belize, watch once-captive orangutans being returned to the wild in Sumatra, dive along the Great Barrier Reef, and camp beneath African skies. A wide range of travel companies, expedition outfitters, nonprofit environmental organizations, and scientific research and education programs specialize in these kinds of tours.

earthTrips describes places you can go and things you can do on your journey that will help protect our delicate world. The trips listed here are only a beginning—a global sampler of the multitude of opportunities that are now emerging for exploring this fragile planet and participating in the conservation of its most threatened ecosystems. Destinations change, and so do expeditions to them. Use this book as a road map to the possibilities. Let it trigger your imagination. Here's how to use it:

Chapter 1 contains information and general hints on what to look for in an ecotourism outfitter, how to pick a tour, and other helpful travel tips, including money matters, packing, photography, and passport and customs regulations.

Chapters 2 through 8 are continent-by-continent samplers of some of the most fascinating and unusual nature destinations serviced by nonprofit and commercial tour operators. Here you will also find "Conservation Alerts," featuring endangered ecosystems on each continent where your travel dollars may make the greatest difference.

Once you've picked your destination, you'll be ready to decide how to travel and with whom. Interested in joining a scientific expedition as a volunteer research assistant? Want to help rebuild a trail in the middle of the Alaskan wilderness? Then turn to Chapter 9, which contains a comprehensive list of volunteer vacation opportunities and the addresses and phone numbers of sponsoring organizations.

Want to increase your in-depth nature knowledge? Chapter 10 lists nonprofit organizations that conduct educational nature travel programs—conservation groups, learning centers, museums, universities. For an even wider selection of possibilities, check out Chapter 11, which lists commercial tour companies and environmentally oriented travel agencies. You'll need to contact these tour operators directly to get additional information about the trips they offer, their costs, itineraries, and departure schedules, and how the tours are conducted to be sure you choose an environmentally responsible operator.

And to help you make the best of your trip, Chapter 12 provides a selection of directories, books, and other publications that will provide you with even more information.

In this day and age, when chainsaws and bulldozers drown out the songs of birds in the rainforests of the world, when human development plunders natural resources from the tundra to the jungle, when dams tame our wildest rivers, your choices of where and how to travel are more important than ever. With *earthTrips* as your guide, you can begin to make a difference.

ecotravel tips

Ecotourism is a chance to explore nature while helping local communities and businesses to develop and conserve the environment. In these treacherous times, when the earth's precious living resources are rapidly being driven to extinction by human activity, responsible ecotourism can serve as an antidote to destruction. In this chapter, you will:

• Learn how ecotourism contributes to local economies and stimulates conservation efforts.

• Find out how to choose a tour operator.

• Check out the pros and cons of traveling independently or with a group.

• Decide how to prepare for your trip and what you'll need to take.

• Learn how to avoid buying "souvenirs of extinction."

• Get information on how to protect your health.

• Learn how to tread lightly on the land with the ecotraveler's Code of Ethics.

ecotravel tips

For my part, I travel not to go anywhere, but to go.
I travel for travel's sake.
                              —Robert Louis Stevenson

The world has become smaller and its ecosystems infinitely more threatened in the century since inveterate wanderer Stevenson penned those words. In that time, half of Earth's tropical rainforests have been obliterated. The remainder are being wiped out at the appalling rate of 55 million acres a year—an area the size of New York State. Along with these rainforests have vanished more species of wildlife than went extinct during the age of dinosaurs. Every hour of every day, two more species disappear, driven off the face of Earth forever. We can no longer afford to be cavalier about travel. Our reasons for taking a journey must have a higher objective, and our methods a more environmentally and culturally sensitive approach.

deciding where to go

The decision of where to go and what kind of nature trip to take largely depends on your interests, temperament, and resources. There is a lot more to choosing a destination than simply spinning a globe, closing your eyes, and pointing your finger. You need to conduct some research beforehand. First, ask yourself some realistic questions. This will help narrow your search.

- How much money do I have to spend?
- What are my time constraints?
- How are my health and endurance?
- What level of participation do I want to undertake, physically as well as mentally?
- Do I want to travel alone or with a group?
- How do I want to travel: by cruise ship, plane, jeep, canoe, camel, bus, bike, raft, on foot, or a combination of these?
- What do I want to see (plants, animals, cultures)?
- In what part of the world can I see them?
- What do I want to learn?
- And, finally, how can I contribute to the protection of Earth's natural resources?

Next, ask your friends, family, and colleagues if they have any recommendations. Find out where they've been and what they've done. Conduct a literature search at your local bookstore or library, leaf through a world atlas, read up on the countries and destinations that have caught your fancy. Learn about their ecosystems and environmental problems. Finally, begin contacting tour operators to find out which destinations they travel to and what kind of trips they offer.

choosing a tour operator

The rising popularity of nature travel has spawned a plethora of enterprises offering trips to every corner of the globe. Their ads now fill the travel sections of major metropolitan newspapers and magazines from *Birder's World* to *Outside*. Many companies advertise "ecotours," but not all of them live up to the name. You need to ask some pointed questions to make sure that the tour operator you select will not only provide you with a quality trip for a reasonable price but, even more importantly, do it in an environmentally responsible way. (See "15 questions to ask a tour operator or travel agent," page 4.)

Generally, there are five qualities you should be looking for in a tour operator: experience, environmental commitment, customer support, cultural sensitivity, and competent on-site staff able to educate and interpret.

Look for a tour operator with plenty of experience in the areas it visits. Travel in the developing world does not always go as planned. Logistics are complex, infrastructure often lacking, amenities mixed, and social and political conditions variable. For these reasons, you need a tour operator that knows the area well enough, should the need arise, to make alternative arrangements on the spot. The experienced operator can turn serendipity into opportunity. Also, you should find out how the operator handles health emergencies.

Ask the operator if it has staff located in the field or close working relationships with local contacts. Partnership with local communities is especially important and can take many forms, from meaningful information exchanges to patronizing the area's businesses. Does the company manage its own trips, or does it only act as a wholesaler for other tour operators? If it is a wholesaler, or a nonprofit organization that relies on a professional tour operator to run its fundraising trips, ask if it requires vendors to subscribe to an ecotour travel ethic.

Environmental commitment should be an integral part of any enterprise offering trips to natural areas. While you usually can be sure this is the case with trips sponsored by nonprofit conservation groups, it's not always so clear with profit-making operations. The most conscientious operators restrict the size of each tour to minimize the impact on the place visited. No more than twelve participants per tour is considered ideal for most tours. Ideally, the operator should also invite tourists from the host country to join as tour participants, even if it means subsidizing them. It is important that the local

conservation alert

15 questions to ask a tour operator or travel agent

1. Could you please describe your trip to... (They should be willing and able to describe the trip in detail.)
2. How long have you been operating tours to this area? (three years or more)
3. What are the environmental/conservation issues in this country? (They should be able to name specific issues: endangered animals/habitats/ecosystems.)
4. How large is each of your tour groups? (no more than twelve people per tour)
5. In what ways do you limit the impact of your tour on the surrounding environment? (use nonpolluting transportation, stay within designated areas and on trails, educate visitors on environmental issues, including what crafts and souvenirs to buy and not to buy, etc.)
6. Do you have staff located in the field? (yes—and/or cooperate with local organizations)
7. How is your staff trained and qualified? (by environmental experts)
8. Do you employ local guides and interpreters? (yes)
9. What other types of local goods and services do you purchase? (locally produced products, transportation, lodging, meals, etc.)
10. Are tourists from the host country also included on your trips? (yes, whenever possible)
11. What kind of accommodations do you arrange? (modest lodgings or locally owned guest houses—not big hotels)
12. How do you handle health or other emergencies? (They should have a plan.)
13. How do your tours support the environment? (tax-deductible contribution to nonprofit conservation group as part of the fee)
14. Could you give me some references of people I might call who have taken this tour in the past? (yes, definitely)
15. If I decide to book with you, will you be able to send me further information on the environment and culture of the region? (yes—advance orientation meeting a plus)

Conservation awareness score:

12–15:	Top-notch operator
8–11:	Stamp of approval—if first eight questions are mostly correct
7 or under:	Better keep looking

people be educated along with foreign visitors. An added advantage is that this provides a cross-cultural experience.

Ask the operator how its tours support the environment. Some companies include tax-deductible contributions to environmental organizations or local conservation programs as part of their fee. Still others promote conservation through environmental awareness. Make sure the operator you are considering employs local guides and service companies for its programs and uses local products. This pumps money into the host country's local economy as an incentive for the local people to protect parklands. Ideal operators hire guides from the community rather than bringing them from outside the country or even from the country's capital city, and arrange lodgings in locally owned guest houses rather than big international hotels.

Customer support should begin with your first call to a tour operator. The outfit's booking agent should have the answers to all your questions, and take the time to fully describe the trip. After all, travel isn't cheap; as a customer, you have the right to know what you can expect before you buy. Don't be afraid to ask questions about how their staff is trained and what environmental regulations exist in the area you are visiting. Their answers will help you evaluate their level of expertise and compliance. And always ask for references.

Once you book, the company should provide you with a comprehensive briefing package containing information on what kind of equipment you'll need, a reading list, natural history overviews, and general travel information. Additionally, the tour operator should provide you with insights into the host country's indigenous cultures, religious beliefs, social practices, languages spoken, and attitude toward foreign visitors. The operator should instruct participants before departure on inoffensive or low-impact behavior. The amount of pre-trip preparation the operator supplies signals the level of service you can expect throughout the trip.

The best indication of a quality tour operator is its on-site staff. Your local guide acts as your window to the world you visit. Not only should guides be knowledgeable about the area you plan to visit, they should also be able to convey their knowledge with humor and enthusiasm. The ideal guide will speak the local language, have lived in the area for some time, be informed about local environmental issues, and be able to answer any questions you may have about the area's natural history—from what makes a flamingo pink (it's the carotene in the shrimp they eat) to whether Mount Everest is getting taller or shorter (taller). Ask the operator to describe the characteristics of the trip leaders it employs. How experienced are they? Does the company train its own field staff? What are their qualifications?

independent travel or group tour?

You don't have to join an organized tour to explore the world's environmentally endangered lands. You can travel on your own to many of the same destinations as the most popular tours. By staying in locally owned hotels and pensions, eating in local cafés or public markets, getting in touch with local conservation groups, hiring local guides, and packing out all your trash, you can still contribute to the environment. But before you venture on your own, remember to do your homework. Study up on cultural traditions so you will be sure not to offend the local people when you get there. (Going nude on the beach is taboo in some countries, for example.) Read as much as you can about the region so you will better understand its natural history and be more sensitive to its environmental heritage. Identify local travel resources beforehand so you can be sure to support them over ones that benefit only absentee owners or foreign-held interests.

Independent travel does have its shortcomings. The first is expense. It's hard to match the economies of scale achieved by organized tours when traveling to the more remote regions of the world. Another question is accessibility. Many national parks and natural areas tightly control access. Tours often receive first priority. Ecuador, for instance, has established a quota on the number of tourists allowed into Galapagos National Park. To visit this region, you must be accompanied by a licensed natural guide. For other destinations, no transportation or infrastructure exists to accommodate independent travelers. You'll find it hard to get to the Antarctic on your own, much less travel around.

Another tradeoff has to do with the level of understanding you can expect to gain about a natural area when you explore it by yourself. Though books and field guides can tell you much about a place, they can't substitute for the cultural insights and scientific explanations that regional experts and professional naturalists provide. All of the best organized tours offer these.

And finally, how great an impact can one person make on a region's conservation practices compared to the influence of a group? When it comes to bringing about positive environmental change, strength definitely lies in numbers. The travel industry is no exception. It responds to consumer demands. If you were to complain to a cruise line about how it dumps its waste at sea, you would probably elicit a shrug and, at best, vague assurances to "look into the matter." But if a commercial tour operator were to threaten to book his clients on a more environmentally responsible competitor, you can be sure the complaint would be taken seriously.

travel insurance
The cost of travel represents a sizable investment. Like any investment, you may want to consider protecting it. The best way to do that is to purchase trip-cancellation insurance through your travel agent. This type of insurance can protect you if you have to change plans due to illness, accident, or other unforeseen occurrences. It will also repay you should the companies you've contracted for tours, airline flights, cruises, or other travel arrangements default or cancel those services.

Just like home, auto, and health insurance, travel insurance coverage varies greatly from company to company. You need to find out exactly what is and what isn't covered. For instance, some policies won't reimburse you for a trip that was canceled because of civil unrest. That might be an important consideration if you plant to travel to areas where political stability is in question.

Before purchasing a policy, check your existing home and health insurance policies. Some offer travel-related expenses. For more information, consult your travel agent or an insurance broker.

The August 1990 issue of *Consumer Reports Travel Letter* compared the coverage and costs of travel policies offered by several large companies. To obtain a copy of that article, send $5 to CRTL, 256 Washington St., Mount Vernon, NY 10553.

Insurance companies that sell travel policies include:

American Express Travel Protection Plan
Amex Assurance
P.O. Box 2070
San Rafael, CA 94912
1-800-234-0375

Travel Assure
Tele-Trip Division
Mutual of Omaha
Box 31865
3201 Farnam St.
Omaha, NE 68131

Travel Guard International
1145 Clark St.
Stevens Point, WI 54481
1-800-826-1300

Travelers Travel Insurance PAK
The Travelers Companies
1 Tower Square
Hartford, CT 06183
1-800-243-3174

money matters

Chances are you will already have paid for your
nature tour before boarding the plane, but this fee won't
cover incidental costs such as souvenirs, drinks, sundries,
and tips for local guides. While traveler's checks and
credit cards will get you through nearly any city in the
world these days—automatic tellers made it to Cuzco,
Peru, by 1984—it's a good idea to exchange some dollars
into the currency of your destination before you leave.
This isn't always possible when traveling to the less-visited
parts of the globe, so be sure to take a reserve of U.S.
dollars, too. Small bills come in handy when you find
yourself making an unexpected layover in a jungle village
that lacks a bank, or having to cover an unforeseen park
fee or departure tax. Invest in a secure money belt or
fanny pack to carry your valuables.

travel documents

Thinking of whale watching in Mexico? For trips of
more than three days, you'll need to obtain a tourist card
before you go, or pick one up at the border. Planning a
Galapagos cruise? Ecuador requires a passport. And
before you can deplane in Cairns for your trek in Cape
York to look for saltwater crocodiles, you'll need to get an
Australian visa. The requirements for official
documentation vary from country to country. Find out well
in advance what you will need. Your tour operator should
be able to assist you. One thing remains the same for all
countries, however: Always keep your official papers in a
safe place about your person; you never know when you
may need to prove your identity, and in some countries,
it's the law.

Passports. Most countries require a valid passport.
You can obtain one through most major post offices and at
U.S. passport agencies. You'll find the addresses and
phone numbers under the government listings in the
white pages of your local telephone directory. New
applicants will need a birth certificate or other proof of
citizenship; two identical passport-size photographs, which
can be taken on the spot at many camera shops; $35 for
the passport itself, plus a $7 processing fee if you apply in
person (no processing fee when renewing your passport
by mail); and proof of identity that includes your
signature. A separate passport is recommended for
children under eighteen (the fee is lower, too). Allow one

month to six weeks for your application to be processed
and the passport mailed to your home. In an emergency,
passport agency offices can have a passport ready in 24 to
48 hours for an additional fee.

It's a good idea to carry a photocopy of your passport
in your luggage—separate from the actual passport—in
case of loss or theft. This can speed the process if you
need to have the passport replaced.

Visas. A visa is official government approval for you
to enter a country; over half the countries in the world
require them. This small slip of paper can easily be
misplaced, so hold onto it because you will need it in order
to exit the country. Visas are issued for a specific length of
time, typically fifteen days, thirty days, or six months.
While some countries will issue a temporary visa at the
border, it's always smart to obtain one prior to entry. Some
countries issue visas free, others charge a fee, typically
$20. You can obtain visas at foreign embassies, consulates,
tourism offices, and international airports. In some cases,
you'll need to send in a completed application form, a valid
passport, and possibly one or more passport-style photos.
Allow two weeks for each visa. Private companies that
offer professional visa procurement services can help you
obtain a number of visas in a hurry. They typically charge
$20 per visa plus the visa fees. Your travel agent or tour
operator should be able to supply you with up-to-date
information about documentation requirements for the
country or countries you plan to visit. You can also obtain
a copy of "Visa Requirements of Foreign Governments"
from any U.S. passport agency, or by writing:

> Bureau of Consular Affairs
> Room 5807
> Department of State
> Washington, DC 20520

health

Nigeria has African sleeping sickness. Brazil has
malaria. The South Pacific, dengue fever. Thailand,
encephalitis. Peru, cholera. Afghanistan, typhus. There are
also hepatitis, tetanus, dysentery, and a host of other
maladies that plague the developing countries of the
world.

Nature travel can expose you to health risks you'd
never find back home. This is especially true in tropical
and rural areas where vaccination programs and public
sanitation and hygiene are rudimentary at best. You can
help reduce your risk of contracting a disease by taking
the necessary precautions and exercising common sense.
Be careful with drinking water and water used for
brushing your teeth and bathing; use water purification

tablets, boil water first, or use bottled water only; avoid eating raw vegetables and fruit except those you can wash and peel yourself; treat cuts and abrasions quickly and aggressively.

While smallpox vaccination is no longer required anywhere in the world, you may need to be inoculated for typhoid, cholera, yellow fever, or tetanus, depending on which countries you plan to visit. Many doctors recommend a prophylactic dose of gamma globulin to help reduce the risk of hepatitis. You may also want to take out extra health insurance for your trip to cover such services as a helicopter ambulance, if your current insurance doesn't include it.

Check with your local community or state health department about immunization requirements a few weeks before your departure (for example, if you are advised to take malaria pills, you will need to start taking them a couple of weeks before you leave), or contact the U.S. Public Health Service for a free copy of "Health Information for International Travel."

The U.S. Centers for Disease Control operate two travel health hotlines with the latest information on diseases and inoculation requirements. Contact:

U.S. Centers for Disease Control
(404) 332-4555 or (404) 332-4559

If you have any kind of medical problem or take prescription medicine on a regular basis, take a Medical Passport; it gives a detailed up-to-date record of your medical history. Write:

The Medical Passport Foundation, Inc.
P.O. Box 820
De Land, FL 32721

For a free list of English-speaking doctors, contact:

International Association for
Medical Assistance to Travelers
417 Center St.
Lewiston, NY 14092

And don't forget to take along your yellow U.S. Department of Health vaccination certificate. You still need to carry this with your travel documents to certain destinations, such as Tanzania.

travel advisories

Before embarking on a trip to any foreign destination, especially the world's political "hot spots," it's always a good idea to check to see if a travel advisory has been issued by the U.S. State Department. The State Department operates a 24-hour travel advisory hot line. It bases its recommendations on such conditions as political instability, war, terrorism, epidemics, and crime. While the information is a valuable piece of travel intelligence, keep in mind the State Department uses considerable caution when making its recommendations. Contact:

U.S. State Department
(202) 647-5225

Another source of information on these matters is the bimonthly World Status Map. Each issue contains a color-coded map of the world exposing trouble spots and listing official government travel advisories. It also provides information on visa and passport requirements. The annual subscription is $36. Contact:

World Status Map
Box 466
Merrifield, VA 22116
1-800-322-4685

packing

Most outfitters and tour operators will supply you with a suggested list of clothing and gear to take on your trip, but the best advice is to pack light. Limit yourself to one small personal carry-on bag—it can also double as your camera bag—and only one more piece of baggage. Soft-sided luggage made of lightweight, durable material such as Gore-Tex® is ideal for nature travel. You want something you can throw onto a Land Rover's roof rack without dislocating your shoulder, a bag so shapeless you can stow it in the bow of a dugout when heading down the Amazon, a tote rugged enough to strap on a camel when caravaning across the Kalahari. Finally, don't take anything you can't replace.

u.s. customs

When you return to the United States, you are required to go through customs and declare any purchases you have made abroad. At this writing, U.S. citizens were allowed to bring in a maximum of $400 in goods duty-free. There are also limits on the amounts of alcohol, cigarettes, and foreign currency you may bring back. Anything over the maximum requires you to fill out a declaration form listing each item and the amount you paid for it. The duty rate is 10 percent up to the next $1,000 worth of declared items. There are exemptions to customs duty. If you plan to take previously purchased foreign goods abroad, such as a camera, bring along the purchase receipt, or fill out a Certificate of Registration for Personal Effects Taken Abroad (U.S. Customs Service Form 4457) in advance so you can get these items back into the United States without paying duty.

You may want to obtain a free booklet from the U.S. Customs Service entitled, "Know Before You Go." It spells out your responsibilities when dealing with customs on your return. Contact:

> U.S. Customs Service
> 1301 Constitution Ave., N.W.
> Washington, DC 20229
> (202) 566-8195

souvenirs

Think twice before you buy that strand of fiery red coral from a gift shop in Belize, or that handmade display of mounted butterflies being sold in the streets of Peru, or that feathered headdress in the open markets of Borneo. You could be pushing an endangered species closer to the brink of extinction.

Purchasing souvenirs is a big part of any trip, but even seemingly innocuous mementos can be harmful to wildlife. Products made from hides, shells, feathers, teeth, tortoiseshell, coral, and ivory not only encourage destruction of wildlife but are illegal in many cases. You could risk government seizure of your souvenirs upon your return to the United States and could incur substantial fines.

The illegal trade of wildlife and wildlife products is a major environmental problem throughout the world. The United States is the world's largest consumer of wildlife, followed by Japan and Western Europe. Despite strong prohibitions, a large percentage of the wildlife trade in these countries still involves protected or endangered species. Wildlife may be "laundered" to conceal its true country of origin. Wildlife is often killed or collected in one country, smuggled into another, and then exported with false permits to a third, making its origins hard to trace.

You can play a significant role in curbing this illegal trade. Combating the problem requires not only increased enforcement efforts but also better-informed consumers and travelers. TRAFFIC (USA), a program of the World Wildlife Fund which monitors the international trade in wild plants and animals, in conjunction with the U.S. Fish and Wildlife Service, offers the following guidelines:

• **Reptile skins** and **leathers** are most commonly used in watchbands, handbags, belts, and shoes. The legality of importing these products depends on the

Tropical wood may be lovely for a dining room table or dresser. But when you purchase furniture made from tropical virgin hardwoods, you may be contributing to the extinction of endangered tree species and the animals that depend on them. Commercial demand for tropical woods is driving some trees to extinction and endangering important forest habitats. Endangered woods to avoid include mahogany, cocobolo, cristobal, guayacan, real, ron ron, and purpleheart.

species and the country of origin. Prohibited imports include products made from most crocodile skins, lizard skins, many snakeskin products, all sea turtle products, and other leather products made from pangolin (sometimes labeled "anteater") skin originating in Thailand, Malaysia, and Indonesia.

- **Birds** and **feathers** may not be imported into the United States except under certain conditions. The survival of many wild-bird species is threatened by habitat destruction and trade. Alarming numbers of birds die during capture, transit, and the required thirty-day quarantine period. For some species, the death rate is as high as 70 percent of the shipment. Prohibited from import are virtually all live birds, most wild-bird feathers, mounted birds, and skins.

- **Ivory** from elephant tusks is traditionally carved into products such as jewelry, scrimshaw, figurines, and piano keys. Imports of ivory from both Asian and African elephants are now generally prohibited. Purchase of ivory abroad is not recommended because at least 90 percent of the ivory sold on world markets in recent years has come from poached elephants. On average, 89,000 elephants per year have supplied the illegal market for ivory—enough to reduce Africa's total elephant population by half since 1979. As long as world demand for ivory remains high, purchases of elephant ivory provide incentive to poachers and illegal traders and threaten the survival of the African elephant. Imports of ivory and scrimshaw from whales, walruses, and narwhals are also prohibited.

- **Furs** from the larger spotted cats such as jaguar, leopard, snow leopard, and tiger, and from most smaller cats such as ocelot, margay, and tiger cat, cannot enter the United States legally, nor can furs of marine mammals such as seals and polar bears.

- **Coral reefs** are the building blocks of important marine communities and serve as natural barriers against beach erosion. Recognizing this, many countries prohibit the collection, sale, and export of corals. Yet corals, often fashioned into jewelry and decorative ornaments, are still sold in enormous quantities. Coral collection is only one of several reasons for the destruction of coral ecosystems. In the Philippines, for example, 70 percent of the reefs have been damaged due to coral collection, harmful fishing practices, and pollution.

- **Plants,** like animals, are subject to illegal trade through laundering, smuggling, and improper documentation. As a result, many plant species are in danger of extinction and receive protection under U.S. law. Species prohibited from import into the United States include many cycads, orchids, and cacti. Whether endangered or not, all imported plants must undergo inspection by the U.S. Department of Agriculture and be accompanied by documents certifying they are free of disease and pests. For more information, contact:

TRAFFIC (USA)
World Wildlife Fund
1250 24th St., N.W.
Washington, DC 20037

Division of Law Enforcement
U.S. Fish and Wildlife Service
P.O. Box 3247
Arlington, VA 22203

photography

The conservationist's chestnut, "Take only photographs, leave only footprints," especially holds true when traveling to the world's wildest areas. Whether you're taking snapshots or magazine-quality photographs, think before you press the shutter. Ask your guide how residents typically feel about being photographed. Some people may ask you to take their picture. If they do, try to get an address and send them a print after you return home. Others consider it a personal affront to be photographed. The capturing of a person's image may conflict with their religious beliefs. Put yourself in their place. How would you feel if you were walking down your own street and a group of wildly dressed foreigners suddenly leaped out of a tour bus, trained their cameras on you, and began whirring away with motor drives? Ask permission first, shoot later.

You should also exercise restraint when photographing wildlife. Animals can suffer from overzealous photographers. Never throw rocks, bang on trees, or make loud noises to make an animal move or react. Don't try to get as close as you can. Odds are you'll probably spook your subject before you get a chance to take its photograph. Worse, the animal could harm itself while trying to flee. It may even turn on you. Let your telephoto lens do your stalking for you.

As for film, take all you think you'll need and then some. It's often difficult to find film in undeveloped regions of the world, and when you do, it is invariably expensive. If you can't decide between taking twenty rolls or twenty-five, just imagine yourself deep in the Monteverde Cloud Forest Reserve in Costa Rica and finally spotting the rare and elusive golden toad, only to find you've just shot your last frame.

Keep your exposed and unexposed rolls in a zippered plastic bag in your camera case for hand inspection when going through airport metal detectors.

▌conservation alert

code of ethics

● The most important item to bring on any trip is your social consciousness. Because you are entering a different culture and your visit may impact on this society in variety of ways both economic and cultural, you have a responsibility to be respectful of your hosts. Keeping the following code of ethics in mind may help ensure that your trip will benefit both you and the country you visit. It was developed by the Ecumenical Coalition on Third World Tourism and is issued by the North American Coordinating Center for Responsible Tourism.

- Travel in a spirit of humility and with a genuine desire to meet and talk with local people.
- Be aware of the feelings of other people, thus preventing what might be offensive behavior. Remember this especially with photography.
- Cultivate the habit of listening and observing rather than merely hearing and seeing.
- Realize that people in the country you visit often have time concepts and thought patterns different from your own. Not inferior, just different.
- Discover the enrichment that comes from seeing another way of life, rather than looking for the "beach paradise" you see in tourist posters.
- Acquaint yourself with local customs, and respect them; people will be happy to help you.
- Cultivate the habit of asking questions instead of knowing all the answers.
- Spend wisely. When shopping, remember that the bargain you obtain is only possible because of low wages paid to the maker.
- Make no promises to local people unless you are certain you can fulfill them.
- Reflect daily on your experiences; seek to deepen your understanding. What enriches you may rob or violate others.

And finally, if you get excited and are tempted to go off the trail or bend the rules "just a little" because you think it won't hurt, think twice—every action, however small, does count.

For more information on responsible tourism, contact:

The Center for Responsible Tourism
2 Kensington Road
San Anselmo, CA 94960
(415) 258-6594

Ecumenical Coalition on
Third World Tourism
P.O. Box 9-25
Bangkhen, Bangkok 0900
Thailand

north america

- Almost 100 percent of Hawaii's invertebrate species and 90 percent of its birds and flowering plants are native to the islands. Hawaii is also the nation's leader in endangered species—55 species and subspecies are officially listed as endangered or threatened.

- The ancient trees in Alaska's Tongass National Forest, one of the world's greatest temperate rainforests, are being cut as fast as the trees of the Amazon rainforest are.

- Wetlands in the United States are disappearing at a rate of 500,000 acres per year, threatening the survival of millions of migrating waterfowl, shorebirds, and countless land species.

- The best place on Earth to catch a glimpse of polar bears in the wild is Churchill, Manitoba, Canada, where tourism has helped rescue this magnificent creature from extinction.

north america

You don't have to travel to the ends of the earth to find spectacular scenery and view exotic species of wildlife. Some of the most biologically important habitats exist right here in the United States and Canada. These ecosystems are also among the most endangered.

the united states

Many nature destinations in the United States offer opportunities for travelers to put their time and money into helping protect them. The potential for using tourism domestically as a conservation tool is promising because, after all, American citizens have greater influence here than they do abroad. To put a present-day spin on an age-old homily, "Conservation begins in the home."

hawaii

The Hawaiian Islands boast more than sunny skies, warm seas, and carefree vacations for the winter weary. A natural history paradise, they claim one of the highest percentages of "endemic" plant and animal species anywhere—species that are native to that particular place and occur naturally nowhere else. Almost 100 percent of Hawaii's invertebrate species and more than 90 percent of its birds and flowering plants are endemic.

Hawaii's globally unique plants and animals resulted from nature's grand experiment in supreme isolation. Only a handful of colonizing species succeeded in crossing the ocean to reach the volcanic islands' shores. The ones that did evolved in strange and mysterious ways. For example, from a single finch-like ancestor, forty-seven species or subspecies of birds evolved, far surpassing the twelve types of Galapagos finches that led Darwin to develop his theory of the evolution of the species. Plants, too, evolved into never-before-seen species. Violets grow on woody trunks 12 feet long, and giant lobelias reach 25 feet.

exploring an eden of endemism

A visit to Hawaii's numerous public parks and private reserves will take you through an extraordinary array of habitats—at least 150 different types of natural communities. They range from coastal dunes to lava-field savannas, from arid scrubland to tropical rainforests, from alpine snowfields to subterranean caverns. Little distance separates the different types. A short hike can be like

! conservation alert

the dwindling natives

● Regrettably, Hawaii has the dubious distinction of being the endangered-species capital of the United States. Fifty-five Hawaiian species and subspecies have been officially listed by the U.S. Fish and Wildlife Service as endangered or threatened. That's about 10 percent of the total number for the entire country. Another 185 species qualify for the endangered list but have yet to be added.

Blame humans. Habitat conversion due to agriculture and development has eliminated virtually all Hawaiian native-plant communities in lower elevations. The introduction of non-native plants and animals has placed even more pressure on endemic species. Rats prey on birds, pigs uproot trees, and goats mow down vegetation.

Still, about one-quarter of Hawaii's natural habitat remains relatively intact. Most is contained within the boundaries of state and national parks, wildlife refuges, and private preserves.

taking a trip from the Archeozoic to the Paleozoic ages. In just a couple of miles, you can walk from a smoldering, lifeless lava field that conjures up images of Hades to a rain-brushed jungle shaded by tropical ferns.

At **Hawaii Volcanoes National Park** on the Big Island of Hawaii, molten lava flows to the sea in rivers of red. In **Haleakala National Park** on Maui, unusual, primeval-looking silverswords that are actually descendants of the daisy grow inside a lunar-like crater. And Mount Waialeale in Kauai is the wettest spot in the world.

Hawaii's shores also have much to offer. You can listen to humpbacks sing off the shores of Maui and snorkel among a kaleidoscope of tropical fish. After witnessing the real Hawaii, you'll come to understand why it is so important that these vital refuges be protected and not plowed under to make room for yet another luxury resort and golf course.

Season: Year-round

The insects of Hawaii's isolated islands have taken on an incredible range of bizarre forms. One species of caterpillar, for example, hides itself in the notches of leaves and preys on other insects as they light. It is the only known ambushing, carnivorous caterpillar in the world. Even stranger are flightless flies and underground denizens called "no-eyed big-eyed jumping spiders."

alaska

"Its grandeur is more valuable than the gold or the fish or the timber, for it will never be exhausted." So Henry Gannett described Alaska in 1899 while working for the U.S. Geological Survey. How prophetic those words have proven. The gold rush has boomed and busted, the oil is being drained, and little has been done to regenerate the forests after decades of logging abuse.

But thanks in part to the Alaska National Interest Lands Conservation Act, a sweeping land bill promoted by environmentalists which created over 100 million acres of new national parks, preserves, wildlife refuges and wild and scenic rivers, Alaska still has plenty of scenery. As a result, tourism is turning out to be Alaska's most valuable and sustainable natural resource.

The forces of nature in Alaska have conspired to create a geological masterpiece, a work of beauty executed with raw and powerful strokes. Glaciers churn and grind and crash into the sea. The tallest mountain in North America, Mount McKinley, holds court over a range of peaks worthy of the same respect shown to the Himalayas. Grizzlies pluck salmon from untamed rivers. Caribou thunder across the tundra. And the sea roils with enormous herds of walrus, seal, otter, and whale. Yet the threat of industrial exploitation hangs over Alaska like the Sword of Damocles. At this writing, the government is contemplating drilling for oil within the sanctified grounds of the Arctic National Wildlife Range, while in the Tongass National Forest, one of the world's greatest temperate rainforests, trees are falling as fast as those in the Amazon.

rafting northern waters

Yukon. Alsek. Copper. Noatak. Stikine. The list goes on and on. Alaska has more than its fair share of mighty rivers. Glacier-fed streams free-fall down mountainsides, hurtle through deep chasms, then broaden and swell with melting snow as they snake across miles and miles of tundra and muskeg on their way to the sea.

Kayaking or rafting down an Alaskan river provides a front-row seat for viewing the Last Frontier State's awe-inspiring landscape. The most popular rivers for running have common denominators: boisterous rapids, cold water, remoteness, and unparalleled beauty. Because rivers act as a lifeline for many wildlife species, you're sure to see such sights as grizzlies fishing in waterfalls, moose foraging along the banks, and eagles soaring above the riverways.
Season: Summer

alaska wildlife discovery

The nation's largest state requires an ambitious itinerary, one that exposes you to several of its multifaceted jewels. Many tour operators offer such trips, traversing a wide range of Alaska's exciting wild areas. Most include stops at the state's finest parks.

A typical tour might include visits to the **Kenai National Wildlife Refuge,** which boasts one of the largest populations of moose in North America. To the south is the **Kenai Fjords National Park,** a coastal

! conservation alert

america's serengeti

● The Arctic National Wildlife Refuge, which comprises 18 million acres in the northeast corner of Alaska, remains a last bastion of unspoiled, vast, arctic wilderness. Located north of the Arctic Circle at the base of the fabled Brooks Range, the refuge protects abounding wildlife. One of the largest herds of caribou in North America, the 180,000-member Porcupine Caribou Herd, crisscrosses the valleys, while shaggy-coated musk oxen looking more like long-lost relatives of woolly mammoths, roam the tundra. Dall sheep cling to the scarps overlooking the rivers while grizzly, wolverine, and wolf hunt along the bottoms. Overhead, peregrines and gyrfalcons put on an aerial display, along with golden eagles and rough-legged hawks. Closer to ground, songbirds flock by the thousands to breed, filling the air with sound around the clock.

The Arctic National Wildlife Refuge epitomizes the very essence of our nation's wilderness heritage. Its unimpacted nature moves visitors emotionally as well as spiritually. To think that the government would allow this place to be sullied and endangered by oil drilling is not only heart-wrenching but maddening. A visit here will have you rallying for its protection, too.

In the frozen world of Glacier Bay, coastal glaciers rush to the sea. A little more than 200 years ago, its entrance—the narrow Icy Strait—was still covered by a sheet of ice. At the furthest inside tip of Glacier Bay, Tarr Inlet, huge, frozen, blue rivers give birth to icebergs. Seals and seabirds hitchhike rides on them.

spectacle where giant glacial fingers of ice poke into the blue tidewaters of the sea. Massive seastacks and headlands serve as noisy condominiums for nesting birds, including puffins, kittiwakes, and glaucous gulls. Pelagic species such as short-tailed shearwaters and fork-tailed storm petrels wing over pods of whales.

The heart of Alaska's wildlands is **Denali National Park**, a 6-million-acre patch of wilderness larger than the whole state of Massachusetts. The crowning glory of the park is Mount McKinley, 20,320 feet tall and still growing. Tectonic action and glacial scouring have created a place of sheer granite domes, brooding mountains, low plains, and polychromatic river valleys.

Hidden in the more remote corners of Alaska are such wonders as **Katmai National Park** and its spectral Valley of 10,000 Smokes; and **Wrangell-St. Elias National Park**, an unending chain of ice-capped peaks and rugged beauty.

Season: Summer

the inside passage

No wonder North Coast Indians call Alaska "the place where the sea breaks its back." The state's 33,904-mile-

natural success

st. paul sanctuary

The Pribilof island of St. Paul in the Bering Sea is home to one of the largest herds of fur seals in the world. Hundreds of thousands of these magnificent marine mammals make their way to island rookeries each year to breed and rear their young. For years, the island's seals were the target of a commercial harvest that supplied the fur trade. In 1984, sealing was outlawed, and the fur seals were given protective status. The ruling, however, put a strain on resident Aleut natives who had become dependent on the commercial harvest as a source of income. To find a replacement, islanders turned to ecotourism.

Today, the island welcomes small groups of visitors from mid-May to September to view the unusual species of birds and animals up close and to experience the Aleut culture. Resident Aleuts act as guides. Besides the huge population of fur seals, St. Paul also hosts more than two million seabirds. More than 210 species have been identified, including puffin, parakeet auklet, red-legged kittiwake, and red-faced cormorant. Many of the species are migrants from as far away as Argentina.

long shoreline contains a hysteria of jagged mountain peaks, churning tidewater glaciers, and sheltered waterways. So powerful is the clash of natural forces here that nearly 2,000 islands have broken loose from a mainland already split by icy fjords that dwarf Scandinavia's in comparison. It is all so wild, so remote that only a handful of roads exists, and access is restricted to boat or float plane.

Discover Alaska's celebrated coastline, the Inside Passage, a protected 1,000-mile marine highway that links colorful fishing ports, Indian villages, and pristine natural areas. Choose from small, expedition-class cruise ships to seagoing kayaks.

Two of the Inside Passage's most popular destinations are **Misty Fjords National Monument** and **Glacier Bay National Park and Preserve.** Misty Fjords encompasses a watery wonderland of towering peaks, shimmering waterfalls, and a maze-like waterways. Low-slung clouds and wispy layers of fog hang over the place like soft blankets, muffling it in total silence. Glacier Bay offers breathtaking views of glaciers drifting seaward.

Season: Summer

washington

If you thought all rainforests were in the tropics, then you haven't visited Washington State. Along Washington's western edge is a temperate rainforest filled with some of the oldest trees in the Pacific Northwest, a forest that covers the Olympic Peninsula. Bounded on three sides by water—the Pacific Ocean, the Strait of Juan de Fuca, and Hood Canal—the Olympic Peninsula catches one of the heaviest rainfalls on Earth. An average of 200 inches a year drenches its highest point, 7,965-foot Mount Olympus.

All this precipitation nurtures thick stands of western red cedar, western hemlock, and Sitka spruce, with graceful shawls of Spanish moss hanging from their branches. A tangled understory of rhododendron, swordfern, bigleaf maple, and huckleberry shadows a lush groundcover composed of a variety of true mosses, ferns, and wildflowers. Not surprisingly, the peninsula supports a bountiful habitat for birds and other wildlife.

Season: Year-round

oregon

You own more than half of Oregon. That's right. Some 15.7 million acres belong to the public. Public lands include national parks, forests, wildlife refuges, and lands managed by the Bureau of Land Management. They comprise a cornucopia of ecosystems: mountain, desert, plain, canyon, river, lake, and wetland. Some of these public lands have been leased to cattle ranchers, but though they may be fenced and gated, you still have the right to enter. By visiting Oregon's public lands, you can see for yourself how the government manages our nation's natural legacy.

on the landing strip

Oregon's public lands contain some of the major wetlands of the Pacific Flyway, offering essential rest stops for huge flocks of migrating birds. Malheur National Wildlife Refuge in the southeastern corner of the state is one of the largest and most biologically important of these areas; it covers more than 183,000 acres. Established in 1908 by President Theodore Roosevelt, Malheur provides an important nesting ground for such notable species as trumpeter swan, Canada goose, greater sandhill crane, western grebe, ruddy duck, Forster's tern, Wilson's phalarope, and black-crowned night heron, just a few of the more than 225 species of birds that have been observed here. The birds share the refuge with nearly sixty known mammal species, including shrew, bat,

pygmy rabbit, bobcat, and chisel-toothed kangaroo rat.

A 42-mile self-guided autotour provides an overview of the refuge's riches, but to really absorb its power, visitors need to get out of their cars, sit quietly in a field or alongside one of the ponds, and listen to the sound of a million birds. And at just the right time of year, waves of Canada geese may be seen swooping down on the marsh in unison, honking loudly as they settle to the ground. Hopefully, their call will inspire action on their behalf.

Season: Spring and fall

running the rogue

Whitewater enthusiasts consider the Rogue River one of the best of rainy Oregon's many rivers. A federally designated Wild and Scenic River, the Rogue slices through a forested stretch of the Coast Range in south-western Oregon before draining into the Pacific Ocean. Rafters bounce down a series of challenging whitewater rapids and past a seemingly endless supply of beautiful sandy beaches.

During your river expedition, take the time to disembark and hike into the surrounding forest. Occasionally you'll spot areas that have been clearcut. The trees

❚ conservation alert

pit stop on the pacific flyway

● The Pacific Flyway is the most westerly of the four main North American "flight lanes" used each year by hundreds of millions of waterfowl, shorebirds, and other migrating birds as they journey between their nesting grounds in the far north and wintering areas of the temperate south. A chain of wetlands that links the tundra to the tropics actually makes up the flyway, for the route across the sky is but a reflection of the stepping stones of water down below.

Regrettably, wetlands big and small are being drained, degraded, and destroyed by commercial development and urban expansion throughout the United States. Nationally, 500,000 acres disappear each year. The destruction of wetlands threatens the survival of not only waterfowl and shorebirds, but countless earthbound species as well. The plight of the nation's wetlands has reached a critical juncture. Citizens need to act quickly if these important habitats and the species that depend on them are to survive.

that once stood there have been mowed down as if by a giant scythe. Compare these to the still-forested areas. The first thing you'll notice is a lack of wildlife in the clearcut sections. It's no coincidence. Clearcutting not only visibly destroys the habitat of many forest animals that depend on the trees for shelter and food, it also affects animal and plant life at the edges of the forest that remains standing.

Season: April through September

The coastal areas of the Olympic Peninsula in Washington State attract dozens of species of shorebirds and waterfowl, including sooty and pink-footed shearwaters, red-throated loons, and black oystercatchers. The forests, in turn, shelter multiple species of woodpecker, owl, chickadee, nuthatch, waxwing, and vireo. The Olympic also supports the nation's largest herd of Roosevelt elk, as well as a large population of mountain lions and mountain goats.

california

From Oregon to Mexico and from the Pacific Ocean to the desert, California offers a range of wilderness experiences that are virtually unequaled in the nation for their extremes of contrast. Big Sur, the High Sierra, Death Valley—the state is as famous for its natural variety as it is for urban sprawl. But because of its continued population growth and increasing demand on wilderness areas as destinations for more and more tourists each year, the wilderness land that remains must be carefully protected.

whitewater victory trip

The fact that it's still possible to take a whitewater raft trip down the Tuolumne River is proof that dedication and determination on behalf of conservation pay off. The fight to keep this Sierra-fed stream running free dates back to 1906 when John Muir and his nascent Sierra Club battled with San Francisco water interests over a dam that would flood Hetch Hetchy Valley, a twin to Yosemite. Conservationists lost that fight, as well as subsequent battles over four more dams, but when a proposal was made to inundate the last stretch of free-running water on the Tuolumne in the 1980s, the war continued anew. This time conservationists succeeded in defeating a new dam, and in 1984 the river was granted official protected status under the Wild and Scenic Rivers Act.

The trophy for the conservationists' efforts is an unrestricted 83-mile stretch between the river's two largest reservoirs, Hetch Hetchy and New Don Pedro. In late spring, the river swells with snowmelt and runoff from four major tributaries and plunges down the granite mountainside, slamming and twisting its way through a canyon strewn with boulders and cloaked in oaks and ponderosa pine.

The steepness of the drop and the sheer volume of water create a series of exhilarating rapids. The grand finale is a plunge over Clavey Falls, an eight-foot drop guaranteed to keep novice and experienced rafters alike humble and ever mindful of what is at stake whenever dams are proposed.

Season: Spring and summer

the varied california desert

The California desert is not just sand and chaparral. In fact, it is actually three deserts in one: the Great Basin Desert, the Mojave Desert, and the Colorado Desert. Each supports a distinct biological community as well as unique geographical features. The Great Basin Desert's most notable biological community, the ancient bristlecone pine forest, grows near Big Pine on top of the White Mountains in eastern California. Thought to be the world's oldest living trees—some of them are more than 4,000 years old—the beautifully gnarled and polished trunks of the bristlecones lure nature photographers from far and wide. The ancient trees stand in stark contrast to the plants most people associate with the desert.

The most famous site in the California desert, **Death Valley National Monument,** provides an unrestricted view of Earth's naked crust. The strange landforms here have been painted with a colorful palette. Their alien shapes disturb and defy. Among the most popular topographical stopping places are Zabriskie Point, Funeral Peak, and Badwater.

Just 100 miles east of downtown Los Angeles lies the **Desert Tortoise Natural Area,** a 39-square-mile corner of the Mojave established to preserve the region's oldest resident wildlife species. The ecosystem ranges in

natural success

discovering the urban wilderness

A two-hour drive from downtown Los Angeles takes you to a place where bald eagles still soar over a lakefront that harbors a vast community of rare and endangered plants. Within commuting distance of Manhattan, a globally threatened species of moth survives in one of Long Island's last dwarf oak brush plains. Not far from Baltimore and Washington, D.C., 2,000 great blue herons find refuge on the banks of Nanjemoy Creek.

These sights provide living proof that you don't have to travel far to get a close-up and uncrowded look at the natural world. These areas are part of a lightly visited system of nature preserves that protects rare and endangered wildlife in its natural habitat. The network of preserves was created by The Nature Conservancy, a nonprofit, nonpartisan, national conservation organization dedicated solely to protecting natural beauty and biological diversity through habitat preservation. Using easements, donations, exchanges, and outright purchases, the Conservancy has quietly acquired a collection of ecologically significant real estate about the size of Delaware and Rhode Island combined.

The Conservancy's active membership currently manages nearly a thousand of these areas as natural preserves, which are open to the public. Understandably, some restrictions do apply. Trails are designed to give visitors a good look at preserves while safeguarding their natural qualities.

It's always helpful to contact the preserve office before arriving to receive up-to-date information on special-use restrictions as well as schedules for guided tours, which are sometimes required. Most of all, plan to explore slowly and you may discover some surprises in the wilderness of your own backyard.

For more information, contact:
The Nature Conservancy
1815 N. Lynn St.
Arlington, VA 22209
(703) 841-5300

extremes—sizzling in summer, freezing in winter. There is little shade from the sun and no shelter from the wind. Yet winter rains set wildflowers blazing across the scrub, and migrant songbirds color the gray-green creosote bush landscape with feathery splashes of red, blue, and yellow. In spring the endangered desert tortoise emerges from its burrow after an eight-month wait and lumbers across the relentless land, as it has for the past two million years, to feed on flowering dandelions and blazing stars.

! conservation alert

desert heart

The future of California's desert rests with the fate of the California Desert Protection Act, an ambitious bill that seeks to protect nearly 9 million acres from a multitude of environmental abuses such as unrestricted mining, off-road vehicle recreation, ranching, urban and industrial development, and military use.

The sweeping bill would redraw the map of southeastern California. Three areas totaling some 4.4 million acres—Death Valley and Joshua Tree national monuments and East Mojave National Scenic Area—would be converted into national parks. An additional 4.4 million acres of public lands currently administered by the Bureau of Land Management would gain wilderness status. All told, the California Desert Protection Act would protect an area nearly twice the size of New Jersey.

At this writing, the bill is still wending its way through Congress, and support from concerned citizens is essential for it to succeed.

When the wind blows across nearby **Joshua Tree National Monument,** you can hear the fringes of leaves on the ancient Joshua trees rustle like a hula dancer's grass skirt. More than 850 square miles of spectacular California desert landscape have been set aside to protect resident wildlife. Among the monument's best-kept secrets are several lovely palm oases. Each is worth a visit. Hiking trails lead the way for a scenic tour of the region's plant and animal communities.

Season: Fall through spring

idaho

The largest wilderness area in the continental United States is the Frank Church "River of No Return" Wilderness in central Idaho. Its 2.23 million acres of rugged mountain beauty include eight national forests and portions of seven others, 10,000-foot peaks, 2,500 miles of trails, 400 lakes, 685 streams, the second deepest gorge in the country, and only about 35,000 visitors a year.

Most people come to whitewater raft on an exciting 91-mile stretch of the Salmon River. This vast and primitive slice of North American wilderness truly deserves the protected status it received with the passage of the Idaho Wilderness Act in 1980. The sides of the canyon alternate between sheer walls and the mouths of tributary river canyons. Forests of ponderosa pine and

At Anza-Borrego Desert State Park, natural and cultural history are linked by more than name alone. At this desert park, 80 miles east of San Diego, guided nature trails and interpretive historic sites offer insights into the plants, animals, and explorers that have populated this unique region. Juan Bautista de Anza was a Spanish captain who led the epic 1776 San Francisco colonial expedition, and *borrego* is Spanish for "bighorn sheep." The curly-horned mammals can sometimes be seen at dawn and dusk when they make their way to strategically placed watering holes. Wildflowers run rampant here in the spring, and the park is a great place for hiking and family camping.

Douglas fir blanket the surrounding mountains. The habitat sustains a wonderland of bird life. More than 240 species have been recorded. Mammals also live here in large numbers, including bighorn sheep, mountain goat, black bear, mountain lion, moose, and mule deer. Numerous wolf sightings reported in past years give rise to speculation that this rare and endangered species has made a stronghold in this wildest of wild places.

Season: May through September

wyoming

Yellowstone is the country's first national park and its most popular. Sadly, it has also been its most abused. For too many years commercial development was given free rein within the park. Cabins, dormitories, golf courses, swimming pools, and tennis courts were built alongside some of the park's most celebrated natural splendors. While much has been accomplished in recent years to remove the worst of these environmental offenders and return the park to its natural state, Yellowstone remains endangered. The threat this time comes from outside the park's borders.

greater than its parts

When Congress drew the park's boundaries in 1872, the science of ecology did not exist. The 54-mile-wide by 62-mile-long rectangle encompassed the region's major geothermal features—geysers, mudpots, and hot springs—but failed to protect the Greater Yellowstone Ecosystem, of which the park is just a small part. Consequently, much of Yellowstone's wildlife and the habitat it depends on for survival actually lies outside the park's boundaries. For example, 40 percent of the grizzly habitat in the area exists outside the park, as does all of the winter range for the six elk herds that summer in the park.

Visitors can appreciate the fragility of Yellowstone by traveling beyond such popular sites as Old Faithful and visiting the park's incomparable backcountry. Here, grizzly bear, moose, elk, bighorn sheep, and bison still forage and migrate across meadows and mountains. It will be up to us to protect them for future generations.

Season: Year-round

The Salmon River in Idaho was aptly nicknamed the "River of No Return" by Lewis and Clark, who, when peering over the edge of the mile-deep canyon and seeing the seemingly endless run of frothing whitewater for the first time, decided discretion was the better part of valor and prudently rerouted the course of their expedition. A week-long raft trip down the Salmon will show you what those intrepid explorers missed.

! conservation alert

beyond old faithful

● The lands outside Yellowstone National Park face enormous pressures. Eighty percent of the nonwilderness lands in national forests surrounding the park have been leased for oil and gas development. Mines operate at the northwest corner. Approximately 26,000 acres of once-pristine wilderness just outside the park has been logged, and the Forest Service plans to build another thousand miles of timber roads over the next ten years. Geothermal development on nearby private land threatens to clog Yellowstone's own natural thermal plumbing system. And, as the result of uncontrolled recreational development at many of Yellowstone's "border towns," problems involving wildlife, such as garbage-addicted grizzly bears, take place with alarming frequency.

It doesn't take much to see that boundary lines offer little conservation value when they don't include the entire ecosystem. Protective management measures for the whole Greater Yellowstone Ecosystem need to be enacted or the United States' favorite national park is doomed.

utah

The completion of Glen Canyon Dam across the Colorado River in 1964 remains the benchmark for which subsequent conservation battles are measured. Beneath the artificial Lake Powell lies a canyon equal in the minds of many to the Grand Canyon just downstream. When the government first proposed damming the canyon, environmentalist David Brower likened the act to flooding the Sistine Chapel. The eventual inundation of Glen Canyon for the purpose of generating hydroelectric power did more than drown a natural wonderland; it mobilized a generation of conservationists dedicated to preventing such a crime against nature from ever occurring again. The passage of the Wild and Scenic Rivers Act several years later owes its existence in part to Glen Canyon Dam.

a clear view on the cataract

Visitors can get a glimpse of what was lost with the construction of the dam by taking a raft trip through Cataract Canyon just upstream. The four-day journey promises more than huge rapids and white-knuckle thrills—though there are plenty of those after the Colorado is joined by the Green River and enters a narrow sluice; 12-foot standing waves result. A raft provides entry to an otherwise inaccessible labyrinth of soaring cliffs, rims of red-rock, razor-sharp mesas, and sandstone spires that has been carved by two million years of water and wind.

The trip ends at the headwaters of what was once Glen Canyon. The contrast between the wild beauty of Cataract Canyon and the dead waters of Lake Powell is irrefutable proof that few causes are as just as the preservation of nature.

Season: Late April through September

arizona, colorado, and new mexico

The sweeping landscapes of the American Southwest contain some of the world's richest archaeological treasures. Towering buttes of red and ocher sandstone and vast, windswept high plateaus cut by deep canyons form an unforgettable backdrop to an even more inspiring collection of ancient dwellings and modern Indian cultures.

Visiting the cultural repositories of the Southwest's earliest human inhabitants divulges insights into how early humans were able to coexist with nature—and where they ran into trouble. There is a lesson here for everyone.

A typical tour includes visits to Chaco Canyon with its dozen or more large ruins and 300 smaller sites from the architectural peak of the Anasazi culture. The highlight, Pueblo Bonito, features a five-story structure that once housed 1,200 people. A three-story 500-room dwelling that dates back 850 years still stands at Aztec, while nearby Mesa Verde National Park in Colorado contains more than 2,000 mesa-top ruins and 300 cliff dwellings built between A.D. 750 and 1100.

Observe modern Southwest Indian culture at Monument Valley; resident Navajos preserve their traditional life-style, building hogans, grazing sheep, and weaving rugs. The Hopi culture still lives in a number of villages, including Oraibi, quite possibly the oldest continuously occupied city in the United States.

At **Canyon de Chelly National Monument,** most famous of all the ancient cliff-dwelling sites in the world, and one of the most magnificent geological sites as well, the Anasazi built houses in caves in the fortress-like walls between A.D. 100 and 1200.

Season: Spring and fall

minnesota

One of the first doorways to the American West for Europeans was a series of lakes that straddles the U.S.–Canadian border in Minnesota. Here, seventeenth-

No one knows for sure why the Anasazi Indians disappeared from their clifftop dwellings of the Mesa Verde some 600 years ago, but some scientists theorize that it might have had something to do with the trees. The thriving population of several thousand inhabitants that built the cliff dwellings near the top of this vast desert plateau were farmers. In order to farm more land for their growing population, they cut down the trees at the top of the mesa—trees that not only held the soil, but also gathered moisture from the clouds and brought rain to the plateau. The loss of the forest, the theory goes, eventually resulted in less rainfall, and the community failed to survive. The moral to this story, if it is true, may still be a lesson to us all.

century voyagers set off to explore the vast, untamed
wilderness in 35-foot canoes made from birchbark. Much
of this wilderness remains in the same condition today as
when the early explorers and Indians first found it.

canoeing on the boundary

On the U.S. side of the border, the Boundary Waters
Canoe Area protects one million acres of clear-water lakes.
Quetico Provincial Park in Ontario preserves an additional
one million acres of water wilderness on the Canadian
side.

Three-hundred-year-old pine forests line a chain of
1,500 interconnected lakes. These forests—islands,
really—provide a home for a stunning array of wildlife,
including moose, black bear, lynx, otter, bald eagle, wolf,
and wolverine. The waters of the lakes teem with aquatic
life. Walleye, northern pike, lake trout, and smallmouth
bass account for just a few of the resident fish species.

As in the days of old, exploration is accomplished by
paddling from lake to lake, gliding over tranquil waters
where rules wisely forbid the use of motorboats.
Beachside campgrounds or comfortable but infrequent
wilderness lodges shelter visitors at night.

Season: Summer

vermont

During winter, the quiet mountains of Vermont offer a
quiet place of solace and solitude for the urban-weary. The
scenery looks as poetic as a line from a Robert Frost
poem. The best way to enjoy the peace and respite is to
strap on a pair of cross-country skis and take to the miles
upon miles of marked trails that wend across hushed
meadows covered with glistening snow and through deep
national forests draped in white.

Charming, homey inns provide a warm refuge from
the rigors of the trail. Visitors can either plot a cross-
country trek that links a different inn each night, or
choose to stay at just one inn and use it as a base camp for
day trips. One of the more popular areas, the Green
Mountains in central Vermont, boasts lodges such as the
Mountain Top Inn. Its 70 miles of marked trails helped
convince the U.S. Olympic Ski Team to designate it as an
official training site in 1986.

Season: Winter

north carolina

Some of the most romantic islands in the world line
the coast of North Carolina. Called the Outer Banks, this
chain of barrier islands acts as a front line of defense
against the wind-whipped waves of the Atlantic.

❗ conservation alert

offshore danger

⬤ Although the designation of National Seashore was intended to ensure that Cape Hatteras in North Carolina wouldn't fall victim to the rampant development sullying much of the rest of the nation's coasts, the Outer Banks are not completely safe. A huge threat lurks just offshore. Recently the federal government opened an area three miles off the tip of Cape Hatteras to oil and gas drilling. Mobil Oil Corporation has already begun exploratory drilling for natural gas.

Many people dependent on the Outer Banks fear energy development will damage the delicate ecosystem and ruin an age-old way of life based on commercial fishing and tourism. One look at these delicate wetlands that act as a nursery for fish and shorebirds reveals how difficult it would be for the Cape Hatteras area to withstand any punishment inflicted by coastal development, oil spills, or the massive amounts of air and water pollution generated by offshore drilling rigs.

Seafaring tales of exploration, piracy, and shipwrecks pepper the history of North Carolina's islands. Little has changed along the Outer Banks from hundreds of years ago when the Italian explorer Giovanni da Verrazano first saw them in 1524, when Sir Walter Raleigh's Lost Colony settled nearby, when Blackbeard pirated the coast, and when the unpredictable waters earned it the reputation as "The Graveyard of the Atlantic."

outer banks, outer limits

The 175-mile-long Outer Banks is teeming with life. Fifty miles offshore lies the Point, a submarine limestone reef washed by the Gulf Stream. The resulting upwellings and currents create a bounty of food for marlin, tuna, king mackerel, whale, dolphin, and sea turtle and also attracts seabirds by the hundreds of thousands. Species include puffin, skua, northern fulmar, glaucous gull, storm petrel, and even albatross up from Antarctica in search of feeding grounds.

The crown jewel in the chain of sandy shoals is the 75 miles of coastline surrounding Cape Hatteras. The Cape's seaside beaches, marshes, lighthouses, and quiet inlet waters are considered so valuable that in 1937 they were designated as the first National Seashore, one of ten such coastal parks in the nation.

Season: Year-round

florida

Just 50 miles west of downtown Miami flows one of the strangest rivers in the world, the Everglades. One hundred miles long, 50 miles wide, and just six inches deep, this shallow, slow-moving waterway covers most of southern Florida in one wide sheet. During the wet season, it brings to life an interdependent web of ecosystems, including fresh-water prairies, sloughs, mangrove swamps, and coastal marshes.

Everglades National Park was established in 1947 and has become one of the country's most visited national parks. This fascinating and fragile ecosystem needs to be seen by water to be fully appreciated. The wonders of the Everglades are best explored by canoe. Visitors can follow a number of well-marked water trails. The rewards of paddling through inland waterways and camping on secluded beaches along the coastal keys or in old mangrove clearings include the opportunity to see flocks of white ibises filling the sky like clouds, hear the slap of an alligator's tail as it breaks the surface of an algae-covered pond, and watch a baby manatee swimming beside its mother in the crystal waters.

Season: Winter

The Florida Everglades nurtures a who's who of wildlife, just as all wetlands do. Only Florida's celebrities are a bit more glamorous. Its most famous residents include the alligator, panther, wood stork, flamingo, spoonbill, and bobcat.

canada

Canada's enormous far north remains one of the most unexplored and least visited regions on Earth. Similar to Alaska, only much larger, the Canadian wilderness consists of mountain scenery, lakeshore serenity, backcountry wildlife, tundra expanse, and great coastal beauty.

polar bear watch

On a map, Hudson Bay looks like something took a big bite out of Canada—something on the order of a polar bear. In winter, hundreds of polar bears live on the pack ice of Hudson Bay. But when summer arrives, the ice begins to melt, and winds drive it south—winds so fierce that onshore only the branches on the southern side of trees survive. Forced into a migratory circle, polar bears are set adrift on rudderless rafts of ice and eventually land on the bay's southern shores. From there, they must trek north along the western shores of Hudson Bay where, once again, they take to the ice to find a plentiful supply of seals, their primary food.

The bear's migration route takes them through the tiny grain port of Churchill, Manitoba. The unavoidable confrontation between polar bears and the human inhabitants of Churchill use to result in many bears being shot every year. But now, with increased tourist interest and a new awareness of the importance of conservation, Churchill's residents allow the great animals to migrate safely through town. In turn, Churchill has become the polar-bear-viewing capital of the world.

Season: October

harp seal watch

Each March, 250,000 harp seals enter Canada's Gulf of St. Lawrence to bear their young on vast floating ice fields just west of the Magdalen Islands. The seal pups are born with white fur, which turns gray within three weeks. For centuries, seal hunters would descend on the ice floes and club the helpless pups for their fur. At the end of 1987, the Canadian government bowed to pressure from conservationists to stop the slaughter. Today, the International Fund for Animal Welfare is working toward creating a tourist industry to replace lost income to the sealing communities.

You can travel by helicopter to the ice floes to get a firsthand look at these enduring seal pups.

Season: February and March

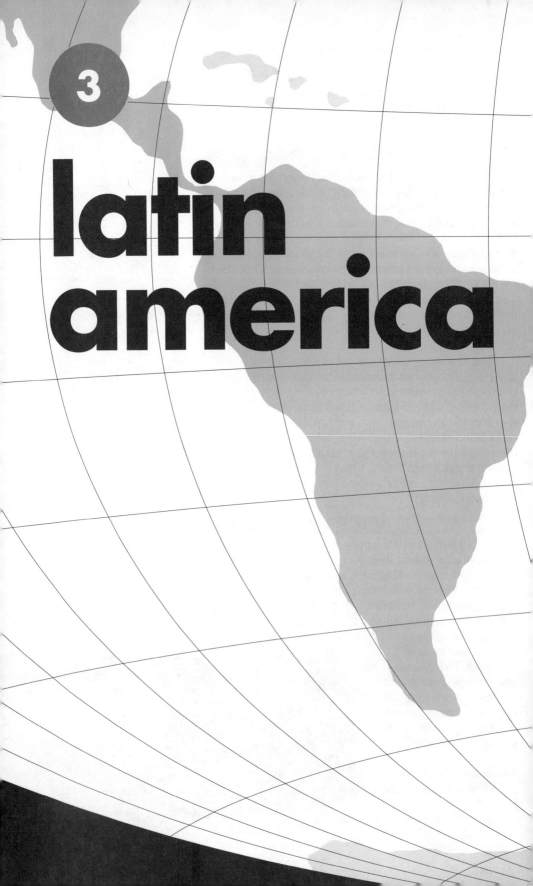

3

latin america

- More than 44 million acres of Amazonian lands have been returned to more than 156,000 indigenous peoples of the Amazon, forming the largest single reserve of its kind in the world.

- Brazil has lost 95 percent of its original forest cover to logging and agriculture, and its unique rainforests remain endangered. Many are working to save it.

- Four hundred years ago, 70 to 80 percent of Mexico's land mass was blanketed by natural vegetation. Today, no more than 35 percent of the land remains in its natural state. New laws have been enacted to preserve Mexico's biological diversity and richness.

- The Pantanal—swampland shared by Brazil, Bolivia, and Paraguay—is one of the most important wildlife habitats in South America, but has been poorly protected. Now, ecotourism is helping.

latin america

Stretching from the Tropic of Cancer to the Antarctic Circle, Latin America encompasses a spectrum of environments and cultures that eclipses most other regions on Earth. Complex and fascinating in their intricacy and diversity, the destinations that make up this part of the world challenge the spirit as well as the mind.

The possibilities for adventure and personal discovery in Latin America are as limitless as the terrain. Great whales give birth in the sheltered seas of Baja California. Jaguars stalk the darkened rainforest of Belize. Flocks of macaws the color of flames streak across Venezuelan skies. Ruins of ancient empires beckon discovery in Peru. And indigenous cultures who defy civilization strive to keep their traditions alive in the heart of the Amazon.

Yet the future of these amazing sights—and sites—is in jeopardy. Explosive population growth, poverty, foreign debt, and multilateral-aid policies have unleashed the environmental equivalent of the Furies. Wave after succeeding wave of migrants sully the Amazon and strip the rainforest of its vegetation and its wildlife. Uncontrolled development crowds the coast of Mexico, while mines pollute the Andes.

mexico

Mexico's proximity to the United States makes it an ideal travel destination. But convenience is not the only reason for the ecotraveler to visit this vast and varied country. Land-bridged between the northern temperate and southern tropical realms, Mexico's biological richness is exceeded only by Brazil, Colombia, and Indonesia. An extraordinary diversity of plant and animal species combine with a dramatic range of topography—lowland and mountain tropical forests, natural grasslands, temperate forests and alpine meadows, deserts, and diverse marine systems—to span the ecological spectrum.

Four hundred years ago, 70 to 80 percent of Mexico's land mass was forested or blanketed by natural, undisturbed vegetation. Today, no more than 35 percent of the land remains in near-natural state. Estimates show that between 700,000 and 1 million hectares (a hectare is about 2.47 acres) of natural plant life are altered completely or severely damaged each year.

Mexico relies heavily on the health and wealth of its natural resources. The nation's economy is based largely on its abundance of land and water. The livelihood of the

❗ conservation alert

preserving the selva lacandona in chiapas

⬤ At Mexico's southeastern tip—tucked between Oaxaca on the west, Yucatan and Guatemala on the east, and the Gulf of Mexico and Pacific Ocean to the north and south—lies Chiapas, one of Mexico's most culturally and biologically diverse states. Chiapas harbors the last major uninterrupted expanses of tropical wet forest in the country—the Selva Lacandona.

The state's wildlands and the Selva Lacandona are changing with rapid rural population growth and increasing demand for land, water, wildlife, timber, and oil resources. With the support of national and local leadership, however, Chiapas' state institutions are becoming more aware of the need to preserve the ecosystems on which they so vitally depend.

Recently, the government has begun a comprehensive program to make education and conservation of natural resources the cornerstones of the area's development. Two pilot projects by Conservation International are also taking place in Chiapas' critical buffer zones. They include butterfly management, agricultural forestry, and ecotourism.

Mexican people also depends largely on the productivity of soils, the abundance of drinking water, and the forest's bounty—including wood for fuel and building materials, wildlife, and a variety of forest products.

Recently, Mexico has adopted a new conservation agenda that recognizes the need to preserve as much genetic diversity as possible, and the country is taking action to preserve the wide variety of flora and fauna within its ecosystems. Not only have new laws been passed, but new conservation units, or extensions of existing ones, have been given the green light—based in part on biological importance. Federal and state governments are working together to protect and manage the nation's wildlife. In addition, the federal government has increased much-needed funding to its Secretariat of Urban Development and Environment and most recently has begun raising loans and grants to help fund its environmental programs.

Conservation International has directly assisted nonprofit conservation organizations to create and expand several protected natural areas. These include the Sierra de Manantlan, Sian Ka'an, and El Triunfo biosphere reserves totaling some 5 million acres.

● Bursting with diverse and abundant marine life and dotted with more than fifty-five pristine islands—most of which harbor unique plant and animal species—the Gulf of California (formerly the Sea of Cortez) is becoming more and more environmentally vulnerable. Nestled between the Baja Peninsula and the mainland of Mexico, this 100,000-square-mile desert sea is increasingly buffeted by winds of social and economic, as well as natural change.

In 1984, Conservation International staff members began supporting a unique, pioneering effort of research and protection of the sea-bird colonies on the gulf's Midriff Islands along with the people of the region. Over the course of a few years, a team of local researchers and committed biologists gathered a wealth of information about the birds' reproductive cycles and the complex web of interrelationships among wild marine life, human environments, and the fragility of the ecosystem. Today, the group has nearly completed the basic inventories and research needed to map out conservation plans for several of the islands.

whale watching in baja california

The azure waters of the Gulf of California (formerly the Sea of Cortez) and the fantastic marine life that inhabit them have been beckoning travelers ever since Doc Ricketts and John Steinbeck celebrated their adventures in Baja California fifty years ago. Schools of bottlenose, common, spotted, spinner, and Pacific white-sided dolphins swim just offshore, while elephant seals mate on deserted island beaches and seabirds by the thousands fill the skies. Along with brown pelicans and Heermann's and yellow-footed gulls, the visitor may spy even more unusual species, including brown and blue-footed boobies, red-billed tropic birds, frigate birds, ibises, and royal terns. Onshore, the uncommon Xantus' hummingbird sips nectar from cactus flowers, while the endemic turquoise lizard scurries across dunes. In fact, 80 percent of the animal species found in Baja and the Gulf of California are native to the region.

But of all the species you can see in Baja, surely the most magnificent and appealing are the whales. Each winter thousands of California gray whales migrate from as far north as the Bering Sea to the sheltered bays and lagoons along this 700-mile-long peninsula. Here they breed, give birth, and nurture their young. In the protected waters of Bahia Magdalena and San Ignacio Lagoon, you may have close encounters with these gentle giants. Board a small skiff or Zodiac and get a water-level view of whales feeding, breaching, and courting. Remember to keep a respectful distance, however. Whales can suffer if watchers don't restrict their actions.

Other whale species inhabit the waters off Baja. Humpbacks sing at the peninsula's tip; blues spout in the southern gulf; and fin, Minke, pilot, and Bryde's whales venture up and down both coasts. Dwarf sperm whales live here, too, but in much fewer numbers. Baja is also home to the totoaba, a large sea bass, and the vaonita, the smallest of the world's cetaceans, both of which are endemic to the region. All in all, 35 percent of the world's marine mammals can be found in Baja California's waters.

The most fulfilling expeditions to Baja include stops at the chain of tiny islets that dot the gulf's waters. These mostly unpopulated islands are home to some of the world's largest seabird nesting colonies. The gulf region is a regular stop along a heavily traveled winter migration route. Take a guided hike and explore spectacular landforms and the unusual plant communities that boast eighty species of cactus and such exotic species as pitaya dulce, elephant tree, Cardons, and devil's claw, along with 570 species of plants. Don't miss an opportunity to snorkel in the warm, clear seas. More than 650 species of tropical fish dot the waters with brilliant color.

Season: January through June

Cloud forests are forests that grow at such lofty elevations that their treetops are in the clouds. The constant moisture in cloud forests is the perfect environment for epiphytes—plants that thrive on the water in the atmosphere and grow on the branches of trees, or on top of one another.

birding in the cloud forest

To travel to El Triunfo Biosphere Reserve in southern Mexico near the Guatemalan border is a step back to primordial times. The reserve contains zones of pristine high-altitude cloud forest protecting neotropical animals. Huge trees laden with orchids tower above the forest floor, and ferns the size of trees reach heights of 40 feet. A rich and varied community of bird life matches the spectacle of plant life, making El Triunfo one of the top birding spots in the world. You can spot such elusive species as the emerald toucanet, blue-throated motmot, and collared trogon. El Triunfo is home to some of the last populations of quetzals and horned guan in Mexico and is the only place one can reliably see the rare azure-rumped tanager.

Besides world-class birding, a trip to El Triunfo affords an opportunity to explore the wilds of the cloud forest on foot, learn about its unique ecology, and enjoy its unparalleled beauty and serenity.

Season: Spring

la ruta maya

Long before Hernán Cortés and his band of conquistadors explored the Americas, a civilization that rivaled the ancient Egyptians flourished from Mexico's Yucatan Peninsula to what is now northern Honduras. During their reign, the Mayans erected stone cities of towering pyramids and elaborately decorated temples in the jungle. These archaeological sites are now the foundation of an ambitious ecotourism project aimed at protecting them and their rainforest setting.

When complete, La Ruta Maya, as envisioned by such noted conservationists as William Garrett, former editor of National Geographic, will consist of a vast network of trails spanning parts of the rainforest inhabited by the Mayans. The trails will take visitors to spectacular ruins of this ancient Indian civilization. Some of these sites date to 250 B.C. The trails will reach pristine beaches as well as dense tropical rainforests.

In the middle of the 7-million-acre network will be a 3-million-acre "peace park"—a park that spans more than a single country. Along the way, research stations will coexist with tourist facilities. Revenues from the new enterprises will provide jobs for residents and will support the guards, park rangers, and other officials needed for park management. The adventurous may hike through the rainforest, raft down rivers, snorkel along coral reefs, and see an astonishing assemblage of wildlife surrounding remote villages where traditions have survived for 3,000 years.

Though full realization of the project remains years off, you can now explore sections of La Ruta Maya. The town of Palenque in the southern state of Chiapas is the perfect gateway. Its hilltop temples, built one thousand years ago, are some of the best-preserved archaeological sites in all of Central America. Particularly impressive is the Pyramid of the Inscriptions and its elaborately decorated Sarcophagus of the Sun God. From Palenque, you can take a raft trip on the Rio Usumacinta into the heart of the Mayan rainforest. The river serves as the border between Mexico and Guatemala, and links several important Mayan sites. Look for colorful birds and monkeys in the trees lining the banks. This region has as many species of birds as the United States and Canada combined.

Season: Year-round

belize

From rainbow-hued parrotfish to gaudy-beaked toucans, from coral islands to dense rainforests, Belize conjures up visions of jungle-covered Mayan ruins, jaguars, and howler monkeys. Located in the Gulf of Honduras next to the southeastern corner of the Yucatán Peninsula, this tiny Caribbean-Creole country the size of New Hampshire was once a British colony. Although it boasts some of the most fascinating natural history in the world, this destination remains among the least known. Because of its size, it's possible to take in the principal environmental attractions of Belize with a single tour.

reefs, ruins, and rainforests

In the turquoise waters that lap the white-sand beaches and mangrove waterways of Belize lies the world's second largest coral reef. Beneath the sea exists a fragile world of coral built by tiny creatures of antiquity more plant than animal. Color-saturated walls of living matter shield eels that spring like ghoulish jack-in-the-boxes. Elegantly armored crabs scuttle after leftovers dropped by sharks. Clouds of translucent, bug-eyed shrimp swirl over coral gardens. And everywhere you look, masses of fish in fluorescent colors and eccentric shapes spin and zigzag in a nonstop carousel of color.

Above the sea, thousands of sea birds flock. Offshore islands provide shelter and rookeries for such species as boat-billed heron, frigate bird, and red-footed booby. Onshore, clear limestone pools and countless unexplored caves dot a lush green tropical highland criss-crossed by cool rivers and noisy waterfalls. Inland borders contain a wide variety of productive habitats and an abundance of dependent wildlife species. Citroline trogons inhabit mangrove swamps, yellow-headed parrots fly in the wild, and East Coast warblers come to winter in paradise—just a few examples of the country's 500 species of exotic birds.

Private reserves and an internationally designated biosphere have been established to protect Belize's rainforest and the species that dwell within it. One of the most popular, **Cockscomb Jaguar Sanctuary**, was established by the Belizean government in 1986 as the first reserve in the world set aside to protect prime jaguar habitat. Four other cats share this richly forested 3,500-acre park with the spotted feline—puma, margay, jaguarundi, and the endangered ocelot. Another fascinating preserve is **Chan-Chich**. This private reserve sits among thousands of

The Rio Bravo Conservation Area in Belize is a birdwatcher's paradise. The 152,000-acre preserve protects the great curacao and orange-breasted falcon as well as such mammals as the tapir, jaguar, and ocelot. Visitors can watch spider monkeys climbing through the trees and listen to the raucous howls of howler monkeys and the cries of margay and jaguarundi.

In 1985, Coca-Cola Foods purchased 200,000 acres in Belize with an eye on using 30,000 acres for citrus groves and building a processing plant.

When a coalition got wind of the deal, they sent a letter to Coca-Cola warning them that they would launch a campaign to boycott the soft drink. Their slogan was "Save the Rain Forests—Stop Drinking Coke."

Coca-Cola Foods soon shelved the project and donated 42,000 acres to the Programme for Belize, a nonprofit group funded by the Massachusetts Audubon Society and others.

natural success

biosphere reserves—more than just parks

The number of parks set aside to protect wilderness and wildlife has been increasing dramatically since the first national park was established in America in 1872. In a race against time, Conservation International and other environmental groups are working not only to continue this trend, but also to assure that these reserves are established and managed to provide sufficient protection for fragile ecosystems and the multitude of life forms that depend upon them.

Ideally, a reserve needs to be very large to support a range of plant and animal life, and some ecosystems, such as rainforests, need more space than others. To maintain biodiversity, reserves also need to be situated in areas that contain as many different species as possible.

The biggest news about how conservationists approach their task in the latter part of the twentieth century lies in the art of drawing boundaries. Traditional parks were like ponds fenced off with a single stroke—wild protected lands within its boudaries and unprotected populated areas outside. Parks set up in this way have been increasingly vulnerable to erosion by social and economic pressures.

During the last fifteen years, however, conservationists have developed the broader concept of the biosphere reserve. This new approach to protection consists of a core of pristine wilderness, large enough for plants and animals to thrive and reproduce undisturbed, surrounded by wide, insulating buffer zones in which some human activity is permitted. This can range from wood-gathering, occasional hunting, and some ecotourism, to the establishment of small settlements and research stations in the outer rings.

Essential to the concept of the biosphere reserve is cooperative management by local residents, scientists, government agencies, and various environmental groups. Developing and managing biosphere reserves is a complex and challenging task for everyone involved. It also may be the most critical challenge of our time.

acres of lush tropical forest. Grass-covered Mayan temples and palaces ring the lodge.

The rainforests of northern Belize conceal more than 600 jungle-veiled Mayan ruins, including such important centers as Lamanai, Cuello, and Altun Ha.

Season: Year-round

costa rica

According to legend, Christopher Columbus gave Costa Rica its name—it means "rich coast" in Spanish—in the belief it contained vast quantities of gold. It turned out that the precious yellow metal wasn't so easy to find, but the country has been blessed with an even greater wealth: an exquisite countryside and a bewildering diversity of plant and animal life.

In recent years, the government of this narrow country half the size of Virginia and sandwiched between the Caribbean Sea and the Pacific Ocean has established an enviable network of national parks and forests—and none too soon. Costa Rica's rich forests had been diminished by more than one-third over the past thirty years, primarily to provide grazing land for cattle. Nonprofit groups and the private sector have responded in kind, adding privately owned and operated nature preserves to Costa Rica's growing inventory of protected areas. Together, their efforts have placed 12 percent of the country's territory off-limits to logging, clearcutting, and slash-and-burn farming. In the process, Costa Rica has become a supernova of conservation, a model of ecotourism, and an unparalleled opportunity for the nature traveler.

exploring costa rica's national parks

Costa Rica's national park system ranks among the finest in the world. Divided into thirty-four units, park lands include coral reefs on both coasts, wet areas such as mangroves, rainforests, tropical dry forests, cloud forests, volcanoes, and high-altitude heaths. The system also protects caves, historic and archaeological sites, and beaches of scenic and ecological importance, including nesting grounds for sea turtles.

The accessibility of these areas, as well as their relative closeness, enables visits to various parks and reserves in the course of just one or two weeks.

Poas Volcano National Park. Overlooking Costa Rica's Central Valley, this site centers around one of the deepest active volcanoes in the world. Poas still emits a continuous flow of steam from vents deep within the main crater. A second crater, located about one-half mile higher in the park, shimmers with an emerald lake rimmed by lush highland jungle. Many of the eighty species of birds reported here are endemic.

Monteverde Cloud Forest National Park. Costa Rica's most famous park, Monteverde preserves what is considered to be the richest and most complex tropical cloud forest in the New World. The abundance of wildlife defies belief. Its boundaries contain six distinct forest

Just when you thought anything you could peel was safe—along come pesticide-laced bananas. According to environmentalists and tour operators, Dole and Chiquita banana plantations on Costa Rica's Caribbean coast near Cahuita National Park have been using pesticides banned in the United States. The chemical is reportedly contaminating groundwater, damaging the nearby coral reef, and may be causing sterility problems for hundreds of plantation workers.

To voice your concern for the health of the people and ecosystems of this region, address your letters to: Luis Manuel Chacon, Ministerio de Turismo, Apdo. 777-1000, San José, Costa Rica; and Hernan Bravo, Ministerio de Recursos Naturales, Energia y Miñas, Apdo. 10104-1000, San José, Costa Rica.

natural success

nature without boundaries in la amistad

La Amistad is the Spanish word for "friendship." Located on the pristine and wild Talamanca Mountain Range of Southeast Costa Rica and West Panama, **La Amistad Biosphere Reserve and International Park** is the most successful peace park established anywhere to date. This is one of Conservation International's flagship projects, and the largest biosphere conservation project in the world.

Designed to promote cooperation, peace, and conservation between two or more countries, peace parks protect plants, animals, and the cultures of indigenous peoples—all of which recognize no national boundaries.

Covering more than 1.5 million acres in Costa Rica, La Amistad accounts for 12 percent of that country's territory. In Panama, the park covers more than 1.2 million acres. Taken together, this area is the largest functioning binational protected area in Latin America.

types. Each supports its own separate yet intertwined plant and animal community. The preserve acts as a gigantic greenhouse, containing more than 2,000 species of plants, including a wide array of orchids, mosses, ferns, and bromeliads.

This lush profusion of tropical plants provides an exotic backdrop for an equally incredible assortment of animals. Monteverde's most famous avian resident, the resplendent quetzal, sports bright plumes and long, colorful tail feathers. Other colorful species include the keel-billed toucan, bare-necked umbrellabird, three-wattled bellbird, and buffy tuffetcheek. At least 300 additional species can be seen. Among the 100 species of mammal are black howler monkey, agouti, and brocket deer. The rare golden toad, the most brightly colored of all toads, was first discovered in the Monteverde Cloud Forest.

Manuel Antonio National Park. The smallest of Costa Rica's famous national parks, Manuel Antonio lies along the Pacific Coast in the transition zone between the southern wet forest and northern dry forest. This meeting of ecozones creates a mix of habitats that sustains a diverse number of species. Towering ceiba trees festooned with colorful orchids punctuate the closed-canopy rainforest. More than 1,500 different types of orchids bloom in Costa Rica. The large and healthy mammal population features such easily sighted species as squirrel and white-faced monkeys, three-toed sloth, and agouti. More than 350 different species of birds wing through the park, including white-crowned parrots and blue-crowned manakins. Along the coast, you'll see brown pelicans and brown boobies.

Tortuguero National Park. Originally protected as a major nesting beach for the Atlantic green turtle, Tortuguero preserves more than 52,000 acres of tropical rainforest in its natural state. Giant 700-pound leatherback sea turtles heave and sigh as they lay up to a hundred eggs in the sand while river otters play in inland waterways. Caimans, iguanas, river turtles, and poison-dart frogs bask on the shores. Among the more than 320 species of birds here are all the kingfisher species found in the New World, as well as toucans, parrots, and trogons.

Braulio Carrillo National Park. Located just north of San José, the capital of Costa Rica, this new park is also one of the country's largest. Rivers have cut steep, vertical canyons through beautiful, thickly forested mountains. Tree ferns, heliconias, and palm trees are among the more than 6,000 plant species that grow here. The park also protects mountain lions, jaguars, ocelots, tapirs, tayras, banded anteaters, sloths, coatis, and three species of monkeys.

Corcovado National Park. Accessible by chartered plane, Corcovado protects the largest tract of tropical rainforest on Costa Rica's Pacific Coast. Jaguars and ocelots stalk tapir and white-lipped peccaries, while scarlet macaws streak the sky red.

Season: December through April, July through August

Mount Roraima rises out of Venezuela's steamy southern jungles, a tabletop mountain bedecked by sculpted rock formations, odd-shaped crystals, and bizarre carnivorous plants. So surreal is this place that, after attending a lecture on Roraima, Sir Arthur Conan Doyle was inspired to pen his tale of prehistoric creatures surviving in present-day South America, *The Lost World.*

venezuela

Besides being home to the world's highest waterfall, Venezuela offers the environmental adventurer a rich tapestry of well-preserved habitats: coral reefs, Caribbean beaches, jungle rivers, rainforests, and sandstone mountains. The mix of ecozones nurtures a diverse array of wildlife, making this country one of the best in tropical South America for observing animals, especially mammals.

llanos and guayana highland

The remote and generally inaccessible interior of the Llanos and Guayana Highlands safeguards some of the world's most exciting wildlife. The Llanos, a vast inland prairie of more than 220,000 square miles, shelters such species as giant anteater, red howler monkey, and giant anaconda. All three New World storks live here—jabiru, maguari, and wood.

The Guayana Highlands comprises nearly half of Venezuela's total area but contains less than 10 percent of its human population. The highlands feature grand savannahs and tepuis—spectacular sandstone mountains that tower thousands of feet above the jungle floor. Angel Falls plummets 3,281 feet down the face of the most famous mountain, Auyan-tepui.

Season: April through June, November through December

cruising the caribbean coast and orinoco

From the undersea gardens of its Caribbean islánds to the lush rainforests of the Orinoco River, northern Venezuela offers a wealth of natural beauty. The Caribbean islands of Bonaire and Los Roques Archipelago harbor some of the finest marine environments anywhere. Their coral reefs invite great snorkeling and scuba diving. On the sheltered islands of **Los Roques National Park**, you can literally walk for miles on sandbars that extend into aquamarine waters so transparent and filled with sea life, you'll feel as if you're walking through an aquarium. Starfish, conches, spiny lobsters, sea turtles, and a multitude of tropical fish species—including the elusive, mirror-bright bonefish—populate these gentle waters.

The mighty Orinoco River constitutes its own ecosystem, one rich in exotic flora and fauna. Orange-winged parrots and blue-yellow macaws brighten the gray sky with mad splashes of color, while snowy egrets and herons dot the shoreline. The indigenous Warao Indians paddle their dugouts along the river, fishing and hunting as they have for generations.

Season: January

ecuador

Straddling the equator, Ecuador is a microcosm of the great biological and geographical variety found in South America. Its backbone, a chain of 21,000-foot-high snow-capped volcanoes, soars above a sea of greenery etched by seemingly countless rivers. The Galapagos Islands lie off its coast. Born of fire, the chain is rightly called the birthplace of evolution. Ecuador's multiplicity of ecozones is matched only by its diversity of wildlife. The influences of colonial Spain and native traditions also make for a vital and colorful blend of cultures.

The Andes Mountains are one of the world's greatest watersheds, hence Ecuador's large number of exciting, navigable rivers. A river raft expedition through the country's lush countryside brings you face to face with wildlife and remote Indian tribes. Such a river is the Toachi, which courses through Valle Hermosa—its name means "beautiful valley" in Spanish. The Cayapas River flows into the homeland of the Cayapas Indians, one of the many indigenous tribes still surviving along the South American equator.

highlands of the andes

The glacier-crusted volcanic peaks of the Andes serve as the top of the world in South America. Ecuador's spectacular mountain scenery rivals that of the Himalayas. Lush highlands flank these towering precipices like enormous patchwork quilts. Squares of cultivated farmland alternate with patches of wild, aromatic vegetation populated by colorful tiny frogs, hummingbirds, llamas, and condors.

Much of Ecuador's large Indian population lives in these remote highlands. The people resist acculturation and retain pride in their dress and customs. They hike down from their mountain homes to trade handmade crafts, such as woven blankets and Panama-style hats, for food and other goods at outdoor markets held weekly in the larger villages. An even more ancient Indian culture once lived here—the Incas. At sites like Ingapirca, archaeologists still excavate the remnants of this once-powerful civilization.

South of Quito, Ecuador's capital city, stretches the Avenue of the Volcanoes, a scenic high-altitude route that runs through incredible scenery and into a network of wildlife-rich national parks and reserves. You can climb a volcanic peak at **Cotopaxi National Park**; trek through the land of Puruha Indians in the foothills of **Mount Chimborazo**; look for rainbow starfrontlets, violet-throated metaltails, and other species of hummingbird at **Cajas National Park;** and ride horses through the **Mazan Forest Reserve**, home of strikingly colorful plant life and equally colorful bird life.

Season: Summer and fall

exploring ecuador's amazon basin

On the eastern slope of the Andes, Ecuador drops precipitously into the upper Amazon basin. Huge rivers course through seemingly endless jungles of tropical rainforests. Strange and wonderful creatures dwell in the thick canopy of trees that shade the jungle floor. More than 1,400 species of birds have been recorded in Ecuador and in the country's eastern rainforests. No doubt more await identification.

However, parts of the Ecuadoran rainforest have suffered greatly from oil development that has left huge chunks cleared and contaminated by oily wastes. Logging and slash-and-burn farming has destroyed still more wildlife habitat.

What remains needs immediate protection. A few preserves have already been established. In the government-protected **Cuyabeno Nature Reserve**, macaws and parrots flock while fresh-water dolphins,

The Amazon is the world's longest and mightiest river. In the time it takes you to read this sentence, the Amazon will pump 4,200,000 cubic feet of water into the sea. The river serves as the surrounding rainforest's lifeline. Countless tributaries flow into it. Around them grow myriad ecosystems, each of them unique, all of them complex.

The river provides the ideal vehicle for exploring the more remote regions of South America from the mountain regions of Ecuador to the vast Brazilian interior. The larger expeditionary-class cruise ships are restricted to the Amazon and the major waterways, but by smaller craft, you can explore the maze of tributaries. This is the only way to penetrate the green wall that lines the banks of the main river.

manatees, and piranhas ply the rivers and lakes. Orchids and bromeliads bloom in mad profusion, providing a stark contrast to the infinite wall of greenery. In the evenings, you can drift along rivers searching for caiman, agouti, paca, and other night-roaming animals.

Season: Year-round

darwin's islands

When Charles Darwin explored the Galapagos Islands aboard the *Beagle* in 1835, he changed the way we view the world. The strange and wonderful wildlife that inhabit this archipelago 600 miles off the coast of Ecuador inspired Darwin's theory of evolution. Today, the islands continue to attract and inspire.

The Galapagos, comprised of six main islands, twelve smaller islands, and forty islets, were never part of the mainland. Instead, they are giant volcanoes that have risen from the sea floor. Volcanic activity still takes place, and you can often see wisps of smoke curling from the fumaroles on the islands of Volcan, Isabela, and Fernandina.

Because of their isolation, most of the wildlife that live on the Galapagos descended from a handful of species that made their way over from the mainland either by flying or riding natural rafts borne by currents. As time went by, the creatures adapted themselves to the islands' harsh conditions and came to differ more and more from their continental ancestors. Darwin's celebrated finches exemplify "speciation"—twelve species of birds all evolved from a single ancestor.

No large land mammals reached the islands, so the dominant species were reptiles, just as they had been all over the world in the very distant past. The largest are giant tortoises. Marine iguanas—the only sea-going lizards in the world—also populate the Galapagos. They survive on seaweed. Land iguanas live here in great numbers as well.

The islands' avifauna is nothing short of spectacular. Unique species include the Galapagos albatross—you can see pairs of these ungainly fliers perform their mating ritual by clacking bills with each other like castanets. You may also see trios of colorful boobies—masked, red-footed, and blue-footed—as well as pink flamingos, frigate birds, and swallow-tailed and dusky lava gulls.

Because of the absence of natural predators and the islands' long-protected status

! conservation alert

rainforests of the amazon

● The Amazon forest is the largest tract of tropical forest on Earth, with roughly 3.7 million square miles spreading over nine countries. Fully 60 percent of the Amazon region falls within the borders of Brazil. These forests are home to the greatest variety of living organisms on Earth, including vast numbers of species that are as yet undiscovered and undescribed by science, especially among the invertebrates and plants. The Amazon region has been targeted as the new frontier for resource exploitation in Brazil, with the result that it has already lost approximately 12 percent of its forest cover.

Already declared as conservation units in this area are: the largest park in Brazil (Jau National Park), the largest river archipelago in the world (Anavilhanas Ecological Station), and Brazil's highest mountain peak (Pico da Neblina National Park). Two reserves for indigenous people are also located in the Amazon: the Ianomani and the Waimiri Atroari.

The future of much of Amazonia's tropical rainforest depends on finding appropriate alternatives to ongoing activities that destroy the forest. A few small-scale projects have shown that multiple use of the forest pays better in the long run than destructive alternatives do, while at the same time conserving biological diversity. These projects include extracting sustainable crops—such as fruits, nuts, oils, rattan, latex, resins, medicinal plants—products that depend upon saving the rainforest from further destruction. The first "extractive reserve" was established in 1988, in Sao Luiz do Remanso, Acre State.

as a national park, the animals remain, for the most part, unafraid of humans. This allows visitors to get excellent close-up views. You won't need a telephoto lens to snap the denizens of this "separate center of creation," as Darwin called this island paradise.

But because of the growing popularity of this destination, the Galapagos Islands also represent an excellent example of the pros and cons of nature travel. As well-intentioned as visitors may be, this truly unique and historic island ecosystem is beginning to suffer under the strain of too many tourists embarking upon its shores. If you do decide to visit the Galapagos, it's especially important to make sure your guides are well-trained, stick to designated trails, and follow the rules of responsible ecotourism.

Season: Year-round

❗ conservation alert

pick up your feet, pick up trash

At the height of the Inca empire, Peru was criss-crossed by a vast network of Inca roads and trails. They followed valleys and traversed the Andes, frequently tracing impossible pathways—narrow routes along precipitous slopes carved out of living rock. The most famous of these roads is the **Camino Inca**, or Inca Trail, a 20-mile footpath built more than 500 years ago, that links the lost city of Machu Picchu with the Inca capital of Cuzco. The five-day hike has become the most popular trek in South America, attracting 6,000 hikers a year. The route passes through rare examples of cloud forest environments, habitat of unique wildlife such as the Andean spectacled bear, Andean condor, and more than ninety species of delicate orchids. Native Quechua Indians, a living legacy of the former Inca culture, live along the way. But most of all, the route connects the only standing system of Inca architectural ruins remaining from the ancient empire.

So important is this cultural resource that it has been designated by the Peruvian Government as the **Machu Picchu National Park** and recognized by the United Nations as a World Heritage Site. Unfortunately, the fragile natural and cultural resources of the park have suffered more damage in the past decade than in the previous four centuries. Inconsiderate and irresponsible trekkers have befouled the trail with trash. Campfires have been built in ruins and caused stones to crack, weakening their structure. Overuse of popular campsites has led to erosion and further structural instability.

Peruvian conservation organizations and local tour operators recently published a trail map with new regulations and suggestions to tell hikers how they can minimize their impact. A new local advisory committee has been appointed in Cuzco. The efforts to make sure that the Inca Trail and Machu Picchu National Park will remain for future generations will only succeed if trekkers help.

If you want to join a tax-deductible cleanup trek, contact Wildland Adventures, 3516 N.E. 155th St., Seattle, WA 98155; (206) 365-0686; 1-800-345-4453. The objective of this service trip is to beautify this sacred area by collecting litter left behind by thoughtless trekkers. Trekkers help collect litter at frequently used camp and rest sites. Extra porters haul out the debris, and horses accompany the group up to the first pass and haul out the garbage collected up to that point. The cleanup trek is co-sponsored by The Earth Preservation Fund and ECCO, a Peruvian conservation organization.

peru

Much of the news about Peru lately has focused on its economic woes, its cholera epidemic, and the terrorist activities of a group of Maoist insurrectionists, the Sendero Luminosa. (Safety precautions, both medical and political, should be strictly observed when embarking on a journey to any foreign land.)

But the real story behind the headlines remains Peru's incomparable geography, wildlife, and cultural heritage. Bisected by a dizzying chain of volcanic peaks and glaciers, Peru is flanked by desert on its western edge and raw jungle on its eastern edge. It is the birthplace of the Amazon River and cradle of one of the most powerful civilizations ever to rule pre–Colombian Latin America, the Incas. Peru's wildlife-rich rainforests, challenging whitewater rivers, and mountain wilderness also helped spawn the concept of adventure travel.

trekking to lost civilizations

Gray stone temples perch in the cloud forest as mute testimony to a race of people who worshipped the sun. The ancient priests and chosen princesses that inhabited the hidden citadel of Machu Picchu have been silent now for half a millennia, but their souls and spirits live on.

Machu Picchu is the proverbial pot of gold at the end of the rainbow when you reach it the traditional way by walking in the footsteps of the Incas through the symbolic Gateway of the Sun. The four-day trek along the Inca Trail takes you through alpine grasslands and cloud forests and over a 14,200-foot-high pass. The rewards include spectacular vistas, close encounters with wildlife, and the opportunity to follow the paths of antiquity.

The popular trail, however, has suffered in the past from thoughtless trekkers. Local trekking associations aided by international conservationists have developed a set of guidelines to limit the damage. Cleanup of the trail and respect for the areas natural as well as cultural resources is the responsibility of all who visit.

Season: Spring and fall

amazonia

The headwaters of the Amazon River begin high on the eastern slope of the Andes, only 100 miles from the Pacific Ocean as the Andean condor flies. From a trickle of glacier water, the Apurimac River builds up volume as its makes a headlong dash down awesome cataracts and canyons. At the foot of the 21,000-foot range, the land levels out into a broad 2.5 million-square-mile expanse of jungle-covered rainforest that stretches 4,000 miles to the Atlantic.

! conservation alert

the disappearing atlantic forest

● The once-magnificent Atlantic Forest region of Brazil's eastern coast was the first part of the country to be colonized. As a result, the area has lost 95 percent of its original forest cover and is now considered one of the most threatened ecosystems on the planet. The remaining fragmented islands of coastal forest shelter an amazing diversity of animal and plant life, most of it native to the area. But these unique tropical forests continue to be endangered by clearcutting for timber, charcoal, and agriculture. Much of the area has already been destroyed or changed forever by the cocoa industry.

Environmentalists are working hard to preserve what remains. The **Caratinga Biological Station** of **Rio Doce State Park** (about 89,000 acres) in the state of Minas Gerais is one of best examples. This station, administered by Fundacao Biodiversitas, has already demonstrated that ecotourism may be one of the region's most important tools to ensure forest protection and create sustainable income for local people. Many animals here—especially the primates—have become so accustomed to human visitors that the animals are easy to see from a short distance. The fact that the park is great for tourists is also a very useful incentive for conservation.

Two other parks in the Atlantic forests—the **Sooretama** and **Nova Lombardia** reserves—serve as ideal locations for bird-watching. More than a dozen species of hummingbird live here.

Travelers to Brazil may also want to pay a visit to another major wildlife conservation center, the 13,200-acre **Una Biological Reserve** in southern Bahia.

Peru's portion of the Amazon basin was first discovered by Francisco Orellana in 1541. He floated down the Napo River from Ecuador to the point where it enters the Amazon before continuing the rest of the way down river. (During his journey, he was attacked several times by savages he believed to be women, hence his reasoning for naming the uncharted river after the female warriors of Greek mythology.)

Since Orellana's time, the Amazon, its tributaries, and the surrounding basin have been penetrated by countless explorers, followed by waves of settlers in quest of free land. Wholesale destruction of the rainforest has resulted from unchecked slash-and-burn farming and logging. Additional efforts need to be made to protect what remains.

A network of preserves has been established. The towns of Iquitos and Puerto Maldonado serve as the two major gateways to the Peruvian Amazon for visitors. From either, you can take dugout canoes along waterways to even more remote locales. Three hours upriver from Puerto Maldonado is the **Tambopato Nature Reserve.** Approximately 545 species of birds, 100 kinds of dragonflies, and 792 types of butterflies live in a space that covers half the land area of the city of San Francisco. And those are only the ones that have been recorded. Scientists identify new species in the Amazon daily.

Season: Year-round

brazil

Brazil is an environmental force to be reckoned with. Sprawling across 48 percent of the South American continent, Brazil's 2.5-million-square-mile expanse makes it the largest tropical country in the world. Brazil's Amazon region contains the largest fresh-water basin in the world, as well as one-third of all the tropical forests on Earth. With the planet's largest river system and the biggest rainforest, it is not surprising to find that this is also one of the top three biologically diverse nations on Earth. Taken together, these countries account for 70 to 80 percent of the entire planet's biological diversity. There may be 1 million species of living things in Brazil, 85 percent of which are as yet undiscovered.

Unfortunately, Brazil is also the world leader in endangered species. The International Union for conservation of Nature and Natural Resources lists 310 species in Brazil that are vulnerable or threatened with extinction. And every day the region edges ever closer to the brink of ecological disaster. Uncontrolled mining, clearcutting, and slash-and-burn farming have left huge areas of the delicate rainforest in smoldering ruin. As the habitat disappears, so do the wondrous creatures dependent on it for survival.

You have to see this amazing cradle of biodiversity for yourself to realize just how much is at risk. Brazil is still a naturalist's dream come true. And it is also a land of extraordinary contrasts, containing areas of dense development as well as some of the most primitive zones known. Deep in the interior are the last unexplored wilderness areas on Earth, insulating tribes of Stone Age Indians from the outside world. In tragic irony, those peoples that have most successfully avoided contact from outsiders are now being threatened by mercury pollution originating from unregulated industrial activity taking place elsewhere in Brazil.

Iguassu Falls creates one of Brazil's most spectacular sights and sounds. During the wet season as much as 400,000 cubic feet of water crash over this mile-long cataract every second. A subtropical forest, home to numerous exotic plants and animals, surrounds the falls.

cerrados and savannahs

Brazil is not all Amazonian rainforest. Nearly equal in size to the United States, the country contains a variety of ecosystems, including dry grasslands, sun-drenched coastal forests, marshlands, and savannahs. Runaway population growth has destroyed huge portions of Brazil's habitats, but you can still find examples of many in protected national parks.

The cerrado (which means "dry grassland") is the second largest ecosystem in Brazil, covering roughly 28 percent of the country's surface. Located in the central portion of the country, it is a mosaic of vegetation, varying between dense grassland and scattered stands of trees. Since the fertility of its soil was finally discovered in the late 1970s, this region has been experiencing severe development pressures. New agricultural advances have transformed this once unspoiled area into a land of soybeans, one of Brazil's principal exports.

Although not as biologically rich as some other regions, the cerrado ecosystem is home to many unique endangered species that depend on it. **Brasilia National Park** in Central Brazil preserves a fine expanse of cerrado. Here you can spot such colorful bird species as the toco toucan, horned sungem, and firewood-gatherer.

To the south, stands a tall-grass savannah reminiscent of East Africa, protected by **Emas National Park**. Like the Serengeti, large numbers of mammals populate this environment—including pampas deer, giant anteater, tapir, and maned wolf. Birds such as the ostrich-like rhea strut across the plain.

At the **Itatiaia National Park**, located halfway between Rio de Janeiro and São Paulo, the country's second highest mountain has also been preserved. Dark tunnels of bamboo lead you to a bromelaid-laden cloud forest that shelters a wide variety of birds, including owls, cotingas, and tanagers.

Season: July through November

Gallery forests grow along riverbanks in areas otherwise devoid of trees. They get their name from the way they appear in aerial views—as long corridors of green.

the contrasts of caatinga

Brazil's Caatinga region is a land of mystery and contrast. It is the location of the largest meteorite ever to strike Brazil and the site of an enormous petrified forest that has yet to be studied by scientists. It was also the site of a great religious war during the nineteenth century. The fourth largest biogeographic zone in Brazil, the Caatinga region covers approximately 10 percent of the country's territory in the northeast, ranging from closed forest to open, desert-like areas.

Caatinga's climate is marked by extremes—from the wet season, when plants flourish, to the dry season, during which only few plants retain their leaves. As many as a dozen plant communities have been described for the Caatinga—some of which appear highly endangered.

Growing demands of agriculture and cattle pasture continues to threaten this ecosystem. Although Caatinga does not possess a great many native species unique to the area, it is home to two of the most endangered macaws in the world—Lear's macaw and Spix's macaw. The Lear's Macaw Project was established here with the objective of saving this species from extinction. With Conservation International support and the involvement of the area's local population, this project has grown.

Season: Year-round

the pantanal wetlands

Near the Bolivian border in southwest Brazil lies the Pantanal, a vast, seasonally inundated grassland and the largest wetland area in the world. One of the most important wildlife habitats in all of South America, the Pantanal contains a wide variety of mammals and reptiles, and literally teems with hundreds of thousands of water birds. The jabiru, a giant stork, can be seen here by the hundreds. Hyacinth macaws, largest of the parrot family, nest in the scattered clumps of forest while the world's largest rodent, the capybara, feeds among the marshes.

This biologically rich 30-million-acre region is shared by Brazil, Bolivia, and Paraguay, although about 80 percent of it lies within Brazil. One of the last refuges for several endangered species, the Pantanal is composed of a mosaic of vegetation types including low-altitude plains, swamp, gallery forest, lake-margin scrub forest, semi-deciduous forest and cerrado.

But as important as the area is to wildlife, the Pantanal is poorly represented in the state and federal protected-area system. The burning of forests to create grazing land has already greatly affected most of its natural vegetation. Even greater threats are posed by uncontrolled gold mining, fishing, tourism, and wildlife poaching.

Pantanal National Park is located mainly on flooded lands. During the rainy season, the local fauna migrate to upper regions, including the area of **Fazenda Acurizal,** which has become a key area for sustainable conservation efforts such as ecotourism and environmental education.

Season: Year-round

At the Punta Tombo Reserve on the coast of the Peninsula Valdes in Patagonia, the barking of southern sea lions mingles with the roars of elephant seals. Hundreds of thousands of Magellanic penguins congregate at water's edge, one of the largest rookeries of its kind in the world. Southern right whales spout within 100 feet of shore, while killer whales can be observed feeding on errant sea lions and penguins.

patagonia

Windswept pampas, stormy seas, granite spires, forested fjords, glaciers, gauchos, guanacos, whales and penguins, fire and ice—Patagonia has challenged the bravest of explorers for centuries. Amerigo Vespuci probably landed here in 1501, as did Ferdinand Magellan nineteen years later. Paleantologists have sought to unlock its mysteries since the days of Darwin.

At the southern tip of South America, Patagonia points to the bottom of the world. Though two countries—Argentina and Chile—actually share this million-square-mile wilderness, Patagonia really is a land unto itself. Nature has created a profoundly beautiful and dramatic backdrop for the staging of life's unending drama.

Yet despite its wildness, Patagonia is threatened. Argentina has considered relocating its capital from Buenos Aires to Patagonia as a means of stimulating growth in the region, although increased population poses serious consequences to Patagonia's fragile ecosystem. Chile has also extended roads into its Patagonian territory, providing easier access to the region's natural resources—its forests and wealth of mineral deposits, including coal and iron ore.

the patagonia express

Patagonia's remoteness, sparse population, and wild beauty make it an ideal destination for travelers seeking adventure and nature travel. The principal stops on any Patagonian journey include national parks, wildlife reserves, and wilderness areas.

At **Lago Argentino**, a glacial wall of blue ice bisects a pristine lake. Occasionally, huge slabs of ice break off and thunder into the water. Except for the squawking of parakeets, the air is utterly still.

At **Glacier National Park**, located at the foot of the Andes, condors soar high over the steppes while tinamous, dotterels, and tyrants stick closer to ground. Other unusual bird species gather around the lakes that punctuate the park. They include the hooded grebe, considered the most beautiful of its kind in the world, and the rare and bizarre Magellanic plover.

Nearby **Torres del Paine National Park** stands like a giant sculpture garden. Hauntingly beautiful, sheer granite faces rise from a land dotted with spectacular glacial tarns. Trek to Grey Glacier and set foot on the

edge of the Patagonian Ice Cap.

Separated from the tip of Patagonia by the famed Straits of Magellan lies the Land of Fires, Tierra del Fuego. The area's various ecosystems harbor such species as the world's largest woodpecker, as well as pink flamingo and the rare and declining ruddy-headed goose. Visit the world's southernmost city, Ushuaia. Explore the coastline for shipwrecks of bygone explorers. And discover the encampments of ancient Indians whose bonfires gave Tierra del Fuego its name.

Season: October through February

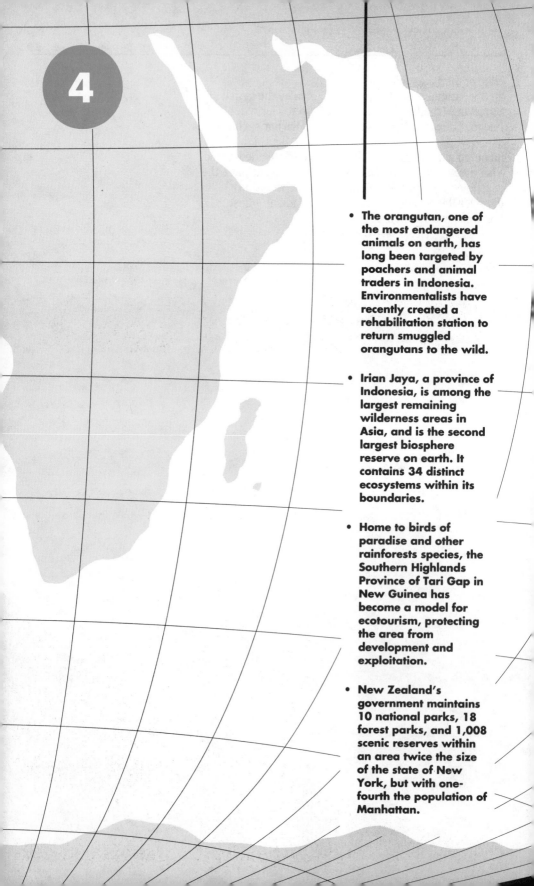

4

- The orangutan, one of the most endangered animals on earth, has long been targeted by poachers and animal traders in Indonesia. Environmentalists have recently created a rehabilitation station to return smuggled orangutans to the wild.

- Irian Jaya, a province of Indonesia, is among the largest remaining wilderness areas in Asia, and is the second largest biosphere reserve on earth. It contains 34 distinct ecosystems within its boundaries.

- Home to birds of paradise and other rainforests species, the Southern Highlands Province of Tari Gap in New Guinea has become a model for ecotourism, protecting the area from development and exploitation.

- New Zealand's government maintains 10 national parks, 18 forest parks, and 1,008 scenic reserves within an area twice the size of the state of New York, but with one-fourth the population of Manhattan.

oceania

oceania

Like a strand of jewels cast upon the sea, the islands of Oceania sparkle with travel possibilities and also are in need of careful protection. One of the largest colonies of orangutans left in the wild lives along the banks of a Sumatran river. Predatory plants lie in wait for unsuspecting insects deep in the forests of Borneo. Sensuous dancers perform in Bali. And in the Eastern Highlands of Papua New Guinea, traditional tribal people adorn body paint and feathered masks to stage living theater, just as they have for centuries. Australia—a continent of extremes—contains the world's largest barrier reef, in addition to saltwater crocodiles, brightly plumed birds, tropical forests, and endless deserts. And New Zealand's countryside alternates between pastoral scenes and alp-like mountains, reminiscent of the best of Europe but without the crowds.

Many countries and cultures comprise Oceania. More than 700 dialects are spoken in the New Guinea archipelago alone, but they all voice a common concern. A sea of environmental problems surrounds the islands of the Pacific. The mounting pressures from overpopulation and runaway industrialization threaten a network of unique ecosystems as vulnerable to human touch as a spider's web. Waves of immigration promise to wash away the traditional way of life for countless tribes of indigenous people. Toxic waste streams from open copper pits and gold mines. And deforestation and attendant erosion have turned many rainforest areas into rutted wastelands.

In too many parts of Oceania, natural resources have been exploited with little regard to sustainable development. While no one expects that ecotourism will alleviate all of the enormous pressures being exerted on Oceania's fragile environment, it is helping out in several instances, as with the orangutans, for example. Support from host governments and foreign visitors alike could improve its chances in other situations as well.

indonesia

Shadow puppets dance on the walls to the mesmerizing lilt of sacred songs and the pulsating clash of gongs. Golden-crowned temples soar to the heavens. Bolts of hand-painted silk stream from exotic marketplace stalls. Flocks of colorfully cloaked birds-of-paradise flap through a seemingly impenetrable wall of trees. And the smell of clove and spice mixes with the smoke of volcanoes. These and myriad sights and sounds make Indonesia a sensory delight.

Indonesia's approximately 17,000 islands are spread across more than 3,000 miles and contain one of the last great wilderness areas in Asia. This biologically diverse nation reaches across two major biogeographic regions: Asia, with its Asian elephants, rhinos, tigers, clouded leopards, and orangutans; and the Melanesian-Australian region, where kangaroos, bandicoots, cuscuses, and echidnas roam. Indonesia's marine ecosystems are also extremely diverse and include some of the world's richest and most productive coral reef, sea turtle, and mangrove habitats.

Indonesia's ethnic, cultural, and religious diversity is also among the greatest in the world. With a total population of about 180 million, Indonesia ranks as the fifth most populated country in the world. Literally hundreds of indigenous societies still depend on forest and marine ecosystems for their cultural and material survival. Eighty percent of the population lives within easy reach of the sea and is sustained largely by a diet of ocean and fresh-water fish.

Komodo dragons, the world's oldest and largest lizards, are protected on a national park on Komodo Island. Tiny islets dot the Flores Sea, ringing coral reefs that bloom like a gigantic submarine garden. And in the highlands of Sulawesi, natives still fashion their homes in the shapes of boats to resemble the legendary ships that carried their ancestors from the stars.

❗ conservation alert

making indonesia's parks count

⬤ Indonesia's strongly centralized government regulates its conservation activities. Following a national conservation plan during the 1980s, dozens of national parks and reserves were decreed, including some of the largest in the world. By 1988, a total of 34.6 million acres (more than 10 percent of Indonesia's lands) were designated as having some form of protection. Marine resources have received less attention than terrestrial systems, with only a small fraction of Indonesia's vast territorial waters under any protected status.

According to Conservation International, no adequate infrastructure exists yet for managing these reserves. Even as new conservation areas are placed under legal protection, existing reserves are diminished by grants to logging and mining concessions and by agricultural encroachment. One of the underlying weaknesses of previous conservation efforts is the failure to involve local communities and governments in the process of defining reserve boundaries. The other is the failure to demonstrate convincingly to Indonesia's political leaders that the conservation of biological diversity is in the national interest. Responsible ecotourism could help.

conservation alert

orangutan rehabilitation station

Deep in the Indonesian rainforest on the island of Sumatra, a conservation group dedicated to saving orangutans by moving them to forests safe from farmers, developers, loggers, poachers, and animal traders has set up a unique rehabilitation station. Orangutans are one of the most endangered animals on Earth. Experts estimate that only 2,000 are left in Sumatra and another 5,000 in Borneo. The worldwide population of red apes has declined drastically in the last decade.

One of the principal causes is the booming illegal animal trade. Though the Convention on International Trade in Endangered Species gives orangutans protected status, officials estimate smugglers take between 50 and 100 orangutans from Indonesia every year. Worse, they say, each smuggled baby represents as many as 15 orangutan mothers and babies that are killed during capture or die in captivity. Babies are typically captured by shooting the mother.

The illegal trade's lucrative nature makes it difficult to halt. Orangutans fetch upwards of $600 each on the black market in Jakarta. Illegal international traders sell the orangutans for $5,000 to wealthy Asians and Westerners. And per capita income in Indonesia averages only $800 per year.

On occasion, alert customs officials have intercepted smuggled orangutans. The World Wildlife Fund then takes the baby apes to the organization's rehabilitation station at Bohorok and teaches them the basic jungle arts of swinging on vines and fending for themselves. Upon graduation, the group's staff reintroduces the orangutans to the wild at nearby **Gunung Leuser National Park**. Another rehabilitation station on the island of Borneo is operated by Orangutan Foundation International.

The rehabilitation stations welcome visitors. The entrance fee helps cover some of the program's costs. Feeding platforms have been set up for the formerly captive orangutans, and you can have a front-row seat to view these rare "men of the forest."

cultural exploration on the islands

Like handmade silk batiks, each of Indonesia's approximately 17,000 islands paints a unique picture. Early explorers such as famed English naturalist Alfred Russell Wallace and Margaret Mead marveled at the archipelago's staggering fusion of cultures and natural heritage. Their tales of dragons roaming the lush countryside, stone deities bigger than life, and Shiva-armed natives dancing

▮conservation alert

keeping the art of the forest alive

●Among the largest remaining wilderness areas in Asia is **Lorentz National Park** in Irian Jaya, the second largest biosphere reserve on Earth. Largely undeveloped and lightly populated, the park presents a monumental challenge for ecosystem conservation, as it contains thirty-four distinct ecosystems within its boundaries. One focus of conservation efforts is on the Bintuni Bay mangrove ecosystem, the largest intact forest of this type in the world.

The park area is also home to the Asmat people whose woodcarving and sculpture is world-renowned. Asmat folk art is used by Indonesia as an artistic flagship, promoted on world tours. However, little is known about what tree species are being used and what their conservation status is as present. Conservation International is examining a proposal to collaborate with local groups on a project to examine the logging of the region's forests and help preserve Asmat art and culture.

in shadows and silk were dismissed as malarial deliriums. But they are real—dragons and all.

The island of Java balances between primordial splendor and cultural extravagance. In the shadow of rumbling volcanoes, islanders hiding behind masks both beautiful and frightening enact legends of magic birds and monkeys. Bali is synonymous with paradise. Palm fronds rustle at turquoise water's edge, while the island's interior looks like a life-sized mosaic whose colorful tiles are made from terraced rice fields and jagged gorges, flooded fields that mirror the sky. On the isle of Sumba, village women weave *ikat* tapestries while men perform the *pasola*, a ritual fought on horseback to appease the gods. On nearby Sawu Island, priests keep a constant vigil at a collection of oracle stones to keep peace with the "upper world."

Season: Year-round

borneo's heart of darkness

Borneo could double as Joseph Conrad's setting for his tale of man's epic battle with nature and his own dark side. The world's third largest island is one of the wildest places on Earth. Borneo lies below the Malay Peninsula. Malaysia governs the upper half of the island, Indonesia the bottom. But the jungle really rules here.

A thick layer of rainforest full of enormous tree ferns, 1,500 species of flowering plants—170 of them orchids—twisting vines that climb and dangle, and troops of human-

▌ conservation alert

the natural riches of borneo

● The third largest island in the world, Borneo contains the most ancient tropical ecosystems on Earth. Borneo's rugged mountainous interior, the Kalimantan, holds the richest number of tree species per unit area ever recorded in a tropical forest and the largest tract of rainforest outside the Amazon.

People have lived and used the resources of the Kalimantan's forests for 40,000 years. Coastal towns arose at the mouths of rivers due to lucrative trade in jungle products, including timber, gums and resins, rattan, nuts, fruit sago flour, aromatic woods, beeswax, animal skins, teeth, claws and horns, bezoar stones from monkeys and porcupines, and edible bird's nests.

With nearly 9 million people now living in Kalimantan, forest resources continue to play an essential role for the regional economy. Borneo's forests contain an extraordinary number of fruit-bearing plants, many of which are cultivated or managed by local people. Species include several kinds of mangoes, bananas, the valuable durian fruit, and a host of others. One recent study found that 10,00 durian fruit were taken to the local market on a single day, yielding about $2,000 in cash income. Medicinal plants, used as an integral part of Indonesian society, also abound in Kalimantan, and trade in these products is a growing export industry to countries such as Thailand where local sources have been destroyed by deforestation.

The two-winged fruit tree, the dominant tree family of Borneo, provides most of the timber rapidly being logged from the lowland forests. However, these trees are also important sources of non-timber forest products, such as the high-quality resins used in art restoration and oil from illipe nuts which is used in cosmetics and as a cocoa-butter substitute.

By helping the people of Borneo to carefully manage their abundant natural resources, conservationists hope to help them preserve the botanical richness and sources of revenue that their environment provides.

Snorkeler's note: Many of Melanesia's coral reefs still thrive in a relatively undisturbed state, and the tropical marine life there is unsurpassed in its beauty and abundance. Marine diversity and especially coral reef diversity reach their global peak in Melanesia with perhaps higher concentrations of species than anywhere else in the tropics. The highest recorded diversity of hard corals and nudibranchs (sea slugs) comes from New Guinea.

The largest island-enclosed lagoon on earth, Marovo Lagoon in the Solomon Islands, is so visibly stunning that author James Michener was moved to call it "the eighth wonder of the world."

sized orangutans who climb the vines like ropes, blankets the island. Within this lush, tropical environment live tribes of indigenous people who continue to observe the ways of their ancestors. Headhunting is no longer practiced here, although it was until the beginning of this century.

Dugout canoes and trekking along footpaths carved by jungle hunters remain the best ways to explore

Borneo's wild heart and experience its hidden spirit.
Season: Summer

rafting the river of the red ape

The Alas River erupts from the highest volcano on the island of Sumatra and courses through jungle gorges beribboned by silvery waterfalls. Along the banks, black-faced gibbons, siamangs, macaques, and leaf monkeys scurry through tangled trees, while more elusive creatures, including monitor lizards, elephants, rhinos, leopards, and tigers, lurk behind a curtain of vines and flowered foliage.

But of all the creatures that inhabit this hidden part of the world, surely the most beguiling and captivating is the "man of the forest," the red ape, the orangutan. Believed by many primatologists to be among the closest relatives of humans living on Earth, orangutans are found along the Alas. Drifting down the Alas on a raft, it is easy to fall under the spell of the timeless beauty of this tropical world where plants and animals still reign supreme.
Season: Year-round

melanesia

The Melanesian region may be small—covering only 0.6 percent of the earth's surface, and sparsely populated—with only about 0.2 percent of the world's population, yet it is culturally unmatched on the planet. Over half of the world's languages—700 or more distinct tongues—are spoken here, and most of the cultures associated with them are still intact. More than 3 million people live here, but because the terrain is so rugged, tribal groups have been kept isolated from one another. Most of its indigenous people have only come into contact with the outside world in the last couple of decades.

Melanesia is also distinguished by containing the largest and highest tropical island on the earth: the island of New Guinea. Of all the world's islands, it is second in size only to Greenland. Many still live much as they did tens of thousands of years ago. Included in the Melanesian region, which sits north of the continent of Australia, just east of Indonesia, are small island nations such as Vanuatu, the Solomon Islands, Fiji, and the French overseas territory of New Caledonia.

And, although largely ignored by the conservation community until recently, Melanesia is extraordinarily rich in plant and animal diversity and endemism. New Guinea has far more undisturbed tropical rainforest than any place in the Asia-Pacific region, and is one of the last significant major tropical wilderness areas on our planet.

! conservation alert

a multicultural adventure

● One of the greatest opportunities and challenges in Melanesia is presented by the fact that, taken as a whole, roughly 80 percent of the land area is still in the hands of its traditional tribal owners through legally recognized systems of customary ownership. The opportunity to work with local cultures and to validate traditional land-use systems is unsurpassed. Standard approaches to conservation, such as those employed in the Western Hemisphere, will have to be redesigned to take the needs of this population into account. And if the challenge can be met, the chances for meaningfully integrating the goals of preserving both cultural and biological diversity here are exceptional.

Local peoples, who control their land and water through customary resource rights throughout most of the region, have a deep sense of the value of maintaining the integrity of their forests and other habitats. However, they have had little or no experience in dealing with increasing pressures from population growth, technologies that could exploit the biological richness of their environment, and proposals from major developers to exploit their land and resources.

Protected areas in Melanesia are for the most part pitifully few, small, inadequately understood by science, poorly managed, and lacking human and financial resources to successfully maintain them. Much effort is needed to identify priority areas for conservation and to work with the people of the region to establish and manage these resources appropriately.

The island has retained at least 80 percent of its original forest cover, a percentage matched by the neighboring Solomon Islands and Vanuatu. In contrast, New Caledonia, on the southeastern end of Melanesia's island string, is one of the most devastated of the world's biologically rich areas.

Marine diversity and especially coral reef diversity reach their global peak in Melanesia as well. The highest recorded diversity of hard corals and nudibranchs (sea slugs) comes from New Guinea. It is likely that other groups of marine organisms are equally diverse, but have yet to be researched.

papua new guinea

Papua New Guinea has a well-deserved reputation of being "The Last Unknown." No other country in the world is more culturally diverse, none more unexpected. New Guinea is the world's largest and highest tropical island. It boasts 15,000-foot mountains topped with snow, even though they're only 400 miles from the equator. The jungle-cloaked peaks shelter large fertile valleys on one side and vast steamy flatlands on the other. Palm trees and mangroves fringe a jagged coastline.

This fantastically complex terrain has produced an equally great habitat diversity. New Guinea's wealth of natural resources is partly due to its location on the globe, strategically straddling the rich and distinctive Asian and Australian biogeographic zones. Its plants and animals have biological links to Asia, Australia, the Philippines, Micronesia, Polynesia, Africa, and even South America.

cultural journey down the sepik

Papua New Guinea's longest and most mysterious river, the Sepik, winds through a fantastic jungle landscape made all the more surreal by the different peoples that live along its banks and in the surrounding highlands.

Many cultures live along the Karawari River, a tributary of the Sepik, including the colorful Arambak, who still practice traditional ceremonies and tell the legends of their ancestors to the accompaniment of flutes. Visitors may explore the river aboard crocodile-prowed dugouts. Crocodiles bask on the banks and herons hunt in the shallows as the standing boatmen paddle their slender dugout canoes with long carved oars. The red-blossomed rainforest resounds with the cacophonous chatter of parrots and cockatoos.

A bird-watcher's paradise, Papua New Guinea is home to more than 700 species of birds, constituting the world's richest island avifauna. Nearly half dwell nowhere else. Ungainly flightless cassowaries strut across the jungle floor as bowerbirds, kingfishers, and fairy wrens flit from tree to tree. And don't forget the birds-of-paradise—thirty-two species in all. The iridescent plumage of the adult males ranges from the exquisite to the unbelievable. When explorers first brought the skins of these unusual feathered creatures home, recipients believed them to be wanderers from a celestial paradise, a belief that persisted until only recently. To see these feathered marvels will leave you questioning their origins, too.

Season: Year-round

The Huli people, renowned for their enormous human-hair wigs and brightly painted faces, dwell in the Southern Highlands of Papua New Guinea. Each village becomes a living stage when the Hulis perform their ritualistic singsing dances. Living in small villages of thatched huts, the Hulis rely on subsistence hunting, agriculture, and gathering in a beautiful moss forest dotted with high-altitude orchids and colored by thirteen species of birds-of-paradise. Papuan men use the birds' ribbon-like tail feathers to make their elaborate headdresses.

!conservation alert

keeping the grim reapers away

● With mineral exploration and timber extraction on the rise in Papua New Guinea, key rainforest habitats need to be protected before they are lost. Grassroots action groups are springing up across the island to assist communities in negotiating for acceptable proposals for resource development by commercial enterprises. As demonstrated by the unscrupulous practices of mineral and timber companies in Papua New Guinea, companies frequently take advantage of local peoples, reap the benefits from resource exploitation, and leave behind degraded forests.

Two areas rich in forest and showing a strong local interest in conservation assistance have been identified as potential models for protection. Both have high ecotourism potential from existing tourist facilities. One of these areas is Tari Basin in the Southern Highlands Province, an area of great beauty and cultural interest (inhabited by the Huli "wig" people) and home to several birds-of-paradise and other important rainforest species. The other site is at Crater Mountain in the Eastern Highlands Province. This area is already a recognized Wildlife Management Area complete with a lodge and nature trails.

The world's largest butterfly, Queen Alexandra's birdwing, lives on Popondetta plain in the eastern lowland region of Papua New Guinea. Conservation International has recently concluded a survey of the butterfly's status in the wild. Local peoples may be able to generate supplemental income from butterfly ranching. Several local ranchers have already been able to benefit from this business, but better strategy and more outreach is needed.

the philippines

The Philippines boasts a robust culture with Spanish and American influences on an Asian base. English is spoken, but Filipino (the national language) and local dialects are often heard on the street. As an archipelago with more than 7,000 islands and an ideal climate, beach tourism has long been a staple in the Philippines. Combining this with world-class snorkeling and diving and delicious fresh seafood, makes the Philippines an enticing base for plunging into an ecotourism adventure.

The Philippines has one of the most unique biotas in all of Asia. Many plants and animals of the Philippines are found nowhere else in the world. Among these gems are the Philippine eagle, the world's largest eagle, and the tamaraw, a dwarf water buffalo found only on the island of Mindoro.

This biological heritage is increasingly rare. The Philippines is ranked among the world's ecological "hot spots," so called because of the value and degree of destruction of its biological diversity. Over 95 percent of the Philippines' forest has been destroyed, leading one expert to call this island nation "the hottest of the hot spots."

natural success

adopt an eagle

For the last twenty years, conservation efforts have focused on protection of the Philippine eagle, the largest and rarest eagle in the world. One of the highlights of a visit to the Philippines is a chance to see one of these magnificent birds—with a wingspan of 7 feet—soaring high above the treetops or nesting in the wild.

Conservation International is working with the Philippine Eagle Conservation Foundation to develop a novel way of involving local people in the preservation of the eagle's habitat. One successful program is the Adopt-a-Nest Program developed by the Eagle Conservation Foundation.

Philippine eagle adventures begin in either Davao or Cagayan de Oro on the southernmost island of Mindanao. From these jumping-off points, eagle-viewing tours may be arranged.

Adult birds may only be seen soaring high in the mountain valleys. But fortunately for adventurers, young eagles stay near the nest for an entire year. And well before the year is up, they are fully grown and have adult plumage. So, if you locate a nest tree, there's a good chance you'll find a young eagle nearby—and it could be a big one. Using special blinds and exercising a little patience, visitors may get a good view of one of the most magnificent birds on earth.

Wonderful ways still exist, however, for experiencing the fullness of Filipino culture along with the country's great natural beauty. Conservation International has been helping the government of the Philippines develop a national ecotourism strategy which will include proper respect for local ecology and culture, return of benefits to local communities, and a strong commitment to conservation. The plan will focus on two major ecotourism attractions and a number of satellite destinations. The two premier ecotourism destinations in the Philippines are the Tubbataha Reefs National Marine Park and the nesting site of the Philippine eagle.

supporting the reefs

Tubbataha is a dual marine atoll in the center of the Sulu Sea. Completely uninhabited, it is renowned as a diving destination, perhaps the best in the Philippines and one of the best in the world. The casual visitor can easily see giant manta rays gliding over the reef, sea turtles approaching sand cays to nest, and a wealth of tropical fish

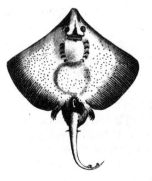

on the huge coral reef.

Tubbataha is reached by dive boat from Puerto Princessa, Palawan, but arrangements should be made in Manila. A short flight to Puerto Princessa is followed by a cruise on fully outfitted dive boat to the atolls. Once there, diving is a several-times-a-day activity. Tired divers are welcomed back on board the boat with cold drinks and freshly cooked meals.

A search for the world's largest and rarest eagle can also lead to destinations that capitalize on miles of white-sand beaches and the area's abundant seafood. A nearly deserted beach and excellent diving are not hard to find within a short walk of an inexpensive but comfortable palm house. Combined with a visit to the Philippine eagle, this is world-class adventure coupled with superbly relaxing beach tourism.

Season: March through June

The duck-billed platypus of world renown shares Australia's Tableland region with tree possums, 16-inch-long leaf-tailed geckos, pythons, and speckled flying foxes. Bioluminescent mushrooms light up the forest floor.

the land of crocodiles and eagles

On the Pacific coast of the largest Philippine island of Luzon is the **Palanan Wilderness Area**, which protects the largest remaining block of lowland forest in the Philippines. This threatened forest formation is linked to intact upland forests and little-disturbed coastal systems in the last integrated upland coastal ecosystem in the country. It is home to the Philippine eagle, dugong, crocodile, and more than ninety species of birds, two-thirds of them endemic. The area is roadless and isolated, and has been a protected wilderness area since 1974. Rapid forest destruction on all sides and total lack of management threaten the future of this important forest area in the Philippines.

A more recently established eagle sanctuary, **Mount Kitanglad National Park,** designated in December 1990, now protects one of the largest remaining areas of Philippine eagle habitat. Community conservation projects are a focus, including a community livelihood/habitat conservation program designed to reduce the clearing of forests by local farmers, thus protecting the eagle. One eagle's nest at the community conservation pilot project has been discovered, and the park is being surveyed elsewhere for more.

Season: March through June

australia

Look at a map of Australia, and the destinations read like a litany. The national parks and nature reserves are among the most lyrical: Kakadu. Dipperu. Ka Mundi.

natural success

park protection down under

Kakadu National Park, made famous by the *Crocodile Dundee* movies, has a wide array of habitats, from salt water swamps to sedgelands to eucalyptus forests and sandstone escarpments dotted with spectacular waterfalls. Aboriginal occupation dates back some 40,000 years. The park wetlands house 260 species of birds, large numbers of crocodiles, kangaroos, wallabies, and other marsupials. All this has earned it global recognition as a World Heritage Park.

But Kakadu also overlies extensive mineral deposits, and for years mining companies have been pressuring the Australian government for permission to dig up land adjacent to the park. In 1986, miners won a cabinet decision that would have allowed them to commence operations at Coronation Hill, a site containing gold, platinum, and palladium.

Alarmed by the prospect of prospectors digging around a natural treasure like Kakadu, environmentalists and Aboriginals began a lobbying campaign of their own. It worked. In 1989 they convinced Australia's Prime Minister Bob Hawke to defer the mining venture. In doing so, he acknowledged he was influenced by "the greatly increasing value of the area in terms of tourism."

The government has now declared that 98 percent of a so-called conservation zone covering 950 square miles adjacent to Kakadu would be incorporated into the 7,300-square-mile national park and become off-limits to further exploitation and development.

Honeycreepers, lyrebirds, birds-of-paradise, and cassowaries make up a small fraction of southern Australia's entire avian assemblage of more than 700 bird species. The array of other animal species includes water buffalo, saltwater and fresh-water crocodiles, kangaroos, and dingos.

Werrikimbie. Wollemi. Mootwingee. And the places are every bit as poetic as their names.

Australia is as large as the continental United States and just as varied. You can't hope to learn all its secrets in a single trip. The opportunities for nature travel in Australia stretch from the famed Great Barrier Reef as far as the island continent's own dusty red Outback. While a two- or three-week cross-country expedition can provide a taste of the land down under, most visitors will want to come back again and again to feast on specific destinations.

a royal safari

If any one of Australia's seven states bespeaks the nation's biogeographical and cultural panoply, than surely Queensland does so best. It not only has plenty of desert-like Outback but also tropical rainforests, rambling mountains, raging rivers, inland meadows, and, most widely visited of all, the Great Barrier Reef. The best examples of each climatic zone are protected as national parks.

The most northern tip, Cape York Peninsula, points like a finger to Papua New Guinea. The land is draped in lush rainforests that have evolved without interruption for some 130 million years. Cape York shelters some of Australia's most unusual species of wildlife. The forests resound with the call of birds. Of the more than 700 birds known to occur in Australia, more than half are endemic. Many are so distinct that ornithologists cannot trace their relationships to other species. Bluewinged kookaburras laugh derisively, galahs and cockatoos chatter incessantly.

The cultural history is also fascinating. Australia's aboriginal peoples trace their ancestry back at least 40,000 years. You can see evidence of this ancient human activity in the rock shelters and superb cave paintings.

To the south, near the city of Cairns, is a land of extinct volcanic lakes surrounded by virgin rainforest, the **Tablelands.** Turbulent streams rush down gorges, fed by spectacular waterfalls. And rolling outback plains and rich red farmland act as the roof over ancient limestone caves. Here, you can spot many unusual species.

Offshore lies a California-sized stretch of coral reef, the 1,200-mile-long **Great Barrier Reef**. It is the largest living structure on Earth. More than 1,400 species of fish have been identified here, not to mention many other marine animals and plants. Weird and wonderful creatures such as unicorn fish with strange snouts, tiny dottybacks, threadfin coral fish, angel fish, groper, sharks, and rays cruise among waving sponges and wandering urchins. Giant clams reach more than three feet across.

Season: Fall and winter (Australia's seasons are the reverse of those in the Northern Hemisphere)

new zealand

At one point in geological time all the continents were grouped together as one. Gondwanaland, as scientists call this singular land, eventually began to split apart into gigantic chunks of land that were set adrift in the world's original ocean, the Tethys Sea. New Zealand separated from the motherland some 70 million years ago, and the only passengers that rode through evolutionary history were plants, insects, fish, and birds—no mammals or reptiles.

New Zealand remains one of the most isolated places on Earth, but its wildlife and geography display a remarkable degree of diversity. The government helps

▌conservation alert

strange birds

● Because endemic bird species originally lived in isolation and without the threat of predators, many unique forms evolved in New Zealand. These included giant flightless moas, kiwis, flightless rails, and even a flightless parrot. But humans brought with them a range of mammal predators to the islands, precipitating a steady rate of extinction which continues to this day.

Estimates show that 10 percent of the world's endangered birds live in New Zealand, including the black stilt, takahe, kakapo, kokako, and saddleback. Many species still inhabit the islands, including three types of penguins, several albatrosses, and the Australasian gannet.

protect the nation's natural legacy by maintaining 10 national parks, 18 forest parks, and 1,008 scenic reserves—all this in a country twice the size of the State of New York but with a population one-fourth that of Manhattan.

new zealand discovery

New Zealand's size makes it easy to experience most of the country's natural highlights in a two-week trip. Featured destinations include the **Kaikoura Range** in the south island, a vaulting group of coastal mountains that runs along a stretch of the South Pacific noted for its wealth of sea life. Sperm whales, killer whales, dusky dolphins, Hector's dolphins, and fur seals are just some of the marine mammals you can expect to see swimming in the adjacent bays. **Kapiti Island**, nesting ground for a variety of seabird species, lies due north.

New Zealand has one of the largest national parks in the world. **Fiordland** encompasses nearly 3 million acres of forested mountains, pristine lakes, soaring cliffs, and monumental waterfalls. The country's most scenic site can be viewed to the north—**Milford Sound**, a body of tranquil water nearly fully enclosed by a ring of pyramid-shaped, forest-covered peaks.

Season: Fall and winter

New Zealand possesses spectacular mountain scenery. More than 250 mountains exceeding 7,500 feet tower over the main two islands, with explorer Captain James Cook's 12,349-foot namesake being the highest. More than 400 glaciers drape New Zealand's lofty peaks.

5

antarctica

- One of the most fragile areas on earth, Antarctica is in danger of being overrun by irresponsible tour operators and industrial exploitation.

- The subantarctic islands of Australia and New Zealand are home to the world's rarest species of penguin, the yellow-eyed penguin of Campbell Island, which breed only here.

- About 730 nautical miles from the bottom of the earth is McMurdo Sound, supporting several permanent research stations. There, National Science Foundation staff are busy unlocking mysteries of marine and terrestrial biology, biomedicine, geology, glaciology, meteorology, and upper atmospheric physics.

- Macquarie Island in southernmost Antarctica was once the site of slaughter. Fur seals, elephant seals, and penguins were nearly driven to extinction by sealers in the 1800s. Now protected, nearly 2 million royal penguins, 140,000 king penguins, gentoo, rockhoppers and sooty albatross safely live on the island.

antarctica

Not quite 200 years ago, the very existence of the planet's seventh continent was mere speculation. Until then, it existed only in the realm of imagination—a theory first conceived by Aristotle. The great Greek thinker postulated that there had to be a southern continent, or the weight of the known world would topple from its own imbalance. It took the daring of such explorers as Roald Amundsen, Robert Falcon Scott, and Ernest Shackleton to finally put the elusive continent on the map. But even now Antarctica remains an enigma.

A frozen desert where less rain falls than anywhere on Earth, yet which holds nearly as much fresh water as all of the planet's rivers and lakes combined, Antarctica is a land of towering mountains, frigid seas, and walls of ice. No continent is higher, less populated, or colder. The ice measures three miles thick in places, temperatures drop to a mind-numbing 128 degrees below zero, and winds reach speeds of 200 miles or more.

For much of its human history, Antarctica has been a place devoted entirely to science. Under the terms of the 1959 Antarctic Treaty, the English, Soviets, Chinese, Poles, Argentines, Chileans, Brazilians, Uruguayans, Australians, New Zealanders, and Americans have built research stations to study the mysteries of the polar world. Now tourists, too, can experience the South Pole's forbidding beauty, unparalleled wildlife, and promise of firsthand discovery and adventure.

Before you rush off to Antarctica, however, keep in mind that it is the one continent on our heavily traveled planet where the environment retains most of its purity, not just vestiges of it. More and more companies have begun operating tours here, so you need to make sure the one you choose to travel with is completely committed to environmental protection and won't make compromises for the sake of commercial gain. The most conscientious tour operators adhere to a self-imposed code of conduct. (See "visitor guidelines," page 80.)

journey to the bottom of the world

Looking southward from the tip of South America, the curling finger of the Antarctic Peninsula beckons across the black waters of Drake Passage. Reaching Antarctica by ship takes one through the Antarctic Convergence. Here the warm seas of the Atlantic collide with colder Antarctic waters, creating an upwelling of nutrients that attract many seabirds and marine mammals.

The Antarctic Peninsula and its adjacent islands

❗ conservation alert

keeping the ice pure

⬤ Without strict limitations, tourism in Antarctica will prove environmentally disastrous. The potential for damage to this fragile reservoir for the world's health has already been realized. In 1989, an Argentinean cruise ship ran aground, spilling 250,000 gallons of fuel in the process. Responsible tourism, however, can benefit Antarctica. Pressure to allow strip mining and oil drilling on "The Ice" is increasing every day. Consequently, the need for long-term protection of Antarctica has never been greater. A possible solution is to designate the entire continent as a World Park and ban all industrial exploitation forever. Tourism can help achieve this end by turning today's visitors into "Antarctic Ambassadors." (See "visitor guidelines," page 80.)

possess an embarrassment of biological riches. Nearly one million chinstrap penguins inhabit Deception Island, one of Antarctica's two active volcanoes. Stark cliffs soar above a sunken caldera where Pintado petrels dance and humpback whales sing. During the height of the breeding season, Paulet Island becomes a waddling mass of feathers and flippers. One-half million Adélie penguins gather here to court and nest. Watch them as they present pebbles to each other as tokens of affection. At Gonzales Videla Station on the Antarctic mainland, gentoo penguins swim through the water like porpoises, the sound of their trumpet-like calls blasting the air with an unforgettable tune. The snowy hills that rise above the beach have been turned into toboggan runs for chinstrap penguins.

At Paradise Bay, hanging cliffs of ice surround a beautiful bay filled with bobbing blue icebergs. The silence of the icy world is broken whenever a glacier calves. As the huge slab of ice thunders into the bay, the nearby rookery of blue-eyed cormorants lets out a collective squawk and ruffles its feathers.

Season: January and February

Coulman Island hosts the world's largest emperor penguin colony. Emperors stretch the tape at four feet and tip the scales at 90 pounds. That's twice the size of king penguins.

the falklands and beyond

The southernmost point of the British Empire lies among the 700 islands 300 miles east of South America and 1,000 miles north of Antarctica. Several expeditionary cruise ships call on these remote outposts on their way to and from the South Pole.

The largest of these windswept southern landfalls are called the East and West Falklands by the British, or the

! conservation alert

visitor guidelines

1. Maintain a distance of at least 15 to 20 feet from penguins, nesting birds, and crawling (true) seals, and 50 feet from fur seals.
2. Be alert while you are ashore.
3. Do not get between a marine animal and its path to the water, nor between a parent and its young.
4. Be aware of the periphery of a rookery or seal colony, and remain outside it.
5. Do not touch the wildlife.
6. Never harass wildlife for the sake of photography.
7. Keep all noise to a minimum in order not to stress the animals.
8. Avoid walking on, stepping on, or damaging the fragile mosses and lichens.
9. Take away only memories and photographs.
10. Return all litter to the ship for proper disposal.
11. Do not bring food of any kind ashore.
12. Do not enter buildings at the research stations unless invited to do so.
13. Historic huts can only be entered when accompanied by a specially designated governmental representative or properly authorized ship's leader.
14. Never smoke near wooden buildings or refuge huts.
15. When ashore stay with the group and/or one of the ship's leaders.
16. Listen to the expedition leader, lecturers, and naturalists.

Developed by Society Expeditions

Albatross Island in the Falklands is appropriately named for its chief resident, the wandering albatross. This ungainly but docile flyer boasts a wing span that measures 12 feet. On this and the other small islands that surround South Georgia, the barks of two million southern fur seals fill the air.

Malvinas by the Argentines. The two countries have disputed ownership of the islands for years. The majority of islanders, whose principal occupation is tending sheep, claim allegiance to Britain, however. Theirs is a starkly beautiful land, shared by dozens of species of wildlife, including elephant seals, southern sea lions, five species of penguins, and such unusual birds as the black-browed albatross.

A number of biologically important nature preserves have been established near the capital city of Stanley, a collection of Victorian-style, weather-beaten houses and shops more British than any found in London. At the **New Island Nature Reserve**, rockhopper penguins perch on

❗ conservation alert

the first world park

● A move to turn Antarctica into the first World Park has gained momentum in recent years. In 1989, the General Assembly of the United Nations called for Antarctica to be declared a World Park with a prohibition on mining. Australia and France have undertaken a joint initiative to have Antarctica established as a wilderness and scientific reserve. Many believe saving Antarctica would be a step on the path to saving Planet Earth.

By designating it as a World Park, exploitation of mineral resources and killing of marine mammals and birds would be prohibited. Nuclear and toxic waste disposal would also be banned. Activities such as tourism, commercial fishing, and construction of logistical and support facilities would be carefully monitored to insure they did not adversely affect the fragile environment.

Park status would enhance scientific research in many ways. By protecting the environment from local sources of pollution, scientists would be assured of a pristine outdoor laboratory for conducting research. Long-term and internationally coordinated planning would lead to more environmentally sensitive research stations.

Finally, World Park status would eliminate the nagging issue of sovereignty. Antarctica could finally become the world's first truly united nation.

The haunting sight of 2,000 reindeer grazing at West Cumberland Bay will leave you scratching your head in wonder. No illusion this, the reindeer are the progeny of a herd brought to the island earlier this century by Norwegian whalers.

rounded boulders in a rookery built along a natural amphitheater overlooking the water's edge. One of the rarest birds of prey also frequents these parts, the striated caracara. Locals call it "Johnny Rook."

Nearby **Volunteer Point Nature Reserve** was created to protect a sizable king penguin rookery. Falkland flightless steamer ducks share the protected area with smaller gentoo penguins. In the breeding season, you can catch sight of the three-foot king parents balancing pear-shaped eggs on the tops of their feet. The trick shields their unborn from the cold ground.

South Georgia Island lies to the east of the Falklands. Rising 10,000 feet out of the Scotia Sea, South Georgia is actually a pinnacle of the Andes that resurfaced as it

natural success

an explorer who cared

The southernmost subantarctic island is Macquarie Island, site of one of the biggest seal slaughters in history. In the early 1800s, sealers drove the fur seal population to the brink of extinction in just one decade. Next, they began decimating the island's resident elephant seals. Finally, they turned their guns and clubs on the island's penguins, which they boiled for oil. By 1900, fewer than 7,000 penguins survived.

The island's native wildlife has made a remarkable recovery, thanks in part to the foresight of explorer Douglas Mawson, who launched a series of effective protectionist measures. Nearly two million royal penguins now cover the southern end of the island, while 140,000 king penguins crowd the shores of Lusitania Bay. Gentoo and rockhopper penguins also live here, along with the light-mantled sooty albatross and both northern and southern giant petrel.

wends its way from the tip of South America to the Antarctic Peninsula. Wild and stormy and gray, South Georgia has changed little since it was first sighted in 1675. Antarctic explorer Ernest Shackleton reposes in his grave in the shadows of its ice-shrouded mountains.

The even more remote South Orkney islands were long known as the "Inaccessible Islands." During the winter, a solid sheet of ice 450 miles long connects these bleak rocks to the Antarctic Peninsula. Along the cliffs lining Coronation Island nest snow and Pintado petrels along with Adélie penguins. Weddell seals also inhabit this oldest of British Antarctic bases.

Season: January and February

antarctica from down under

The other approach to Antarctica begins at the southern reaches of New Zealand. Follow in the footsteps of Scott and Shackleton, who pioneered this route. You can even visit their expedition huts that have been frozen in time. Perhaps you'll find yourself drawn by the same power that made them risk their lives to reach the nadir of Earth.

Cape Adare is the site of the first confirmed landing on the mainland—a feat achieved a little less than 100 years ago. Behind a sandy beach stands the hut built by the British Antarctic Expedition in 1898. A huge rookery of Adélie penguins exists in the shadow of the Admiralty Mountains. Herds of Weddell, leopard, and crabeater seals

Cape Royds and Cape Evans are frozen museums. At Cape Royds you can visit the simple wooden structure that served as Ernest Shackleton's base camp for his 1908 Nimrod Expedition. He and three companions slogged 800 miles only to turn back a maddening 97 miles from the Pole. Robert Falcon Scott's hut still stands at Cape Evans. Scott left its warm security for his fatal race to the Pole in 1911. Perfectly preserved groceries and scientific instruments still sit on the shelves in the wooden hut, literally frozen in time. They seem to await his return.

share the sea.

A series of landfalls south through the Ross Sea—gateway to the Antarctic—supports past and present scientific expeditions. Dominated by the 13,000-foot-high Admiralty Mountains, Cape Hallet guards the entrance to a iceberg-filled sound that terminates at the convergence of several glaciers. An abandoned New Zealand research base sits here, now inhabited by thousands of Adélie penguins.

The farthest south any ship can sail is McMurdo Sound. The Sound abuts the Ross Ice Shelf, a dramatic 400-mile-long wall of ice that rises above the sea as high as 200 feet. The scenery is staggering, surreal, and downright breathtaking. The 12,450-foot steaming summit of Mount Erebus punctures the blue horizon and ice-chilled air. The dozing volcano has been used as a navigational beacon for many a dash to the Pole.

About 730 nautical miles from the very bottom of Earth, McMurdo Sound supports several permanent research stations. The U.S. McMurdo Station outsizes the others by far; it has a summer population of 1,200. On a tour of the facility, National Science Foundation representatives, time permitting, will explain ongoing projects in marine and terrestrial biology, biomedicine, geology, glaciology, meteorology, and upper atmospheric physics.

Season: January and February

King George Island houses a remarkable collection of international scientists. Some of the research stations welcome visitors. At the Polish facility, you'll find a greenhouse, one of the tour's more unexpected sights. Imagine tomatoes ripening on the vine and daisies in full bloom in a frozen world without trees.

the islands in between

The subantarctic islands of Australia and New Zealand harbor a wealth of wildlife, including the world's rarest species of penguin, the yellow-eyed penguin of Campbell Island. Snares Island, home to up to 60,000 Snares Island penguins, marks the first landfall heading south from New Zealand. These waddling beauties breed only here; you can watch them as they march solemnly back and forth between their nests and the sea.

A team of a dozen or so meteorologists inhabit Campbell Island to the south. Near their weather station, huge southern royal albatrosses launch themselves from rolling hills as they head out over the ocean to fish. The birds live here and on nearby Aukland Island, another stop for several of the expeditionary cruises to and from the Antarctic.

Season: January and February

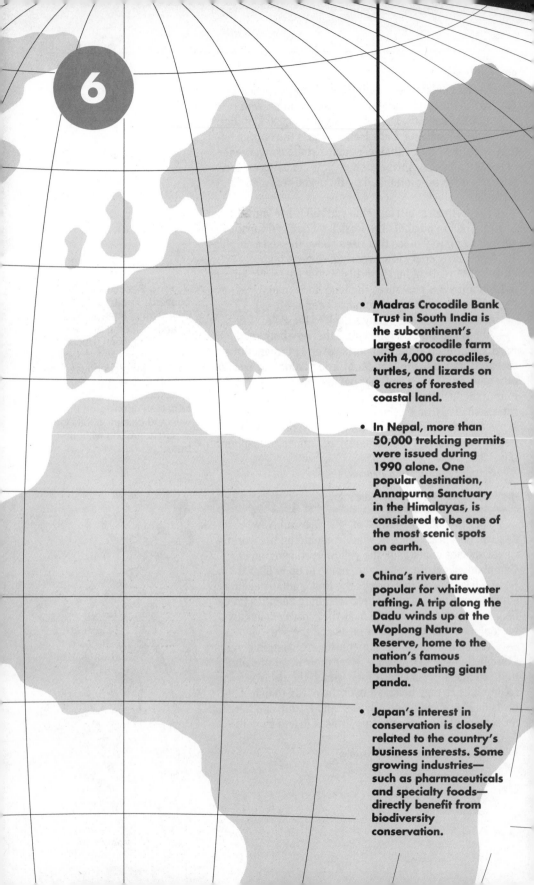

6

- **Madras Crocodile Bank Trust in South India is the subcontinent's largest crocodile farm with 4,000 crocodiles, turtles, and lizards on 8 acres of forested coastal land.**

- **In Nepal, more than 50,000 trekking permits were issued during 1990 alone. One popular destination, Annapurna Sanctuary in the Himalayas, is considered to be one of the most scenic spots on earth.**

- **China's rivers are popular for whitewater rafting. A trip along the Dadu winds up at the Woplong Nature Reserve, home to the nation's famous bamboo-eating giant panda.**

- **Japan's interest in conservation is closely related to the country's business interests. Some growing industries—such as pharmaceuticals and specialty foods—directly benefit from biodiversity conservation.**

asia

An ancient Sanskrit proverb says, "A hundred divine epochs would not suffice to describe all the marvels of the Himalaya." The same wisdom holds true for all of Asia. To adequately characterize the vast array of landscapes and cultures that make up the Far East would require the soul of a poet and the stamina of a Marco Polo.

But for the traveler interested in experiencing exotic cultures while exploring natural environments, Asia offers the ultimate "movable feast." The adventurous traveler can trek up the tallest mountain in the world, visit the bamboo forests of China's **Wolong Nature Reserve**, view rhinos in Nepal's famed **Royal Chitwan National Park** from the back of an elephant, worship in the golden temples of Bangkok, and look for tigers in Ranthambhor.

Besides being the world's largest continent, Asia is also the most populous. Two out of every five of our planet's citizens live in either China or India. The pressures of overpopulation are literally tearing the environment apart at the seams. The Himalayas bind Asia like a gigantic piece of stitchery, but deforestation has unraveled this once pristine ecosystem. The lion-tail macque and other rare and endangered species in India live on the brink of extinction, pushed by farmers in quest of new lands to till. Japan and the Western nations are fueling their economic growth at the expense of Malaysia's virgin rainforests and the plants, animals, and indigenous peoples that live within them.

The magnitude of Asia's environmental woes runs so deep, one could never suppose that ecotourism alone would be enough to solve all the region's problems, but it can at least bring us closer to an awareness of them. And at this precarious point in our fragile planet's evolutionary journey, every small step counts.

nepal

High above the clouds, wrapped in mystery and mysticism, Nepal perches on the rooftop of the world like an ascetic, offering insight and enlightenment to those willing to scale its heights and listen.

Nepal may be the world's fifth poorest country but it has a wealth of human culture. Buddhist in the north, Hindu in the south, Nepal comprises many peoples: Tamangs, Newars, Gurungs, Limbus, Rais, Thakalis, and the sure-footed Sherpas, well-known for their climbing and guiding skills.

Nepal has only been open to the outside world since 1950. Sir Edmund Hillary and Tenzing Norkay put it on

▌conservation alert

trekking with care

● The boom in tourism in Nepal has given the country a new source of income, but at a steep environmental price. Foreign visitors, combined with the country's exploding population—the populace has doubled in thirty years—tax Nepal's already scarce natural resources. Agricultural terraces rise higher and higher on the flanks of mountains. Forests fall to provide fuel and heat. Hillsides erode. Traditional cultural practices disappear under the influence of a new economy. And cigarette packages and used toilet paper mark the most well-trodden trails.

Does this mean Nepal has been ruined? Not yet, but the country has reached a crossroads, and it is up to tourists to make sure that they don't repeat the mistakes of the past. Sir Edmund Hillary probably said it best. In his foreword to Stephen Bezruchka's authoritative *A Guide to Trekking in Nepal*, he cautions:

> Nepal is still very beautiful—surely one of the world's great trekking paradises. But those of us who take advantage of these charms have great responsibility. We can play an active part in Nepal's future by making positive efforts to leave the mountains and walkways cleaner than we found them, taking care not to abuse local customs and traditions, and limiting our use of energy to a minimum so there may be something left for future generations. Nepal must be saved—and we can help do it.

the proverbial map in 1953 when they became the first humans to set foot on the highest point on Earth, Mount Everest. Since then the trickle of visitors making the pilgrimage to this mountain sanctuary has turned into a flood. More than 50,000 trekking permits were issued in 1990 alone.

trekking on the summit of the world

Trekking means traveling by foot along ancient mountain trails for many days. Typical treks in Nepal take anywhere from ten days to a month. The different styles of trekking range from going alone without benefit of a guide to organized treks where porters carry your gear and wake you in the morning with a cup of steaming tea. You can opt to sleep in tents or stay in lodges and guest houses.

Along with the multiple styles of trekking to choose from in Nepal come a variety of paths to follow. Some of the more popular treks include:

Mount Everest. Who hasn't dreamed of a journey to

natural success

the world's highest landfill

What goes up doesn't necessarily come down. This is especially true when it comes to equipment carried up the Himalayas by trekkers. With trekkers now numbering 50,000 per year, the world's highest mountain range has also become the world's highest dumping ground.

Loboche, the highest campsite along the approach route to Mount Everest, has been especially hard hit by thoughtless trekkers. A few years ago a landfill was built there to contain the waste left behind by tourists, but it was situated in such a way that high winds often blew its contents all over the mountain.

Alarmed by what was happening, Cambridge, Massachusetts–based Overseas Adventure Travel sought to remedy the situation. Working with the Nepal government's Department of Parks and Wildlife and private nonprofit groups in Nepal, OAT established the Loboche Conservation Project. Construction of a windproof landfill and sanitation facilities was begun in 1990. The project also involves an educational component: multilingual signs instruct tourists and guides in techniques in "low-impact" tourism. Educational literature that underscores the importance of environmental responsibility is distributed through the Trekking Agents Association of Nepal. For more information, contact:

> Overseas Adventure Travel
> 349 Broadway
> Cambridge, MA 02139
> (617) 876-0533/1-800-221-0814

Nepal is a tiny country, but packed within a region the size of California's Central Valley tower eight of Earth's ten tallest peaks, examples of most of the vegetation zones in the world, and a surprising variety of wildlife.

the apex of the world? This quintessential Himalayan trek follows the route to Mount Everest—a trail that takes you through valleys strewn with garlands of azaleas and rhododendrons, along cascading waterfalls and bottomless chasms, over mountain passes where a thousand prayer flags snap in the wind, and to the base of the noble mountain itself. You can choose from several different approaches to the massif. The Gokyo route winds through the relatively untrodden Gokyo Valley, a colorful wonderland of glaciers, turquoise lakes, and rugged mountain scenery. The Classic route follows Hillary's footsteps and ventures east from Jiri and across two major passes to the Dudh Khosi Valley and beyond into the sacred domain of the mountain gods. Delightful Sherpa villages, Sagarmatha National Park, and Lobuche, the high camp at 16,200 feet, line the route.

Annapurna Sanctuary. One of the most scenic spots imaginable, Annapurna Sanctuary unveils the full grandeur of the Himalayas. The trail takes you through thickets of bamboo, along the deep Kali Gandaki Gorge to a beautiful 13,000-foot-high meadowed uplands surrounded by no fewer than five massive mountains, all but one soaring 23,000 feet and higher. Truly, it is the throne room of the gods.

Dolpo. Called the "Hidden Kingdom of the Himalaya," the Dolpo region of Nepal was long forbidden. Open to foreign visitors only recently, it appeals to trekkers looking for journeys off the beaten path. The route provides a nonstop panorama of remote peaks, pristine lakes, and traditional villages.

Season: October to May

river rafting in nepal

Ice and water carved Nepal's great peaks, and the mountains serve as a source for several major rivers. The most popular for rafting is the glacial **Trisuli.** Fairly gentle but with some rousing rapids, it courses through a series of gorges and into the jungle-covered foothills of Royal Chitwan National Park.

The **Sun Kosi** is even more exhilarating. Springing from the flanks of the high Himalaya, the Sun Khosi flails down tortured gorges before spilling out onto the tropical plains. The river cuts through a veritable cross-section of Nepal, passing under vertigo-inducing suspension footbridges and within view of the cobbled squares of Newari villages. Reaching the put-in point of the river requires an eight-day trek through the Himalayan foothills.

Season: October through May

nepali safari

When most people think of Nepal, they picture a jagged skyline of stark and windswept mountaintops. But Nepal also has a lush and densely vegetated side. In addition to its alpine regions, the country has subtropical and temperate habitats, and a rich and varied plant and animal community thrives within these jungle lowlands.

Nepal's most prized wildlife region is the **Royal Chitwan National Park**. Here, more than 450 species of birds fill the sky. Within the forests and grasslands live two of the world's most spectacular and rarest species, the royal Bengal tiger and the greater one-horned rhinoceros. Several species of deer, sloth bear, leopard, wild boar, fresh-water dolphin, and gharial share the park with them.

Royal Chitwan National Park in Nepal contains an unusual lodge, Tiger Tops Jungle Lodge and Tented Camp. As its name implies, the lodge perches on stilts at treetop level. The height prevents the park's royal resident, the Bengal tiger, from making uninvited visits to rooms. It also provides visitors with a bird's-eye view of the surrounding terrain. The park's thatch-grass protects river banks from erosion and is also a useful crop for local villages.

In the field, visitors ride elephants to view wildlife. The elephants provide a safe and advantageous viewpoint from which to look for rhinos and other species in the park's tall grasslands.

Season: October through May

india

India. The name brings to mind maharajahs, the British raj, the Taj Mahal, ancient cultures, and huge cities teeming with people. True, India is crowded by our standards—one-third the size of the United States, its population is almost four times greater—but it encompasses a surprising wildlife heritage. Not all the lions, elephants, and rhinos of the world live in Africa. India has these exotic creatures and more, including tigers, panthers, four species of antelope, nine species of deer, and more kinds of bear than any other country in the world.

A multifaceted subcontinent, India's geography ranges from the towering mountain passes of the Himalayas to the barren sweeps of the Thar Desert. This topographical variation has produced an incredible diversity of habitats, from semi-tundra to tropical forests, from salt deserts to coastal mangroves. In turn, this abundance of ecological realms supports a remarkable spectrum of wildlife species—350 species of mammals,

natural success

thriving tigers

When conservationists discovered the population of the Bengal tiger had been reduced from 30,000 to 2,000, they were able to convince the Indian government to create nine tiger reserves. As a result, the Bengal tiger was spared extinction, and some of the best jungles were protected. Today, the Bengal tiger population has more than doubled.

1,250 kinds of birds, 130 different reptiles, and a plenitude of plant species.

India also has a long and colorful social history. Five thousand years of civilization has resulted in an extraordinary complexity of ethnic origins and cultures. Here, East truly meets West, and practicality and spirituality share a common ground. The result is a land of contrast and counterpoint, a nation where business executives and engineers walk the same ground as snake charmers and mystics.

the national parks of india

India is unique in many ways, but surely its most remarkable characteristic is the fact that nowhere else on Earth do such large populations of people and animals coexist in the same environment. Despite the pressure to devote more and more of its land to agriculture in order to feed its burgeoning population, India maintains an ambitious national park and wildlife preserve program. Foreign visitors help support their maintenance. Visiting India's parks, preserves, and sanctuaries on a motorized safari will put you face-to-face with some of the most exotic species on the planet.

Dachigam National Park. Located in Kashmir, India's most beautiful reserve sprawls over 55 square miles of riverine, coniferous, and broadleaf forests. The park provides sanctuary for many endangered species, including the Himalayan black and brown bears and the Kashmir stag. In fact, it is the only park with a significant population of this highly endangered stag. Bird life includes golden oriole, streaked laughing thrush, and koklas pheasant. Another common species found in Dachigam is the long-tailed blue magpie with its dramatic foot-long tail feathers.

Gir National Park. Located on the crowded western edge of India, Gir is under siege by farmers seeking new lands. Still, it protects the last remaining habitat of the

Kashmir has been called the "Switzerland of Asia" for good reason. The quiet lakeside villages, wildflower-strewn valleys, pine-scented forests, and snowcapped peaks in this far northern corner of India resemble the alpine land of chocolate and red-handled army knives. The Vale of Kashmir became a coveted hill station during British rule. Its cool weather and serene charm offer a welcome respite from the scorching plains below. You can still laze about in a luxurious houseboat in grand colonial style on Dal Lake, just as Queen Victoria's viceroys did a century ago. Adjacent Nageen Lake is far less crowded and even more appealing to Western visitors.

Asian lion. The huge cat preys on spotted deer, antelope, and chinkaras.

Kanha National Park. The most famous four-legged resident of this deciduous forest park is the massive gaur, or Indian bison. Timid and retiring, this distant relative of our own buffalo can be seen at dawn and dusk feeding in the park's grassy meadows. Striking black-and-white blackbucks fence with one another using their long, spiraled horns as foils. Kanha is also known for its sambar deer (the largest deer in India) as well as the swamp deer and a four-horned antelope, the chousingha. Another of the 366-square-mile park's more unusual creatures is the Indian wild dog, or dhole. The exotic calls of racket-tailed drongo, red junglefowl, and Indian peafowl fill the air.

Kaziranga National Park. Located near India's border with Burma, its horizon dominated by the lofty Himalayas, Kaziranga is a classic example of wetland savannah. You can ride atop elephants to view one-horned rhinoceros. More than 1,000 rhinoceros are protected here. Traveling by elephant provides a safe and ideal vantage point for wildlife viewing and photography. Elephants can also approach wildlife much closer than a human hiker can. The gharial lives in the streams and marshes that fill the park, as do smooth Indian otter and Gangetic dolphin.

Keoladeo Ghana National Park. This World Heritage Site lies near the marbled walls of the Taj Mahal south of Delhi. Once a duck-shooting preserve for the Maharajah of Bharatpur, who created these fresh-water marshes. Birds come here by the thousands to nest and feed. After the monsoons fill the ponds and shallow meadows, you can spot nesting painted storks, sarus cranes, and jacanas. Raptors flock here in great numbers, too, including fishing eagles, spotted eagles, and dusky horned owls. More than 370 species of birds can be found here. Other denizens of the swamp include mongoose, flying cat, hyena, and python.

Ranthambhor Tiger Reserve. Tigers loll around ancient ruins at this 153-square-mile preserve. The arid land produces a savannah forest dotted by a central lake and scattered watering holes. Because they provide the only water for wildlife during the dry season, they attract large herds of sambar, chital, nilgai, chinkara, and wild boar. These in turn support a large population of tiger, leopard, and jackal. Many birds also thrive here. At sunrise you can see several species of parakeet as well as

natural success

ecotourism in little tibet

Ladakh's traditional Buddhist culture and stark mountain scenery have earned it the well-deserved nickname, "Little Tibet." Its colorful culture, mystical monasteries, and dramatic Himalayan vistas have been attracting visitors ever since the region was opened to international tourism in 1974.

While tourism has brought economic benefits to the region, it has also caused a host of environmental and cultural problems, including increasing demand on already scarce water and energy resources. Inadequate waste disposal has led to the spread of pollution and disease.

Several nonprofit organizations have been established in Ladakh to promote sustainable development through tourism that harmonizes with and builds on traditional Ladakhi culture. One is The Ladakh Ecological Development Group (LEDEG). Associated with LEDEG is the Ladakh Project, which distributes guidelines for responsible behavior for tourists and has initiated a program aimed at developing souvenirs based on traditional crafts and designs.

Another locally based group is the Students' Educational and Cultural Movement of Ladakh (SECMOL). Its goal is to improve education and preserve Ladakhi culture, generating funds through responsible tourism. SECMOL sponsors nightly shows during the tourist season, featuring traditional dances, songs, and music. It also conducts excursions to popular tourist sites, trains local guides who accompany tourists to the monasteries, and sells postcards, cassettes, and local handcrafts to raise money. For more information, contact:

The Ladakh Project
21 Victoria Square
Clifton, Bristol BS8 4ES
England

the golden-backed woodpecker, red-vented bulbul, treepie, and red-wattled lapwing.

Season: Spring and fall

china

The lure of the Orient has never been stronger as China opens more and more of its doors to Western visitors. The first waves of tourists had to content themselves with city tours of Beijing and Shanghai and brief side trips to the 1,500-mile-long Great Wall. Now, the sky is the limit. You can follow in the footsteps of Marco Polo along the Silk Road, ride a train across the great Gobi Desert, raft down rivers fed by the Himalayas, and search for such exotic and endangered creatures as the panda, golden monkey, takin, trogopan, and snow leopard near the eastern edge of the Tibetan highlands.

bicycling in china

The most Chinese way to see China is to do what one billion locals do—ride a bike. Pedaling through the countryside takes you beyond the Great Wall and offers a taste of the daily life of one-fifth of the planet's inhabitants.

Support vans usually accompany most bike trips. They carry gear and transport winded riders. Tours typically overnight at local hotels. Popular bicycle routes include a trip through Guangdong Province, a region noted for ancient temples, pagodas rising above misty lakes, and friendly people. Another follows the Yangtze Valley and along the Grand Canal. Still another loops through southern China to Guilin; the countryside here comprises some of China's most photogenic scenery.

Season: June through February

spring blossoms

At the southern tip of Yunnan Province, in the Prefecture of Xishuangbanna is a tropical botanical garden with an incredible variety of plant life. Yunnan Province contains the greatest plant biodiversity in the nation, as this garden so vividly demonstrates.

Season: Spring

thailand

A nation of jungles, beaches, delicious cuisine, and shimmering golden-domed temples, Thailand is the delight of the Orient. Part of its charm has to do with its friendly people and their allegiance to a long and uninterrupted cultural tradition. Unlike the rest of its Southeast Asian neighbors, Thailand has never been colonized by a foreign power. The hill tribes in the north, for example, still maintain their unique way of life, including colorful costumes, customs, and crafts.

Though its tropical beaches and bigger-than-life emerald statues of Buddha attract most travelers, there remains a side of Thailand waiting to be discovered—a wild side.

Whitewater rafting on one of China's famous rivers is an adventure of a lifetime. The Yangtze, the fourth longest river in the world, stretches 3,600 miles. The Huang Ho and Mekong also run over great distances. However, China's relatively shorter rivers provide the most whitewater thrills. Raft trips also present the most unique perspective on China's natural heritage.

The Dadu drains the eastern edge of the Tibetan Plateau. Representing a side of China that has yet to be tamed by decades of industrial and socialist revolution, the Dadu flows through deep canyons still inhabited by minority tribes who farm terraced hillsides. A trip here winds up at the **Wolong Nature Reserve**, home to China's famous bamboo-eating giant panda.

thailand's national parks

Some fifty national parks exist in the country, and many are well worth visiting.

Khao Yai National Park. The nation's oldest national park and one of the world's finest, Khao Yai protects some of Southeast Asia's largest remaining areas of rainforest. You can listen to monkeys scramble in the trees and white-handed gibbons wail, and hear the whoosh of wingbeats as pied hornbills take to the air.

Tarutao National Park. This unique marine sanctuary lies off the tip of Thailand and preserves a group of fifty mostly uninhabited islands, palm-shaded white-sand beaches, and stunning coral reefs. The park headquarters includes an outdoor museum and turtle-rearing ponds.

Nam Nao National Park. Though the bizarre fur-coated Sumatran rhinoceros was last spotted here in 1971, rumors that it still exists persist. The variety of flora and fauna makes this one of Thailand's most beautiful and biologically important parks.

Season: November and December

japan

Above Japan's crowded cities rises a graceful mountain range whose gentle scenery provides a soothing backdrop to the country's otherwise high-tech facade.

trekking in japan's alps

Nature-loving Japanese hold a special reverence for the Kita Alps. While trekking in these moderately elevated mountains is not as physically demanding as, say, the Swiss Alps, the sensory rewards are no less fulfilling. Grand vistas and serenity are coupled with the rarest of all commodities in Japan: open spaces.

The Japanese have imprinted trekking in the Kitas with their own indelible style. A chain of handsome and elegantly provisioned huts lines the well-graded trails that loop through the range. Scaling Mount Hodaka makes for a challenging adventure. The reward is an unobstructed view of Japan's most famous peak, Mount Fuji.

Takayama, an ancient mountain village, appears to have leapt right from the scroll of a Japanese *ukiyo-e,* or woodblock print. Skilled artisans dedicated to the preservation of time-honored folkways craft pottery and delicate latticework carvings. Generation upon generation of Takayama wood joiners have been tapped by the Imperial Court to build shrines around the country. A visit to the Kita Alps will show you from whence they draw their inspiration.

Season: Spring through fall

africa

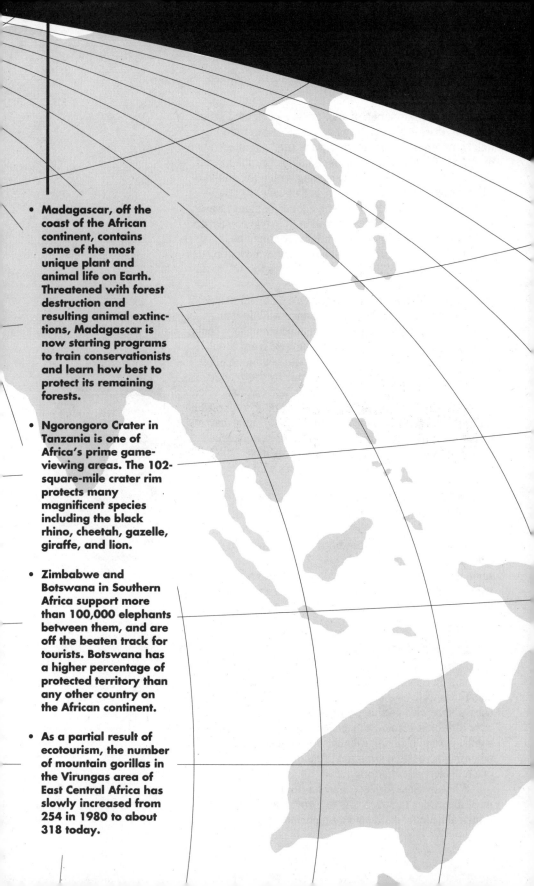

- **Madagascar, off the coast of the African continent, contains some of the most unique plant and animal life on Earth. Threatened with forest destruction and resulting animal extinctions, Madagascar is now starting programs to train conservationists and learn how best to protect its remaining forests.**

- **Ngorongoro Crater in Tanzania is one of Africa's prime game-viewing areas. The 102-square-mile crater rim protects many magnificent species including the black rhino, cheetah, gazelle, giraffe, and lion.**

- **Zimbabwe and Botswana in Southern Africa support more than 100,000 elephants between them, and are off the beaten track for tourists. Botswana has a higher percentage of protected territory than any other country on the African continent.**

- **As a partial result of ecotourism, the number of mountain gorillas in the Virungas area of East Central Africa has slowly increased from 254 in 1980 to about 318 today.**

africa

Many have dreamed of taking a classic, tented safari through Africa—traveling by Land Rover from watering hole to watering hole, watching wave after migratory wave of zebra, wildebeest, impala, elephant, and giraffe stream across the grassy plains, and sleeping within the sound of a lion's roar, separated only by a wall of canvas.

An African safari remains the apogee of nature travel. But while it's still possible to travel in the style popularized by Isak Dinesen and Ernest Hemingway, much has changed in recent years. A mood of urgency now pervades every safari—to see Africa's animals before they all disappear.

Africa is blessed by nature but cursed by humans. The number of people living in the once wildlife-rich regions of East Africa is growing by more than 3 percent a year. In Kenya, the population has jumped from about 10 million in 1964 to some 25 million at the beginning of 1990. That number is expected to triple by the year 2025. Where herds of antelope, zebra, rhino, and elephant once roamed, cattle, sheep, and goats now graze. The Great Rift Valley, once blemished only by hoofprints, is now marred by onion farms and tin-roofed villages. If left unchecked, cultivation and civilization will continue its inexorable spread, eventually dooming all of Africa's wild places and animals.

While the growth of tourism in Africa has its drawbacks—viewing wildlife on your own without a throng of other safari buses crowding around may be difficult—plenty of opportunities for exploring wild Africa still remain. Visitors can glimpse chimpanzees in the same forests where Jane Goodall studied them, look for lemurs in Madagascar, climb Mount Kilimanjaro, and raft down the mighty Zambezi River from Victoria Falls.

east africa

Safari means "journey" in Swahili, a common language in East Africa. Beneath the blue dome of Kenya and Tanzania lives a wild animal population that sets the spirit ablaze with its sheer numbers and variety. Picture a river of zebras, elands, and sable antelopes pouring across a grassy plain. Listen to the thunder of a million hoofbeats pounding across the savannah. And experience the thrill of a bull elephant charging through the acacia trees.

While an East African safari has endless variations, most itineraries include visits to Kenya's and Tanzania's principal national parks and game reserves.

!conservation alert

a call for help

Although human population growth in Africa poses serious problems for both people and animals, an even more brutal end may take place much sooner for many of Africa's wild creatures. Rampant poaching in Africa has taken a gut-wrenching toll. The decline of elephants tells the grim tale. Ivory poachers, armed with automatic rifles, have decimated Africa's elephant population from 1.3 million to fewer than 600,000 in less then a decade. Kenya alone has lost more than 85 percent of its herd in the past twenty years. Black rhinos have fared even worse. The species has been virtually exterminated throughout the continent, killed for its horns, which fetch up to $50,000 apiece in Asia and the Middle East. Buyers grind them into powder for aphrodisiacs and carve them into ceremonial dagger handles.

Fortunately, many African governments are taking steps to protect their countries' wildlife. A key motivation is the revenue generated by foreign tourists who come to view the animals. In Kenya, for example, wildlife tourism has become the leading source of foreign currency. More than 700,000 tourists—mainly German, British, and American—spend about $390 million a year in Africa. As a result, huge tracts of land have been set aside as national parks, the ivory trade has been declared illegal, and park rangers shoot poachers on sight.

When traveling in Africa on a properly managed, environmentally responsible tour, you help pay to protect wildlife. Many local conservation programs virtually depend on funding from tourists.

kenya

Kenya attracts more wildlife enthusiasts than any other country in Africa, and for good reason. It is home to a diverse assemblage of large mammals. In addition, more than 1,000 species of birds have been recorded there. The myriad ecological habitats encourage highly varied species, gaudy plumages, and bizarre shapes and sizes.

Roughly the size of Texas but similar to Arizona in topography, Kenya is a land of dramatic natural beauty. Palm trees shade the coral

beaches of its tropical eastern shore along the Indian Ocean while desert covers the north and a seemingly endless sweep of plains the south. To the west lies the shore of Lake Victoria, Africa's largest lake and the source of the Nile. And down the middle, a huge chasm—the Great Rift Valley—bisects the land from north to south. Shouldered by mile-high escarpments and bejeweled by soda and fresh-water lakes, the Great Rift is actually a mammoth fault zone 15 million years in the making. This gigantic weak spot in the earth's crust is visible from outer space, 90,000 miles away.

Kenya has sixteen national parks and twenty-three wildlife preserves. The most popular include:

Nairobi National Park. Nairobi—in the Maasai language it means "place of cool waters"—is the nation's capital city. Just five miles from its cosmopolitan heart, the black rhinoceros finds protection in a 44-square-mile park, one of the few places in Kenya where the rare rhino survives. Herds of impala, Thomson's gazelle, Coke's hartebeest, giraffe, Burchell's zebra, and wildebeest graze in the open plains and scattered acacia scrub.

Mount Kenya National Park. Located on the equator, Mount Kenya is the nation's highest mountain and rises to 17,058 feet. Elephant, cape buffalo, and bushbuck live on its lower slopes. Higher up, the scrub lands give way to mountain bamboo and hagenia forests festooned with old-man's beard. Open moorlands mark the next highest vegetation zone, and feathery strands of giant green lobelia highlight the grassy alpine zone just below the perpetually snow-cloaked peak. More than 150 species of birds can be spotted in this park.

Samburu and Buffalo Springs National Reserves. Located on either side of the Uaso Nyiro River—a lifeline for one of Kenya's most important elephant herds—these two reserves comprise dry scrubland interspersed with acacias and doum palms. Besides encompassing some of the most beautiful countryside in East Africa, Samburu and Buffalo Springs sustain a remarkable variety of animal life. Some of the more exotic creatures living here include the rapier-horned Beisa oryx, narrow-striped Grévy's zebra, reticulated giraffe, diminutive dik-dik, and graceful gerenuk.

The Great Rift Valley. A necklace of soda and fresh-water lakes hangs down the middle of this immense yellow plain. Volcanic activity has left lava flows

In Kenya, a profusion of herd animals usually indicates a large population of predators as well. The stealthy stalkers in Kenya's game parks include lion, cheetah, and leopard, and more than fifty species of birds of prey. Visitors to Samburu and Buffalo Springs game reserves frequently see martial eagle, pale chanting goshawk, pygmy falcon, and bateleur.

thousands of feet thick, and water—some of it fresh, some of it briny—has collected in the depressions. The lakes attract huge numbers of birds, including millions of flamingos. **Lake Nakuru National Park** also supports black rhinos and leopards. Two fresh-water lakes, Lake Naivasha and Lake Baringo, nurture a wide range of waterfowl, including Jackson's and Hemprich's hornbills, goliath herons, malachite kingfishers, white-breasted cormorants, yellow-billed storks, and African spoonbills. More than 480 species of birds stop over at Lake Baringo alone. Hippos wallow in the reed beds lining the shore.

Maasai Mara Game Reserve. Deservedly one of the most famous wildlife reserves in the world, the Mara is part of the fabled Serengeti ecosystem. Seven hundred square miles of parkland savannah, acacia woodland, and riverine bush provide a home for large numbers of big game animals, including hartebeest, wildebeest, topi, giraffe, and gazelle. Surely the reserve's star resident is the lion; some prides number more than forty. Visitors can also see cheetahs, hyenas, jackals, and bat-eared foxes. Banded and dwarf mongoose use giant termite mounds for homes. You can spot the endangered African wild dog in the Talek River area near Kichwa Tembo, and bird-watching excels in the Mara River area. The hundreds of resident species include the world's largest living bird, the ostrich, in addition to the prehistoric-looking marabou stork and the elegant crowned crane.

Amboseli National Park. Though this popular national park resembles a parking lot at times, it still has much to offer in the way of wildlife viewing. With Mount Kilimanjaro providing a stunning backdrop, Amboseli's sprawling plains serve as the crossroads for migrating animals in search of water. Two swamps guarantee remarkable game viewing. You may see lion, cheetah, elephant, buffalo, rhino, and leopard.

Tsavo National Park. At 8,000 square miles, roughly the size of Massachusetts, Tsavo is one of the largest wildlife parks in the world. Divided into two areas, Tsavo West and Tsavo East, the park contains a vast semi-arid expanse of savannah, acacia woodlands, riverine forest, and palm thickets. At dusk, 2,000-year-old baobab trees stand silhouetted against the sky. Tsavo is famous for its large elephant and Nile hippopotamus populations, as well as its legions of herd animals.

If flamingos are among your favorite birds, you won't want to miss Kenya's Great Rift Valley. Be prepared for a sea of pink. More than a million flamingos live on the valley's soda lakes. Because of this and the multitude of other species that flock to this spot, Roger Tory Peterson unabashedly describes Lake Nakuru as "the greatest bird spectacle on earth."

tanzania

Tanzania lies on the East African coast, with Kenya on the north, Zaire on the west, and Mozambique on the south. Although often not identified specifically with Tanzania, the country's biological assets are well-known.

! conservation alert

monkey business

⬤ Jane Goodall's thirty-year study of the chimpanzees at Gombe Stream Reserve has taught us many things about primate behavior, including an invaluable lesson about the pitfalls of uncontrolled tourism.

Goodall's highly acclaimed research has inadvertently turned Gombe Stream Reserve and its resident chimpanzees into a major tourist attraction. Though the 30-square-mile research site was designated as a national park in 1968, it has never been equipped to handle the problems that come with a flood of visitors.

Part of the problem, as reported in *Audubon*, has to do with the fact that one-third of Gombe's chimps have been habituated to humans as a result of a feeding program initiated by Goodall. This has made the chimps dangerous. Unescorted tourists wandering through the park are vulnerable to attack from chimps looking for food.

Uncontrolled exposure to humans also proves unhealthy for the chimps. In one viral epidemic, for example, thirteen of the habituated chimps died of a flu-like disease complicated by pneumonia. Six infants were left orphaned.

This has helped convince the Tanzanian government that something must be done to protect the chimps while keeping Gombe as an important tourist attraction. With help from the African Wildlife Foundation, a plan has been developed. It calls for building a hotel to accommodate tourists, limiting the number of visitors, and training guides.

The hope is that, with tight controls, Gombe can continue to be a source for education as well as economics.

The greatest animal migration on Earth takes place on Tanzania's Serengeti. The migrating mammals of the Serengeti, including globally important elephant and black rhinoceros populations, make up what is probably the greatest concentration of large mammals in the world. In wave after undulating wave, the animals fan out across this 5,700-square-mile reserve in search of water. The migrants include 1.5 million wildebeest, 200,000 zebra, 18,000 eland, 500,000 Thomson's gazelle, and 50,000 Grant's gazelle. The peak seasons are February, when about a million wildebeest calve, and June, which is mating season for many species.

They include the famous chimpanzee population at Gombe Stream Reserve and the extraordinary diversity of animals at lakes Tanganyika, Victoria and Malawi. The mammals that migrate across the Serengeti plain are legendary as well as biologically significant.

In addition to these already celebrated areas, the Malagarisi Swamps form one of the largest wetlands in Africa. At 19,340 feet, Mt. Kilimanjaro is the highest free-standing mountain in the world, as well as home to its own collection of endemic plants and animals.

Tanzania's human population of 26,343,000 in a country of 365,000 square miles (70 people per square mile) belies the extent of pressure on the area's natural resources. More than half the country is too dry for cultivation, the population is largely rural and agricultural, and the population growth rate of 3.6 percent will double the number of Tanzanians in nineteen years.

Although one of the poorest nations in the world, with a gross national product of $183 per person, Tanzania's commitment to conservation is unsurpassed. Twenty-five percent of the country is contained within conservation areas. Serengeti National Park, Ruaha National Park, and the Ngorongoro Conservation Unit each protect large areas of East African woodland/savannah. Gombe Stream, Kilimanjaro, and Arusha national parks protect important highland ecosystems.

Serengeti National Park. Bordering Kenya's Maasai Mara Game Reserve, the Serengeti is justly one of the most famous wildlife areas of the world. Its 5,700 square miles of acacia savannahs, grass plains, and woodlands support enormous herds of animals. Because of its critical location on the migration routes of so many species, the Serengeti plays a vital role in the preservation of Africa's wildlife.

Ngorongoro Conservation Area. The world's largest unflooded caldera, Ngorongoro is a renowned World Heritage Site. Many regard it as Africa's most unique game-viewing area. An oasis of tranquility, the rim of this 102-square-mile crater protects a remarkable concentration of species, including black rhino, cheetah, gazelle, giraffe, and lion. Flamingos live in an alkaline lake in the crater's center, along with a plethora of other avian species.

Lake Manyara National Park. Located at the western edge of the Great Rift Valley, this 127-square-mile lake is a haven for naturalists. Flamingos and hippos inhabit the lakeshore. The density of elephants is said to be the highest in Africa; they may be viewed at very close range. Nowhere else can you find cape buffalo with russet red coats. The unique tree-climbing lion perches in acacia trees, waiting for unsuspecting prey to pass beneath. The park also supports monitor lizards, two species of baboon, and a plentitude of birds.

Tarangire National Park. At 1,000 square miles, Tarangire is Tanzania's third largest national park. Immense populations of herd animals migrate from the Maasai Steppe. Resident animals include elephant, black rhino, several antelope species, leopard, cheetah, and lion. The more than 260 species of birds include bateleur, secretary bird, ostrich, ashy starlings, and orange-bellied and brown parrots.

Season: Year-round except in April and May

Olduvai Gorge in Tanzania is famous for being the cradle of humanity. It is here that Louis and Mary Leakey made their archaeological discoveries, including the remains of a 2-million-year-old human-like creature. Olduvai serves as the world's foremost outdoor museum, showcasing the origin of our species.

the snows of kilimanjaro

Mount Kilimanjaro soars above the East African savannah like a white-capped sentinel. The 19,340-foot "White Mountain" offers breathtaking views of the richest game lands in East Africa.

Kilimanjaro was first climbed in 1889 by Hans Meyer. It has become a favorite destination for African travelers seeking a different point of view. The ascent to Uhuru Peak (Swahili for "freedom") passes through a stepladder of vegetation zones from equatorial rainforest to grassland to glacial ice. Climbers pass animals and flowering plants along the way.

Season: June through December

off the beaten trail

While the interest in Tanzania's more famous parks is well-deserved, one result is that little attention has been paid to Tanzania's most biologically diverse and unique ecosystem: the Eastern Arc Mountains. Listed by the United Nations Natural Resource Council as one of the eleven most important areas for biological diversity in the world, the Eastern Arc Mountains are comprised of a series of forested mountain islands dotted across the dry woodland/savannah of Eastern Tanzania.

Throughout their long history, these isolated and geologically ancient mountains have served as a laboratory for the development of new species. Although these high-elevation forests make up less than 2 percent of the land area of Tanzania, they contain 15 percent of the plant species known in the nation. In addition to the inherent value of such diversity, many scientists consider the region to be of major global importance for the clues it might offer to the pursuit of biogeography and evolution.

African violet fanciers, as well as bird-watchers, may well consider a visit to the Eastern Arc. The region contains eighteen of the twenty known species of African violets, as well as sixteen species of wild coffee, three endangered primates, including the Sanje crested mangabey and the Uhehe red colobus, which are endemic to the Uzungwa forest. Sixteen threatened bird species live in the Eastern Arc. They include five that are native to the region, among them the unusual Usambara eagle owl.

Season: June through December

The Usambaras in the Eastern Arc Mountains was once a major vacation destination for British colonialists. The nickname "Little Switzerland" refers both to the cool mountain air and the German colonial architecture of Lushoto, the district capital. Trout that were stocked in the streams more than 60 years ago continue to provide an angler's sport, and the unique bird life attracts the serious bird-watcher.

rwanda

This Maryland-sized nation lies sandwiched between Tanzania and Zaire in East Central Africa. Though the most densely populated country in all of Africa—with more than 750 people jammed into every square mile and a growth rate expected to double within twenty years—

Rwanda has set aside more than one-tenth of its total land area as national parks.

Kagera National Park is a sea of grass, savannahs, marshes, and lakes, home to a wide variety of animals, specifically zebra, eland, oribi, and topi. **Parc National des Volcans** is actually Africa's first national park—it was originally Parc National Albert, established by the colonial Belgian government in 1925. The park protects more than ninety species of birds and such unusual animals as the tree hyrax, black-fronted duiker, buffalo, elephant, forest hog, and bushbuck. But it is best known for its most extraordinary and captivating inhabitant, the mountain gorilla. Visitors to Parc des Volcans must be in good physical condition to go on a gorilla-viewing expedition. The terrain is rough, weather can be nasty, and one may hike for hours before seeing the animals—although the rewards are great.

gorillas in the mist

An encounter with any primate in the wild is exciting, but few experiences can match the thrill of observing mountain gorillas up close in their natural habitat. The opportunity to see these magnificent creatures in the wild proves that ecotourism can and does work.

Mountain gorillas are sociable animals and live in family groups of three to thirty. They move about frequently during the day as they search for food. At night they retire to sleeping nests. Huge, six-foot, 400-pound, graying mature males, known as "silverbacks," preside over their families. The sight of a family of gorillas feeding, playing, and napping in the forest is an unforgettable experience.

Season: Year-round

monkey hiking

One of the few places in Africa where it is possible to see wildlife and enjoy a forest hike at the same time is **Nyungwe Forest Reserve**, which has recently been developed for tourism. In the first year of operation (1989-90), 5,000 visitors came through, including those brought by well-known United States-based tour agencies. The forest offers about 22 miles of well-groomed nature trails passing through a variety of vegetation types: dense forest, rocky ridges, wetlands, and forest openings. Although good physical condition is necessary for any wildlife hike, these trails allow for short or long hikes on easy or difficult terrain, as you choose. Hikers may have the opportunity to see some of the thirteen types of primates that inhabit the forest. In addition, guided hikes run twice a day for viewing of the black-and-white colobus

natural success

tourists in the mist

The mountain gorilla remains one of the most endangered animals on Earth, but thanks to a unique ecotourism program, its future is brighter than it has been in decades. Human incursion has restricted the mountain gorilla's range to the 9,000- to 15,000-foot volcanic slopes of the Virunga Mountains in East Central Africa. The gorilla population plummeted mainly in Zaire as a result of outright killing during the country's civil war in the 1960s. And in Rwanda, poaching was a serious factor in driving the population down as well.

The plight of the gorillas received international attention due to the writings of renown primatologist Dian Fossey, specifically her book, *Gorillas in the Mist*. Though Fossey's approach was heroic, it has really been ecotourism that has helped secure the huge primate's future. The gorilla tourism program was begun in 1979 by Bill Weber and Amy Vedder, two American researchers who came to the conclusion that the only way to save the gorilla was to find a means of helping it earn its keep. Four gorilla groups were slowly habituated to the presence of humans. Then, small groups of tourists were taken up the mountain to view them.

The tourism program had an immediate impact on poaching. Today, according to Vedder and Weber, approximately 7,000 foreigners per year visit the gorillas in their natural habitat. Park regulations keep groups small and provide instructions to visitors to keep the human impact as low as possible. The program has become an important source of income, boosting park revenues some 2,000 percent and helping make tourism Rwanda's third largest producer of foreign capital. As a result of ecotourism, the number of mountain gorillas in the Virungas is increasing, climbing from 254 in 1980 to around 318 today.

monkey or gray-cheeked mangabey. The reserve is a great attraction for birders, especially those interested in birds native to the mountains of Africa.

Season: Year-round

southern africa

While most Americans and Europeans target East Africa for their safaris, a bounty of wildlife and natural adventure remains nearly undiscovered in southern Africa, specifically in three adjoining countries: Zambia, Zimbabwe, and Botswana. You can follow in the footsteps of such legendary explorers as Sir Henry Morton Stanley, David Livingstone, and Sir Richard Burton. In some cases, the wildlife is even more abundant than in East Africa. Zimbabwe and Botswana have more than 100,000 elephants between them, the landscape is more spectacular, and, best of all, the tourists are far fewer.

zambia

Zambia is a predominantly flat land with some low undulating hills and a few isolated mountains. Two national parks showcase the best of Zambia's natural heritage.

South Luangwa National Park. Covering more than 3,500 square miles, this huge park encompasses the game-rich Luangwa River. Considered one of the finest wildlife-viewing areas in Africa, it has a variety of species. One of the few parks where walking safaris are possible, you can see elephant, hippopotamus, leopard, lion, zebra, Lichtenstein's hartebeest, Cookson's wildebeest, the scythe-horned sable antelope, and the unique Thornicroft's giraffe. South African crowned crane, saddle-billed stork, and wood ibis share top billing as the park's largest and most spectacular birds.

Lochinvar National Park. Located in southern Zambia on the floodplain of the Kafue River, this vast, treeless flatland is a successful example of a former cattle ranch restored as natural habitat. More than 40,000 unique Kafue lechwe, a semi-aquatic antelope, populate the park, along with 400 species of birds, including the wattled crane, sacred ibis, and the African fish eagle, Zambia's national bird. The park encourages visitors to explore on foot.

Season: Year-round

zimbabwe

The former British colony of Rhodesia is a naturalist's surprise. Despite decades of intensive farming and pressure from an increasing population, huge areas of national parkland have been set aside to provide a haven for a wide range of species, from large carnivores to hoofed animals. Compared to the beleaguered herds in East Africa, Zimbabwe's elephants continue to thrive.

Matusadona National Park. Situated on the banks of Lake Kariba, the park covers 585 square miles of low flatland, bush, and a range of mountains. The reserve is famous for its walking safaris, where you can see the elusive and endangered black rhinoceros and cape buffalo. Matusadona hosts a remarkable number of bird species, including such bizarre spectacles as the yellow-billed hornbill.

Hwange National Park. Hwange is Zimbabwe's largest national park and one of the last great sanctuaries for African elephants left on the continent. The size of the park has enabled the interdependent wildlife system to remain relatively pristine. As a result, it supports a prolific animal community. More than 100 species of mammals and 400 species of birds can be seen here.

Zambezi National Park. Large herds of cape buffalo, elephant, sable antelope, and cheetah make this a prime area for wildlife viewing. The mighty Zambezi River, which forms the border between Zimbabwe and Zambia, cuts through the park, so you can also explore it by boat. The animal life is so rich, it harkens back to the old days of Africa before the pressures of runaway population and uncontrolled cultivation took their toll.

The Zambezi River's steep descent and endless whitewater washboard proved too much for the intrepid David Livingstone. He took one look over Victoria Falls and turned back. What a journey he missed. The 70-mile run to Lake Kariba promises adventure, thrills, and a unique perspective into the wild heart of Africa.

rafting the mighty z

If it's whitewater adventure you're after, than take a plunge down the Zambezi River. It boasts more than 100 rapids, 10 of them ranked the biggest in the world—on par with the biggest the Colorado River has to offer.

A raft trip down the Zambezi begins at the base of Victoria Falls, or Mosi-Oa-Tunya, the local name that means "the smoke that thunders." This mile-wide curtain of falling water is one of the Seven Wonders of the World.

Season: June through December

botswana

Botswana is one of the least-known places on Earth, yet it ranks among the greatest wildlife strongholds. A landlocked nation about the size of Texas, Botswana spans two diverse biomes: the arid Kalahari and the wetlands of the Okavango. These meet in the north, where a vast savannah wilderness is supported by the Okavango delta. This wilderness represents some of the best-preserved habitat within the Zambezian regional center of endemism, a biogeographic region with more

▐ conservation alert

saving the wild dogs

● African wild dogs are the most social of all the canid species. They live in extended family groups, called packs, of up to fifty individuals. Each dog has a unique coat color pattern of white, black, and brown, which helps identify it. In the Okavango Swamp, the dogs range over large areas of at least 310 square miles, hunting small antelope species they find as they travel. In Botswana, their primary prey is impala, although they also kill reedbuck, kudu, and wildebeest.

Botswana's Wild Dog Research Project, begun in 1988 in cooperation with Botswana's Department of Wildlife and National Parks, and the University of California at Davis, is surveying the population and habits of the wild dogs that remain in Botswana. A recent survey estimated the population throughout the continent to be 2,000. Wild dogs have disappeared entirely from most African countries where they were once common. In others, they survive only within the confines of national parks. In Botswana, the majority of wild dogs live partially or entirely outside of protection. Despite this fact, Botswana may be home to Africa's largest wild dog population.

Wild dogs are currently being monitored in the Okavango Swamp, including areas within and near the **Moremi Wildlife Reserve.** Ten packs are known to live in this area, and nine of these are being monitored by Conservation International with the help of radio collars. This subpopulation represents the core of Botswana's wild dog population, and the health of this core is likely to dictate the species' future.

plant species than all the lowland rain forests of West and Central Africa combined and with a comparable number of bird and mammal species.

Having both one of the lowest population densities in the world and valuable diamond deposits, the democratic country of Botswana offers a great hope of delivering intact this ecosystem into the next century.

Season: Year-round

the okavango is better than ok

The world's largest inland delta at 6,200 square miles in area, the Okavango is one of Africa's last undeveloped wetlands. A remarkable, sprawling eco-complex of inland marshes and isolated isles, this intact ecosystem supports more than 80 species of fish, more than 400 species of birds, and more than 100 species of mammals. The mammal species cover the full spectrum of Africa's rapidly diminishing large animals: wild dogs, cheetahs, lions, leopards, zebras, giraffe, a dozen species of antelope, as well as hippos, buffaloes, and Africa's largest single population of elephants. Wildebeest, resplendent oryx, roan antelope, and red lechwe roam this wildlife wonderland in large numbers. Waterbirds which can be spotted here at one time or another include such unusual species as black egret, rufous-bellied heron, wattled crane, and pygmy goose.

The Okavango is surrounded by 100,000 square kilometers of wilderness. To the north is **Chobe National Park**, home to the largest herd of elephants of any African park. The gray giants come down to the river en masse to play and cool off. You'll also find numerous lions as well as cheetahs and wild dogs.

Season: Year-round

madagascar

Few other places in the world have produced as many unusual species of life as Madagascar has. It is Earth's fourth largest island and a living laboratory for evolution. When the 226,000-square-mile island tore away from Africa 165 million years ago, only a few types of plants and animals were on it or were able to drift to it before the Mozambique Channel became too wide to cross. This ensured that those few types could flourish and diversify relatively free from competition. Diversification was further encouraged by the variety of ecological niches available, including mountains, deserts, and rainforests. It is estimated that some three-quarters of the country's 200,000 native flora and fauna are found nowhere else.

Consider the Aepyornis, or "elephant bird," which laid the largest known egg, big enough to hold more than 2 gallons. Or the lemur, a primitive primate displaced elsewhere in the world by monkeys, but found on Madagascar in at least twenty-five different varieties. Or the baobab tree; six species grow on Madagascar compared to only one in all the rest of Africa. Of the island's 130 species of palms, all but two are endemic. Thousands of flowering plants bloom here, including many orchids. Of the 3,000 species of butterfly, 97 percent live nowhere else. Madagascar is also the chameleon capital of the world, with more than one-third of the world's species.

Sadly, Madagascar has suffered a tremendous loss of wildlife in recent years. Growing poverty is exacerbated by a population that has doubled in twenty-five years, giving it

Chameleons, found in Périnet Special Reserve on the island of Madagascar, are great camouflage artists. This special kind of Old World lizard can change color to blend in with its surroundings or according to its mood. Parson's chameleon, for example, goes from turquoise to jade to emerald. Chameleons come in a range of sizes, from the gecko-sized leaf-tailed lizard to the ultra-tiny dwarf chameleon.

one of the highest population growth rates in Africa (over 3 percent). Sixty percent of the population is under the age of twenty. This growth has pushed the Malagasy, as islanders are called, into an increasingly ferocious assault on the island's natural resources. Although the problems are complex and will not be easily solved, the government of Madagascar is very committed to improving the standard of living for its people and is turning to a number of conservation-based activities, including ecotourism, to bolster its economy. And, fortunately, there is still a lot of wildlife to see.

Zahamena Reserve in Madagascar is one of the largest rainforest reserves in the country, and much of its 180,000-plus acreage remains unexplored. On the outskirts of this largely undisturbed primary forest are rural villages that will be included in conservation plans to preserve this important ecosystem.

looking for lemurs

Named for the ghosts of the Roman dead that are said to have roamed the night, lemurs are the closest living descendants of the common ancestor of monkeys, apes, and humans. This primitive, squirrel-sized primate, known as a prosimian, lived in subtropical forests throughout the world 50 million years ago. But it could not successfully compete with the smarter monkeys and so were displaced—everywhere, that is, except in monkey-free Madagascar, where a handful of prosimians rode the island into evolutionary history.

It is still unclear just how many different species of lemurs existed in Madagascar before the arrival of humans 1,500 years ago. But about thirty species survive, including the reclusive aye-aye; the more common ring-tailed lemur; the mouse lemur, smallest of living primates; and the indri, largest of the dwarf lemurs, which looks like a cross between a teddy bear and a grown panda. Scientists rediscovered a species thought to have gone extinct: the hairy-eared dwarf lemur, one of the world's tiniest known primates. And in 1986, the golden bamboo lemur was discovered to live here.

Madagascar's lemurs and other prized wildlife species can be seen by visiting the island's national parks and reserves. The most accessible of these are:

Berenty Reserve. Located on the banks of the Mandrare River in the ultradry spiny desert of southern Madagascar, this internationally acclaimed reserve of mostly gallery forest abounds with rare flora and fauna. Ring-tailed lemurs can be seen in troops of about twelve to twenty-five animals. Other species include white-coated sifakas and lepilemurs. More than fifty of Madagascar's 251 unique bird species have been recorded here.

Périnet Special Reserve. This tropical rainforest reserve is one of the most accessible in the country. Just 90 miles east of the capital city of Antananarivo, it protects nine different species of lemur, including the indri, a child-sized, nearly tailless lemur that grasps the sides of trees with powerful legs and arms and leaps from treetop to treetop.

The reserve is also home to a variety of chameleons, an unusual kind of lizard that can alter its pigmentation.

Ranomafana National Park. Another tropical rainforest reserve located on the east coast, Ranomafana is the site of the 1986 discovery of the golden bamboo lemur. Soothing thermal springs are an added attraction.

Montagne D'Ambre National Park. This tropical rainforest, located in the northernmost tip of Madagascar, boasts well-kept paths, labeled trees, and a huge waterfall. Orchids, reptiles, and many species of birds share the park with several types of lemur.

Lokobe Natural Reserve. This tiny reserve, located on Nosy Be, a beautiful resort island off the north coast, has a picture-postcard beach and nearly perfect weather year-round. The black lemur, a primate considered sacred by the native islanders, lives here and can be easily observed. An outrigger canoe ride to an isolated village with tourists themselves doing the paddling is a special attraction.

Season: Spring and fall

cruising the enchanted isles

In addition to Madagascar, the Indian Ocean holds other island surprises. Visiting these islands makes for an ideal natural history cruise.

The **Comoro Islands**, an archipelago of four volcanic islands, lie between East Africa and Madagascar.

Featured attractions include bird watching, swimming, and snorkeling. A barrier reef shelters the island of Mayotte, enclosing one of the largest lagoons in the world. The island's interior has more scents than the perfume counter at Bloomingdale's. The comingling of jasmine, patchouli, palma rosa, lemon grass, ylang ylang, and basilic violet fills the air and the senses.

To the northeast of the Comoros are the Seven Sisters, or **Seychelles**, a last outpost of peace and tranquility. The islands produce a paradise for ornithologists. Several rare species live on La Digue Island, including the unusual black paradise flycatcher. Black parrots, blue pigeons, and sunbirds flock to the nature reserve on Praslin Island. On Praslin, a forest of coco-de-mer and other palms thrive in the Vallée de Mai, a valley so lovely that British General Charles Gordon of Khartoum believed it to be the original Garden of Eden.

Cousin Island is a 70-acre nature reserve. Held in permanent trust for the International Council for Bird Preservation, it was the first internationally sponsored reserve in the Indian Ocean. Its fauna includes white terns, lesser noddies, white-tailed tropic birds, shearwaters, and several endemic land birds, specifically the Seychelles warbler, fody, and sunbird. The island's beaches also provide an important nesting site for the hawksbill turtle.

Giant tortoises inhabit the island of **Aldabra.** No wonder this "Galapagos of the Indian Ocean" was designated as a UNESCO World Heritage Site. The island serves as a home for 150,000 tortoises as well as drongos and frigate birds.

Bird Island is aptly named. The beaches are awash in a sea of gannets, while the branches of island trees are so covered with noddies that they appear brown, not green. Little red Madagascar fodies wing across the hills, while snow-white fairy terns fill the sky like living clouds. At dusk, millions of sooty terns turn the sky dark.

Season: Spring and fall

! conservation alert

rush to save endangered madagascar

The entire island of Madagascar is an environmentally threatened area. Estimates of forest destruction show that as much as 80 percent of the country's original forest cover has been destroyed in the 1,500 to 2,000 years since the arrival of humans, and the destruction continues today. Threats to the environment include slash-and-burn farming, uncontrolled ranging of livestock, timber exploitation, charcoal burning, and uncontrolled hunting. The denuded hills hemorrhage red clay whenever it rains. From the air, the face of the island appears pockmarked, as if ravaged by a virulent form of terrestrial smallpox.

It's already too late to save many of Madagascar's evolutionary wonders. Gone forever are fourteen species of lemur—including one 200-pound giant—along with a pygmy hippopotamus, two species of giant tortoise, an aardvark, and the "elephant bird," one of the largest birds ever to walk the Earth.

In a rush to save what remains, several major environmental initiatives have been created. They include an ecosystem management program at the **Zahamena Reserve**, an effort to establish a university-level training program for Malagasy conservationists, and a pilot study to reduce the problems caused by fuelwood collection and charcoal production.

Madagascar was one of the first countries in the world to establish a national park system—in 1927. Most of the wildlands that remain in Madagascar are still protected. In 1984, when the bottom fell out of the market for the country's main crops—vanilla and coffee beans—the government turned to these parklands as a new source of income. Spurred on by media attention to the country's environmental problems, the government of Madagascar is now very committed to conservation-based development for its people.

A blueprint for low-impact, environmentally conscious tourism was recently developed with help from the U.S. Agency for International Development, and Madagascar's nature reserves are now open for business. If you wonder where your travel dollars might be best spent, check out this extraordinary country.

west africa

The West African region has long been noted for its rich cultural diversity. However, until now information about places to visit has been difficult to find, and little has been done to accommodate tourists.

Recently, however, the state government of Ghana's Central Region has begun to recognize the tourist appeal of its natural and cultural resources as a source of economic development. In a project with Conservation International, the Smithsonian Institution, the International Council on Monuments and Sites, and the Midwest Universities Consortium for International Activities, the Central Region is developing a package of tourist attractions that should be enjoyable for its vacation value as well as educational interest for visitors from other countries.

The tourist package centers on three main attractions: a tropical forest national park, a series of historic forts and castles dating from the 15th century which were used in the slave trade of the 18th century, and an undeveloped strip of pristine beaches.

nature and history meet in ghana

Kakum National Park and Wildlife Reserve, an area encompasing 260 square miles, contains populations of forest elephants, five species of monkeys, and a mix of forest and savannah birds native to the West African region. In addition, the park is surrounded by twenty villages whose residents count on the park for clean water supplies, and who are an integral part of the tourism planning for the area. Located 18 miles north of the seaside town of Cape Coast, Kakum will be available for day trips as well as overnight stays beginning in 1992.

Three forts and castles, originally built by the Dutch, Portuguese, and British, are scheduled for renovatation and restoration as part of the tourism project. Part of a group of 26 structures perched on the Ghanaian coast and classified as World Heritage sites, the buildings stand as grim reminders of the slave traffic that emanated from the Ghana coast under colonial powers during the 1700s.

The third area targeted for protection is a stretch of pristine beaches. A limited number of small-scale hotels are to be built nearby. Unlike much of the West African coast, some of Ghana's beaches are not subject to the strong undertows that limit beach tourism elsewhere in the region.

Although this three-fold project is in its early stages, Ghana's emphasis on tourism has already begun to attract visitors.

Season: December through June

8

europe

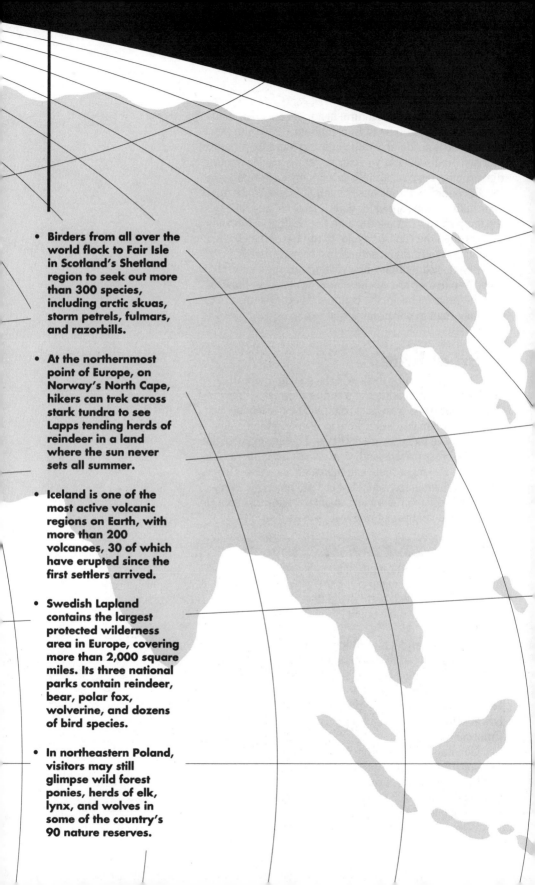

- Birders from all over the world flock to Fair Isle in Scotland's Shetland region to seek out more than 300 species, including arctic skuas, storm petrels, fulmars, and razorbills.

- At the northernmost point of Europe, on Norway's North Cape, hikers can trek across stark tundra to see Lapps tending herds of reindeer in a land where the sun never sets all summer.

- Iceland is one of the most active volcanic regions on Earth, with more than 200 volcanoes, 30 of which have erupted since the first settlers arrived.

- Swedish Lapland contains the largest protected wilderness area in Europe, covering more than 2,000 square miles. Its three national parks contain reindeer, bear, polar fox, wolverine, and dozens of bird species.

- In northeastern Poland, visitors may still glimpse wild forest ponies, herds of elk, lynx, and wolves in some of the country's 90 nature reserves.

europe

Europe's arresting cultural history is only part of its attraction. Within hours of Buckingham Palace and the Louvre exists a side of Europe little explored by American tourists. To discover it, you can forget the package tours that promise ten capital cities in as many days, and leave the air-conditioned tour buses behind. Instead, lace up your hiking boots, shoulder your knapsack, and take to the footpaths. On a walk through the Scottish Highlands, a trek through the Alps, or a hike to the top of the Caucasus Mountains, you'll find a natural history surprise.

Pay close attention when visiting Europe's natural areas. While they are nowhere near as exotic as those of, say, the Amazon basin, the continent's ecosystems are no less important to our planet's well-being.

great britain

The "kingdom by the sea" is laced with more than 100,000 miles of walking trails and bridleways. Many of these public paths were first trampled by the feet of prehistoric humans. Later, Roman legions added roads, which survive today as grassy lanes. Though many of the footpaths cross private land, visitors still have the right to use them. Picking a route and following it is easy. The British Parliament passed a law in 1949 requiring every county council to prepare and maintain maps that show all the public footpaths and bridleways in its district.

walkies

The real United Kingdom reveals itself on a walking tour. While you can camp along the way, most people choose to spend each night in a different historic inn or public house. The most popular districts for walking tours include:

The Peak and Lake districts. Historic paths lead through a picturesque countryside that seems torn from the pages of a coffee-table picture book. Quaint villages set off by grand estates highlight the Peak District, while the Lake District suggests the poetry of Wordsworth—a lyrical setting of peaks and ridges rising above the lakes of Cumbria County.

Coastal England. England's longest trail—the 500-mile-long Southwest Coastal Footpath—rings the island's southwest peninsula. From Somerset to Devon, from Cornwall to Dorset, it passes through colorful seaside villages and a string of nature reserves.

Western Ireland. Most of Ireland has left its native

natural success

the green airline

Now you can fly the "environmentally friendly skies."

London-based Virgin Atlantic Airways is incorporating conservation into its everyday business practices. It began by issuing biodegradable plastic shopping bags for duty-free goods purchased by passengers. The airline stocks only biodegradable toiletries in the planes' lavatories. Not only are the soaps and lotions made from all-natural ingredients, but they also haven't been tested on laboratory animals.

For the May 16, 1990 inaugural flight of its new route from Los Angeles to London, Virgin Atlantic held a silent auction for charity—people bid through the mail for plane seats—and the proceeds went to the Environmental Conservation Organization. The airline also planted a tree for every passenger who traveled on the Los Angeles/London flight in 1990.

Virgin Atlantic also became the first airline to begin recycling its in-flight scrap. The trash is separated and recycled. The airline is considering using recycled paper for its tickets.

Virgin Atlantic serves London from Los Angeles, New York, Miami, and Boston. It also flies to Moscow and Tokyo.

John Muir, the famed conservationist and naturalist, must have crossed the East Lothian dunes in Scotland more than once. Follow in his footsteps to the John Muir Trust Preserve. Begin at his birthplace in Dunbar, then walk west across the Highlands to the preserve named in his honor on the Knoydart Peninsula. This is true Scots wilderness—a land of desolate moors and haunting bagpipes.

tongue behind as well as much of its past, but not the district of Connemara. Locals here still speak Gaelic, and the countryside looks as undisturbed as it did a century ago. Nearby Mount Mweelrea offers plenty of vistas and solitude for those willing to climb it.

Season: Spring and summer

cruising and birding

The rugged islands that dot the coast of Great Britain hide a bounty of cultural and natural surprises. Not only do they support some of the greatest colonies of seabirds anywhere, they also cloister a repository of archaeological treasures and religious artifacts. Expeditionary-class cruise ships call on the most important islands.

The **Skellig Islands** off Ireland rise out of the sea like forbidding black haystacks. Tens of thousands of gannets nest among the stone ruins of a ninth-century monastery.

The **Aran Islands** off the western coast of Ireland also shelter cultural antiquities. Dun Aengus is a prehistoric fort built, the legend goes, by the mythical Fir

Bolg people. It is said to be the most magnificent barbaric monument in Europe.

Farther north lie the **Hebrides Islands.** The Scots call Iona, in the Inner Hebrides, the "Holy Isle of Scotland." Scottish Christianity traces its roots to this burial place of Viking, Irish, and Scottish kings, including Macbeth. On the Isle of Skye, golden eagles soar in front of the dark and brooding silhouette of Cuillin Hills.

A Stonehenge-like cluster of gray stone monoliths pokes out of the peat on the **Isle of Lewis** in the Outer Hebrides. These unearthed bones of a long-forgotten religion were famous throughout the ancient world. Greek historian Herodotus called it "the great winged temple of the northern isles."

The **Orkney** and **Shetland** islands rest on the northern horizon of Scotland. In 1850, a gale unveiled the 5,000-year-old neolithic village of Skara Brae near Kirkwall. Birders from all over the world come to Fair Isle in the Shetlands to see more than 300 species, including such cliffside denizens as arctic skuas, storm petrels, fulmars, and razorbills.

Season: Summer

On Norway's **Lofoten Islands**, large colonies of puffins, sea eagles, kittiwakes, guillemots, and auks cling to sheer cliffs above desolate beaches and rustic fishing villages. A formidable tide-race known as the maelstrom—inspiration of stories by Edgar Allen Poe and Jules Verne—churns the sea.

norway

Norway is Europe's longest country and, with the exception of Iceland, also its least populated major nation. Mountains cover more than 72 percent of its countryside, and less than 4 percent has ever been cultivated. Norway possesses 150,000 islands and 12,500 miles of astonishingly scenic shoreline, much of it in the form of rugged fjords that slash their way deep into the interior, leaving steep mountain walls to shoot straight up from water's edge. The majestic juxtaposition of natural elements is unforgettable—sea against mountain, forest against glacier, rainbow against waterfall.

steaming in the land of the midnight sun

Exploring Norway's coast and fjords by coastal steamer takes you to small seaside villages where, centuries ago, high-prowed Viking longboats set sail for England, Greenland, and across the Atlantic to North America. These coastal stopovers provide the perfect jumping-off points for hikes on the elaborate trail system that penetrates deep into the interior mountain ranges.

The sea lanes to the north cross the Arctic Circle. Farther north lies North Cape, the northernmost point in Europe. You can hike across the stark tundra, where Lapps tend herds of reindeer and the sun shines continuously from May through August.

Season: Summer

Norwegians invented cross-country skiing 4,000 years ago. It's both the national sport as well as the national pastime, so it should come as no surprise that the country also boasts the world's biggest and best Nordic trail system. A 1,200-mile-long groomed track called the Nordmarka winds through thick stands of spruce trees, across frozen lakes, and up and down gently rolling hills before dropping into the outskirts of the nation's capital, Oslo.

A well-planned trip on this fabled route reveals a side of Scandinavia seen by few outsiders. The Norwegians have strategically placed small, cozy ski lodges about every 12 miles along the route, providing warm and comfortable places to spend the night after a full day on the trail.

Season: Winter

iceland

Borne by fire, Iceland remains one of the most active volcanic regions on Earth. More than 200 volcanoes can be counted here; thirty of them have erupted since the first settlers arrived. There is no escaping the island's fiery volcanic heritage. Fumaroles, craters, geysers, hot springs, and bubbling mudpots create an uneasy mood among ancient lava flows scoured and sculpted by rivers and glacial ice.

This is geology in the making—an embryonic terrain where the earth undergoes creation right before your eyes. Volcanic eruptions constantly add to Iceland's 39,709 square miles of territory.

A tour that circumnavigates Iceland's interior and coastal reaches takes in such hot spots as the nation's most famous volcano, Mount Hekla, which has blown its top at least seventeen times in the last 900 years, and Eldhraun, the world's largest lava field.

Iceland is not all rock and fire, however. As its name implies, plenty of ice exists as well. Glaciers and ice caps cover some 12 percent of the land. Vatnajökull ranks as the largest ice cap in the world behind Greenland and Antarctica. Beneath its frozen mantle, numerous volcanoes simmer. Look out should they boil over. Past eruptions have produced torrential glacial floods.

Season: Summer

The Arctic fox may be Iceland's only native land mammal, but plenty of marine mammals ply the waters offshore, including seventeen species of whale. Huge colonies of seabirds nest on the coastal cliffs, including guillemots, razorbills, puffins, kittiwakes, fulmars, and gannets. The Iceland gyrfalcon and rare white-tailed eagle, two of the country's most notable species, are protected by law.

sweden

Sweden boasts more wildlands and forested expanses of any European country outside the Soviet Union. About half the nation is covered by forests. As befits this progressive nation, Sweden takes a very enlightened approach to wilderness protection. Sixteen national parks have been established, along with dozens of nature preserves.

Swedish Lapland contains the most intact wilderness areas. Three national parks and several adjacent nature reserves cover more than 2,000 square miles, making it the largest protected wilderness area in Europe. The land is rugged and wild. Steep mountains tower above narrow valleys and deep glacial basins. Bogs, marshes, and lakes dot a land marked by dense willow thickets and tundra-like heaths.

The largest of the three is **Padjelanta National Park**. The wide-open mountain plain and its large lakes protect some of the most botanically important species in Sweden, such as the endemic arctic cinquefoil, creeping sandwort, and pale gentian. Resident mammals include reindeer, bear, polar fox, wolverine, and lemming. Bird life is also diverse. Dozens of species, including gyrfalcon, hooded crow, grey shrike, and song thrush, dwell here.

Nearby **Sarek National Park** boasts nearly 100 glaciers and eight peaks topping 6,000 feet. The abundance of wildlife allows easy viewing of reindeer, mountain elk, moose, lynx, golden eagle, rough-legged buzzard, snow bunting, and long-tailed skua, among others.

The third contiguous Lapland national park, **Stora Sjofallet**, features virgin pine covering its lower elevations. This is actually the western reach of the Eurasian taiga, the world's most extensive pine forest. For the past 7,000 years it has been left undeveloped and unmolested.

Sjauna Bird Sanctuary, one of Europe's largest wetlands, serves as a breeding area for numerous species, including whooper swan, bean goose, spotted redshank, osprey, white-tailed eagle, red-throated pipit, and broad-billed sandpiper. Wolf, bear, and lynx have all been spotted ranging within the sanctuary.

Season: Summer

Sweden believes in granting access to its public lands and maintains one of the most extensive networks of footpaths in the world. Under the centuries-old tradition known as Everyman's Right, all people in Sweden, including foreign visitors, have the right to wander freely anywhere in the country, as long as they don't enter private homes, damage croplands, litter, pick plants, cut trees, drive off public roads, or hunt.

the alps

The Alpine region of Europe is an 84,942-square-mile expanse of peaks, high meadows, idyllic valleys, and icy lakes that stretches from the French-Italian border to southern Austria and northwestern Yugoslavia. Seven

❗ conservation alert

a mountain of problems

⬤ Until Hannibal crossed them on the back of an elephant, the Alps proved to be an almost insurmountable barrier. No longer. Some fifty airlines, seven railroads, and thirty major highways now service the mountainous region, delivering more than 40 million tourists a year. This vacation invasion has not been without its casualties, the biggest being the mountains themselves.

The felling of trees on steep mountainsides to create ski slopes has also set the stage for avalanches in the winter and mud slides in the summer. The loss of habitat has driven forest animals away. Tons of detergents and wastes flushed from hotels and condominiums have fouled water supplies. Contamination of mountain streams in lower Bavaria in Germany is so heavy, in fact, that 70 percent of the native fish there have wound up on the endangered list. In parts of Switzerland, more than half the space traditionally used for grazing and farming has been lost to tourism. Tourist spoor can be found in even the most rugged and remote reaches of the Alps. In one year, litterers left behind nearly 5,000 tons of trash in the Austrian Alps. Some of the most popular Alpine footpaths have been buried beneath a trail of candy wrappers and beer cans.

The environmental costs of uncontrolled tourism have aroused local preservation groups, such as the Society for the Protection of the Alps, to oppose new development. Theirs is an uphill battle in every respect. Many towns in the Alps are completely dependent on tourist dollars. In some areas of Switzerland, for example, travelers' spending accounts for up to 80 percent of the economy. Other regions are eager to cash in on the boom. It's projected that Switzerland will build another 300 ski lifts and add another 750,000 guest beds by the year 2010. However, by doing so, Switzerland may doom the very natural resource it sells. In that case, Switzerland's fairy-tale image of storybook villages, pristine mountains, and uncrowded spaces will be just that—a fairy tale.

European nations share the Alps, with Switzerland as its heart.

Though they attract plenty of visitors and have suffered significant environmental degradation in the process, the Alps continue to hold plenty of opportunities for outdoor recreation and close encounters of the natural kind. It is up to tourists to help convince local authorities that more needs to be done to protect this global resource.

tour du mont blanc

Hiking around Mont Blanc—at 15,781 feet, it is the highest peak in western Europe—has become one of the great walks of the world. Besides stunning alpine scenery, unparalleled views, and rugged geography, Mont Blanc provides the trekker with entré to the distinct culture of the alpine region.

Hikers travel through three different countries—France, Italy, and Switzerland— on a circumnavigation of the "White Mountain," but they actually visit seven distinct cultures—one for each of the magnificent seven valleys that surround the massif.

Tumbling glaciers, green mountain meadows, and towering peaks provide a dramatic backdrop to the glacial ridges and rocky moraines. Sharing overnight accommodations in rustic chalets and mountain lodges with trekkers from other countries lends this experience an international flavor.

Season: Summer

the swiss crisscross

Switzerland encompasses three major cultural regions—German, French, and Italian—and a trek across the Alps from north to south is a triptych of language, architecture, culture, and cuisine. The German-speaking **Bernese Oberland** region boasts some of Europe's most celebrated mountains. Storybook villages perch on impossible mountainsides, surrounded by plunging glaciers and waterfalls. Sheer cliffs, icy peaks, and bucolic pastures epitomize the beauty of the Alps.

Next stop, the orchards and vineyards of the **Rhône Valley**, mark Switzerland's French sector. Above the headwaters of the Rhône River lie the challenging Nufen and Corno passes. The route that leads from here has been popular with travelers since Roman times.

The cross-alpine trek then passes through the Italian **Ticino region** before culminating at picturesque Lake Maggiore. Quiet forests, flower-filled meadows, charming mountain lodges, and lovely scenery line the way.

Season: Summer

Tuscany has left its indelible stamp on Italian culture and, for that matter, all of Western Civilization. The province is the birthplace of the Etruscans. The Renaissance came of age in Florence. And in Pisa, Galileo unlocked the mysteries of the universe.

italy

The Italian countryside offers a range of experiences steeped in natural beauty as well as cultural history. Here are just two to whet your appetite.

a trek in tuscany

Culture and nature intertwine in the rich wine-country region of Tuscany. This historically important province lies in the northern range of the Apennine Mountains, the geological seam of Italy that runs north and south through the entire length of Italy.

No doubt the spectacular landscape of the region helped inspire the likes of Leonardo da Vinci, Michelangelo, Dante, and a host of other artists who lived here. You'll see why if you follow in their footsteps on a walking tour of Tuscany. Beneath dazzling white peaks pressed against the blue sky stretch forests of beech and chestnut; high alpine meadows lie in between. Mountain huts, small hotels, and quiet pensions provide solace and comfort during a walk that invigorates the spirit and stimulates the mind.

Season: Summer

doing the dolomites

The Dolomite Alps tower over the northeast corner of Italy. Carved by wind and sculpted by ice, snow-dusted spires stretch skyward. Reminiscent of some of the granite faces of Yosemite National Park in California, these limestone pinnacles have been luring rock climbers for years. The barren peaks provide stark contrast to flower-strewn alpine meadows and peaceful hamlets. Alpine *refugios,* homey family-run hotels in the villages, offer shelter in the heart of the mountains.

Season: Summer

spain

Little known to many who have yet to discover their abundant surprises are the gallant mountains of eastern Spain. Hikers take note.

traversing the pyrénées

A chain of crystalline mountain lakes, glacier-fed waterfalls, and wildflower-strewn alpine meadows marks the border between Spain and France. These natural wonders are hidden in the folds of the Pyrénées, a range of mountains not as massive nor as steep as the Alps but still spectacular and far less visited. The Pyrénées satisfy hikers in search of alpine adventure and cultural exploration.

A 350-mile-long trail traverses the entire mountain range, which stretches from the Atlantic Ocean to the Mediterranean Sea. The start of the trail links together

A Basque country trek could well include the "witches' cave" at Zugaramurdi, where Paleolithic human beings once dwelled; the historic town of Roncesvalles and its beautiful Gothic cloister; and Montserrat, a strange and mystical holy spot that has attracted ascetics since the fifth century.

several enchanting Basque villages whose residents have a reputation for hospitality, hearty food, and tangy wine. The Basque culture spills over into both Spain and France, and so does the trail. It zigzags between the two countries, allowing hikers to spend nights at charming village inns on either side of the border.

Season: Summer

picos de europa

A crown of limestone crags known as Picos de Europa adds to one of Europe's best-kept secrets. Spanish hikers and climbers have long favored this jagged mountain range of towering spires and fang-like pinnacles, but few outsiders know of it. Rugged trails promise challenging hiking. Limestone peaks rise out of deep forests of oak, beech, and pine dotted with meadows full of brilliant wildflowers that bloom for much of the year.

The trail links remote mountain villages, many reachable only by foot. The inaccessibility of the towns has left inhabitants sheltered from the modern world—an anomaly in this day and age. The people living here hold to traditions as old as the proverbial hills themselves. Shepherding remains the principal occupation in these parts, and the local delicacy, *cabrales,* a tangy blue cheese made from goat's milk, is still made in the same way as it has been for centuries.

Season: Summer

yugoslavia

Not all of Europe's alpine mountains exist in France,

The **North Albanian Alps** rise dramatically in the southern corner of Yugoslavia and are an excellent destination for those interested in both alpine ecosystems and cultural variety. The countryside exemplifies the ethnic diversity that exists within the borders of this patchwork nation—actually eight countries in one. The clothing, architecture, and rhythms of life in the mountain villages take on an Asian air while the topography is downright otherworldly.

Switzerland, and Italy. In the northern part of Yugoslavia stretches a formidable range of peaks known as the Julian Alps. The high point of this jagged range is Mount Triglav. Scaling to its triangular top 9,393 feet above the surface of the Adriatic is a much sought-after goal of mountaineers from all over Europe.

The countryside leading up to Triglav offers plenty of rewards of its own. Thick forests, bucolic meadows, and glacial streams enrich the trail. Mountain huts and lodges provide a comfortable place to pass the night and meet hikers from around the world.

Season: Summer

turkey

Past and present, East and West, converge in Turkey. Straddling Asia and Europe, Turkey truly deserves its reputation as the crossroads of the world. At the Strait of Bosporus, where two continents meet, you can feel the ebb and flow of history. This ancient land has been the scene of monumental struggles between some of civilization's mightiest empires. At one time or another, Assyrians, Greeks, Romans, Byzantines, and Ottomans laid claim to Turkey. Present-day life reflects the overlay of these great cultures. You can see it in the tiny rural villages on the plains of Anatolia as well as in the great city of Istanbul.

Equally as exotic is Turkey's natural history. The country is crammed with rugged mountains, wilderness areas, and undeveloped coastal stretches. Sample both Turkey's cultural and natural diversity on a cross-country trek. Highlights include the Grand Bazaar at Istanbul; Cappadocia, where a thousand years ago people carved underground cities in the soft tufa rock; the final resting place of Noah's Ark, 17,000-foot Mount Ararat; and the Pontic Mountains, a seldom-visited land of 10,000-foot passes, cobalt-blue lakes, thickly wooded forests, and colorful tribespeople.

Season: Spring and summer

poland

In the northeast corner of Poland lies a land of dark forests and a thousand lakes. Ninety nature reserves have been set aside in the region to protect the rare habitat and the even rarer wildlife species that dwell within them. In the **Borecka Forest**, for example, you can see a wild herd of wisent (European bison) 300 members strong.

At Popielno, tarpan ponies still gallop in the wild. These smallest forest ponies in the world were on their way to extinction before the reserve was created. The largest herd of elk in Europe — about 300 head — live in the **Czerwone Bagno Reserve**. Lynx, roe-deer, fox, and beaver are just a few of the other large mammals that inhabit this former Prussian territory.

But of all the animals, surely the most elusive yet sought-after by wildlife viewers are the wolves that inhabit the ancient forests near **Puszca Romincka**. Winter is the best time to look for them. You can stay at historical hunting lodges and ride in horse-drawn sleighs across fresh snow as guides keep a lookout for tracks. Blinds have been set up in the trees at places frequented by the wild canines.

Bialowieza National Park to the south offers an additional opportunity to find wolves. At 480 square miles, the park protects the last primeval lowland forest remaining in Central Europe. Ancient oak, spruce, and pine trees comingle in a shadowy tangle, prime habitat for many species of birds. Europe's only wild bison herd lives here, as do wild boar, moose, and tarpan pony. Occasionally bears wander across the border from Byelorussia.

Season: Year-round

czechoslovakia

Numerous castles, refined cities, colorful villages, and fascinating architecture lure most tourists to Czechoslovakia, but its greatest national treasure could be the Tatras, an all-but-forgotten wilderness deep in the Carpathian Mountains. The Czechs divide the Tatras into two ranges. The Low Tatras encompass beautiful valleys, extensive caverns, and near-mythical villages steeped in folklore. Huge castles dating back to the fourteenth century rise like pinnacles above rivers that cut through the folds of the foothills.

The High Tatras have been attracting a small but fiercely loyal group of international mountaineers ever since British climbers discovered the region back in the late eighteenth century. Climbers relish the region's granite pinnacles and sheer rock walls that rise 4,000 feet above timberline. The highest peak is Gerlach, which soars stoically above the East Slovakia countryside and offers stunning views into Poland and beyond. Alpine meadows, silvery waterfalls, and mirrored lakes make this exquisite hiking country.

Season: Summer

soviet republics

The doors to the Soviet republics' natural side are now open wider than ever. And despite Chernobyl and a host of other environmental woes, Russia and the other Soviet republics contain some of the finest wildlands found anywhere. While few Western tourists have ventured beyond Moscow and Leningrad, a number of nature travel opportunities now exist. The Soviets take pride in these natural resources and eagerly show them off. Travel restrictions still apply in many areas, however, so touring by group is recommended. The republics span two continents—Europe and Asia—and so do some of these trips.

hiking the caucasus mountains

The Caucasus Mountains belong to the world's premier class of mountain ranges, right alongside the Himalayas, Andes, and Alps. More than a dozen peaks surpass the 15,000-foot mark, and Mount Elbrus, a 18,510-foot-high mountain, is Europe's highest.

Little-visited trails wind through valleys dotted with clumps of wild strawberries and raspberries and scented by wildflowers. The climb to the summit is long but does not require special equipment. It spirals upward past isolated tarns, around rugged couloirs carved by glaciers, and beside silvery waterfalls. Climbers claim as their reward a chance to stand at the top of Europe and look into a mountainous realm explored by few.

Russian guides accompany each trip. Expect to meet the region's famous mountain people, the Balkars, who like to invite visitors to their camps for fresh-baked bread and *arian*, a homemade yogurt.

Season: Summer

Ussuriland, a vast stretch of wilderness that escaped the ravages of the last ice age, lies near the border between the Soviet republics and China. You can raft down the Ussuri, its main river. A remarkable abundance of exotic wildlife lives here, including such species as the Far Eastern fire-bellied toad, lungless newt, Horsfield's sparrowhawk, jungle nightjar, and the majestic Siberian tiger.

a soviet sampler of nature reserves

Shortly after the Revolution, the Soviets began establishing nature reserves to preserve habitat and wildlife. Together, they represent a wide range of ecosystems. Recently, a few have been opened to foreign visitors.

The **Caucasian Biosphere Reserve** was established in 1924, just two years after the U.S.S.R. was officially formed. Located in the northern part of the Caucasus Mountains, it protects 300 endemic plants and 192 species of birds. Mammals include cubanian goat, chamois, Caucasian bison, wolf, and the highest concentration of brown bear in the whole country.

The **North Ossetinsky Reserve** is also located on the northern slopes of the greater Caucasus Mountains. Few outsiders visit this lush area of alpine meadows, high peaks, and many glaciers. Located on the eastern shores of the Caspian Sea, the **Krasnovodsky Reserve** was established in 1932 to preserve the breeding grounds of more than 200 species of birds, many of them waterfowl. A wetland covers three-quarters of the preserve. Terns, flamingos, swans, and ducks depend on it for survival.

The Repetsky Reserve is found in the southwestern part of the Kara-Kum Desert. In spring, the desert blossoms to life with wildflowers, including iris, tulip, and poppy. Bird species include Pander's desert jay, desert sparrow, and black kite. The reserve also sustains many unusual mammals, including long-eared hedgehog, Afghan pika, and goitered gazelle.

The **Alma Atinsky Reserve** in the Talgar Mountains to the east contains four different ecozones: steppe, forest, subalpine, and alpine. That makes for quite a wide range of wildlife. Ibex inhabit the alpine areas, while goitered gazelle live on the steppe. Bird life features bearded vulture, Caucasian blackcock, and blue whistling thrush.

The **Bargdisinsky Reserve** rims the northeastern shore of Lake Baikal, the world's deepest freshwater lake and one of the most clear. The lake is more than 5,000 feet deep. One hundred thousand freshwater Baikal seal dwell in the lake, along with more than twenty-five species of endemic fish. The white-tailed sea eagle, black-billed capercaillie, and three-toed woodpecker account for just a handful of the more than 240 species of birds found in the preserve. The endangered bargaisin sable lives along the shores of Lake Baikal.

The **Far East Sea Reserve** protects a string of islands in the Sea of Japan off the coast of Vladivostok. The subtropical environment supports myriad species of birds, plants, mammals, and marine life.

Season: Spring and summer

russian rivers

Bouncing down rowdy rapids in the company of fellow Soviet rafters is not only a unique way to explore the wilderness, but a good way to make friends and prove that people have a lot in common despite cultural differences.

The quick-paced **Rioni River**

in the Caucasus Mountains passes through deep canyons and over boulders the size of houses. Its Class III rapids ensure plenty of thrills, and the nonstop scenery promises a fantastic slide show as well as lifelong memories.

Out of the mysterious Tien Shan mountains to the east pours the **Chatkal River**, a challenging whitewater roller coaster that boasts Class IV rapids and at least one Class V drop. The stunning scenery and isolated riverside Moslem villages lend the trip an otherworldly feel.

Further east rise Siberia's **Altai Mountains**. Towering over the region is 14,600-foot Mount Belucha, with a glacial shroud that turns into a rollicking run, the Katun River. The topography dispels the notion that Siberia is all endless tundra, and the hospitality of the riverside villagers will remain with you long after you return.

The **Zhumpanova River** flows through the Kronotsky Nature Preserve on the Kamchatka Peninsula. This is the Soviets' answer to Yellowstone National Park— a land of volcanoes, geysers, and wildlife, including Siberian bighorn, sable, marmot, and brown bear.

Season: Summer

9

volunteer
vacations

If traveling to an exotic location to paddle down a river, take a hike, or snap a few photographs isn't enough environmental involvement for you, you may want to volunteer for scientific research or community service. Here are a range of ideas . . .

• Assist scientists in the field—in every area from archaeology to primatology, entomology to ornithology.

• Learn new skills— from identification of species to mapping natural terrain and restoring habitat.

• Provide a service in exchange for an experience of the natural world as few tourists ever experience it.

• Do something positive for the planet.

volunteer vacations

Volunteer vacations give a whole new meaning to the term *working vacation*. The kinds of trips offering ecological or scientific opportunities fall under two general categories: research expeditions and service trips. On a research expedition, you help scientists in the field to obtain a better understanding of our world and to find solutions to the problems facing our planet. On a service trip, you volunteer your efforts to rehabilitating streams, improving trails, and other constructive projects that contribute to the environment.

Most programs of either type build in plenty of free time and are much less costly than organized tours. What's more, most of the organizations that sponsor trips are nonprofit and tax-exempt, so you can deduct your expenses and contributions. Finally, you get the satisfaction of actually doing something positive for the planet.

Contact the agencies and organizations listed below to obtain information on current offerings. Remember to ask the same types of questions you would ask a tour operator (see Chapter 1) to determine whether the trips are being managed in the most environmentally responsible manner.

research expeditions

Research projects cover a wide range of academic disciplines, from archaeology to primatology, from entomology to ornithology. The venues for these kinds of trips are equally diverse. You can board a ship researching whales in the South Pacific, conduct wildlife surveys in the national parks of Kenya, or search for rare monkeys in Peru.

When you join a research expedition, you become a labor force and a funding source for conservation all in one. Some trips require special skills, such as scuba certification, but you don't need to be a scientist to sign on, just a willing and able participant.

Typically, you pay a share-of-cost contribution that covers your meals, lodging, and ground transportation and provides for the chief researcher's expenses as well, including equipment and supplies. The work you do makes it possible for scientists to conduct their research in this day and age of personnel and funding shortages. In exchange, you receive an opportunity to experience the natural world as few tourists ever do.

◆ **CEDAM International**
Fox Road
Croton-on-Hudson, NY 10520
(914) 271-5365

CEDAM International is a unique, nonprofit
organization devoted to conservation, education, diving,
archaeology, and museums. Novice and experienced
scuba divers assist professional archaeologists, biologists,
scientists, and naturalists to conduct meaningful
exploration and research in the seas and oceans of the
world. One of the principal goals of the organization is to
promote marine biology and stimulate public interest in
conservation programs.
Sample projects:

Belize Reef Study Project. An expedition to study
the flora and fauna of the outer islands. Information
gathered will be submitted to Wildlife Conservation
International and the Belize Department of Fisheries.
Dates: April and July
Cost: $1,700

Galapagos Guide Book Project. Working with
local conservationists, participants will gather data for
conservation-oriented guide book.
Date: June
Cost: $3,000

Bermuda Flora/Fauna Study Program. Based at
the Bermuda Biological Station, team members assist
scientists in their study of local fishes, corals, and
plankton.
Date: August
Cost: $1,350

Australia Fish Collecting Expedition. Accompany
Ernie Ernst, Director of Education at the New York
Aquarium, to collect live fish for display at the New York
Aquarium.
Date: December
Cost: $4,000

◆ **Earthwatch**
680 Mount Auburn St.
P.O. Box 403
Watertown, MA 02272
(617) 926-8200

Earthwatch is a tax-exempt, nonprofit institution that
sponsors scholarly field research by finding paying

volunteers to help scientists on research expeditions around the world. Since its founding in 1971, it has mobilized more than 1,000 field seasons of more than 700 projects in 87 countries and 36 states. The mission of Earthwatch is to improve human understanding of the planet, the diversity of its inhabitants, and the processes that affect the quality of life on Earth. The coalition of citizens and scientists work to sustain the world's environment, monitor global change, conserve endangered habitats and species, explore the vast heritage of our peoples, and foster world health and international cooperation.

Sample projects:

Australia's Rainforest Canopy. Using nets, lights, traps, bait, and sticky paper, teams at two study sites capture and catalog insects as part of Australia's University of New England's study to determine how insects interact with their plant and animal neighbors. Accommodations in comfortable lodges.

Dates: November through December
Cost: $1,695

Tropical Forest Invaders. Based at a modern research station in a beautiful Costa Rican botanical garden adjacent to pristine cloud forests, teams of scientists plant and care for plants and observe hummingbirds and herbivores as part of a University of California study to test the impact of introduced species on tropical forests.

Date: April
Cost: $1,500

The Orangutan Project. Volunteers mix orangutan-sitting with tracking wild adults to document foraging, reproductive, and maternal behavior in Borneo as part of the longest-running study of orangutans in the wild.

Dates: August, September, October, November (four teams)
Cost: $2,050

Diamondback Terrapins. Volunteers work from boats and shore to capture, study, and release terrapins on Kiawah Island, South Carolina to assist University of Georgia–sponsored investigation. Accommodations at rented houses.

Date: August
Cost: $1,000

Kaikoura Seabirds. Against the backdrop of New Zealand's spectacular coastal mountains, peaceful fields,

and bracing surf, volunteers help capture and band red-billed seagull chicks and record gull behavior to assist New Zealand Science and Research Directorate study.
Date: October
Cost: $1,460

Bush Wildlife in Zimbabwe. Volunteers help trap and track small animals such as zebra mice, elephant shrews, and bush babies as part of a University of London study in Gosho Park Nature Reserve, Zimbabwe.
Dates: August, September, April, May
(multiple teams)
Cost: $1,495

Coastwatch Britain. As Britain considers several large coastal development projects, volunteers assist in mapping coastal habitats to help Nature Conservancy Council scientists determine how development will affect fragile habitats. Accommodations in rented cottages.
Dates: August, September
Cost: $1,425

Alpine Life of the Caucasus. As part of a five-year collaborative U.S.–Soviet study, volunteers help scientists determine plant community composition in the Soviet republics' Caucasus Mountains.
Date: August
Cost: $2,200

◆ Foundation for Field Research
787 S. Grade Road
P.O. Box 2010
Alpine, CA 92001
(619) 445-9264

A nonprofit organization founded in 1982, the Foundation meets the needs of scientists conducting research by finding members of the public interested in working as volunteer field assistants. Research projects cover a variety of academic disciplines, including geology, archaeology, paleontology, biology, primatology, ornithology, and ethnography.
Sample projects:

From Belugas to Blues. Volunteers help conduct a long-range whale census in the St. Lawrence River estuary of Quebec, Canada, to determine the abundance, geographic distribution, and concentration of each principal whale species. Accommodations in modest lodges.

Date: August
Cost: $1,022

Saving the Caguama. Volunteers help marine
biologists at the Marine Turtle Project in Baja California,
Mexico as part of an ongoing project aimed at saving the
endangered sea turtle. Accommodations in comfortable
huts 150 feet from the edge of the Gulf of California.
Date: July, September, or October (multiple teams)
Cost: $625

Tool Use Among Chimpanzees. Chimpanzees are
our closest living relatives. Among the most fascinating
behaviors of chimps is their use of tools. In this project,
volunteers observe wild chimp tool use in the Loffa forest
in Liberia, Africa.
Date: January, February, or March (multiple teams)
Cost: $1,485

The Quetzal Quest. The quetzal is one of the New
World's most magnificent birds. It is also one of the most
endangered. Volunteers work with biologists from the
Chiapas Natural History Institute in censusing the birds of
the El Triunfo Cloud Forest in southern Mexico.
Accommodations in tents.
Date: February or April (multiple teams)
Cost: $982

A Rejuvenated Rainforest. How fast does a
rainforest rejuvenate? Researchers are trying to find out
on the island of Grenada in the West Indies. Volunteers
help botanists observe and collect plants from each of the
major habitats.
Dates: June, July (multiple teams)
Cost: $1,163, first week ($234 each additional week)

◆   Hawkwatch International
    P.O. Box 35706
    Albuquerque, NM 87176
    (505) 255-7622

Volunteers are needed to assist field researchers with
bird migration surveys in several western states for four to
fifteen weeks. Programs includes bird counts, capture, and
banding. Experience preferred.
Dates: Year-round
Cost: Expenses

◆ International Research Expeditions
140 University Drive
Menlo Park, CA 94025
(415) 323-4228

International Research Expeditions is a nonprofit
organization that brings together field research scientists
and interested members of the public who wish to assist in
research covering a wide range of disciplines, including
ecology, animal behavior, entomology, marine biology,
and zoology.
Sample projects:

Elephant's Appetite. Zambia counts wildlife as one
of its most important natural resources, but with nineteen
national parks, there are quite a few animals to manage.
Park officials need help to find out the dietary
requirements of their resident species. Volunteers assist
in the study of population dynamics, forage, and nutrition
at Kafue National Park. Animals to be studied include
elephant, buffalo, lion, leopard, kudu, and wildebeest.
Accommodations at park headquarters.
Date: May 15 through September
Cost: $1,090 for one-week session; $1,790 for two
weeks

Bahamas Birdbanding Project. The major thrust of
this expedition is to study and band North American
migratory birds on their wintering grounds on Andros
Island, Bahamas, including searching for the elusive
Kirtland's warbler. Accommodations at Forfar Field
Station.
Dates: February and November
Cost: $750 for one-week session;
$1,400 for two weeks

Jungle Monkey. Of the thirty species of primates
which inhabit the Peruvian rainforest, the uakari is one of
the few species for which ecology and distribution are
almost totally unknown. Volunteers travel by canoe up the
Rio Tapiche and other tributaries of the Amazon to assist
scientists in mapping uakari territories, identifying and
censusing populations, and recording behavior and social
interactions.
Dates: February through November
Cost: $1,590 for two-week session

Oil Spill in Patagonia. The supertanker *Metula* lost
50,000 tons of oil in August 1974 in the Strait of Magellan,
Chile. The study of the spill site provides a unique
opportunity to determine the long-term impact of oil on

the coastal environment. Volunteers assist with photographic surveys, mapping, and digging trenches to determine extent of buried oil, and make observations on the impact on wildlife.

Dates: February, March
Cost: $1,520 for 10-day session

Galapagos Finches. Volunteers help ornithologists record the bird songs and calls of Darwin's famed Galapagos finches in long-term study to determine why these birds have evolved the way they have. Volunteers will travel between islands aboard chartered yachts.

Dates: March, May, August, January (multiple sessions)
Cost: $1,790 for 11-day session

Cape Cod Marine Biology/Socioeconomic Study. Volunteers help scientists study the fishing industry in New England and how it affects both the marine organisms hunted commercially and those animals inadvertently impacted as part of the ecosystem. The base of operations will be the world-famous Woods Hole Oceanographic Institution.

Dates: June through August
Cost: $790 for one-week session; $1,390 for two weeks

◆ **Intersea Research**
P.O. Box 1667
Friday Harbor, WA 98250
(206) 378-5980

Intersea conducts humpback whale research in southeast Alaska during the summer and around the Hawaiian Islands and South Pacific in winter. Volunteers join researchers aboard the 93-foot brigantine *Varua* or the 126-foot classic fantail yacht *Acania* to collect evidence on the feeding behavior of whales and to photograph tail flukes for use in identifying individuals. Participants help sail the boats.

Dates: June through September for Alaskan trips; December through February for Pacific trips
Cost: $1,400 to $2,300 for 11-day Alaskan session; $950 for 7-day Hawaiian session

◆ **Pacific Whale Foundation**
Kealia Beach Plaza
Suite 25
101 N. Kihei Road
Kihei, Maui, HI 96753
(808) 879-8860

The Foundation is a research, conservation, and education organization that specializes in the study of marine mammals and their ocean environment. It was founded by scientists and concerned environmentalists who felt a common need for an organization to support benign research projects that would benefit marine ecosystems. Volunteers—research interns—are trained in areas such as photography, boat handling, equipment maintenance, behavioral data collection, and field data analysis to help researchers. Small, inflatable boats with outboard motors are used to maneuver near and among the animals.

Sample projects:

Humpback Whale Recovery. In 1905, some 15,000 humpback whales lived in the North Pacific Ocean. They were commercially harvested until 1966, when they became internationally protected. The current population is estimated at 2,500. At present, it is not known how fast the North Pacific humpbacks are recovering. Volunteers are needed to determine humpback distribution and movement patterns within the Hawaiian breeding grounds as part of a long-term study of human-activity impact on recovery. Research teams observe and photo-identify individual whales and use hydrophones and tape recorders to record songs and social sounds. Accommodations in modern houses on the island of Maui.

Dates: December through April (multiple sessions)
Cost: $1,395 for two-week session;
$2,495 for four weeks

East Australian Humpback Whales. Humpbacks along the east Australia coast were not seriously hunted until 1950; but by 1962, the population of some 10,000 was reduced to fewer than 1,000. Since 1984, the Pacific Whale Foundation has conducted research to determine the abundance and behavioral characteristics of these humpbacks. Research interns assist scientists in photo-identification, sound recordings, and land-based tracking with computers and theodolites. Accommodations in comfortable house across from white-sand beach at Hervey Bay, Queensland.

Dates: June through September (multiple sessions)
Cost: $1,395 for two-week session;
$2,495 for four weeks

Tropical Reef Dynamics. Human activities threaten to destroy the once-pristine reef communities in Maui and Lanai, Hawaii coastal areas. Volunteers are needed to help scientists assess the effects of human activities and natural disturbances on tropical reef communities and to determine coral recovery rates. Work includes scuba diving and swimming along predetermined transects in near-shore reef areas, documenting the fish species, systematically deploying quadrant grids, and studying coral species and abundance. Accommodations at the Foundation's research facility in Kihei.

> Dates: June through November (multiple sessions)
> Cost: $1,395 for two-week session;
> $2,495 for four weeks

◆ Smithsonian Associates
   Research Expeditions Program
   The Smithsonian Institution
   Fourth Floor
   490 L'Enfant Plaza
   Washington, DC 20560
   (202) 287-3210

The prestigious Smithsonian Institution arranges for volunteers to assist Smithsonian scientists, curators, and research associates in projects that result in exhibitions, publications, and collections for the institution. Projects cover a wide range of disciplines including archaeology, volcanology, photographic documentation, folk culture, wildlife ecology, and archival research.

> Dates: Year-round
> Cost: Contributions range from $1,000 to $1,500 for one- to two-week expeditions, which include accommodations, some meals, and all scheduled activities.
> *Sample projects:*

Excavating a Caribbean Plantation. Volunteers help scientists excavate a cemetery on the island of Montserrat. The information will be used for the Smithsonian's 1991–1992 Quincentenary exhibition, "Seeds of Change," which commemorates the 500th anniversary of the landing of Christopher Columbus in the New World.

> Dates: July through August (multiple two-week sessions)
> Cost: Call

Fossil Forests of Wyoming. Volunteers assist paleobiologists in Bighorn Basin, just east of Yellowstone National Park, in excavating a fossil site, collecting compressed leaves, fruits, and flowers, and noting how the composition of the flora changes over millions of years.

> Date: July
> Cost: Call

Costa Rican Volcano: Reshaping the Landscape.
Volunteers help geologists and botanists monitor
eruptions and study volcanic samples using sensitive
photographic and seismographic equipment, as well as
study the impact of lava and ash debris on the region's
vegetation and the effect of acid rain on local plant life.
Date and Cost: Call

◆ University Research
Expeditions Program (UREP)
University of California
Berkeley, CA 94720
(510) 642-6586

Since 1976, UREP has been sponsoring field
expeditions in which volunteers help University of
California scientists conduct important research projects.
In 1989, more than 400 people participated as expedition
volunteers. The research opportunities allow paying
volunteers to make a direct contribution in helping to
preserve Earth's dwindling resources by working on
projects that improve the lives of people in developing
nations and searching for clues to the past at
archaeological sites from California to Ireland. On UREP's
SHARE (Science Serving Humanity and Research for the
Environment) projects, UC researchers work in
cooperation with scientists from developing nations. In
1990, UREP formed a partnership with UNICEF to share
information and resources on expeditions in Brazil. Plans
are also underway to develop cooperative environmental
projects in Ecuador to continue UREP's research for
rainforest management plans.
Sample projects:

The Faithful Fire Goby of Polynesian Waters.
Monogamy is only one of several possible mating systems
in the animal kingdom. In the tropical paradise of the
French Polynesian islands, the brightly colored fire goby
fish darts among the coral reefs in monogamous pairs. By
observing the goby's underwater environment and
breeding habits, scientists can broaden their
understanding of mating patterns and how they fit within
an organism's strategies for survival. Volunteers will scuba
dive in the calm waters of Cook's Bay to map the features
and location of goby burrows, collect specimens, and
release them for observation. Accommodations at UC
Berkeley Gump Field Station on Moorea.
Dates: January through March (multiple sessions)
Cost: $1,425 for two-week session

Marine Birds in the Gulf of California. The jutting peninsula that separates the Gulf of California (formerly the Sea of Cortez) from the Pacific Ocean once provided sanctuary for millions of migrating and native marine birds. Development of highways has increased tourism and recreational use of the shorelines once inhabited primarily by wildlife. Volunteers will assist scientists in documenting the marine habitat of Gulf of California seabirds as part of a long-term study of the marine ecology of the area. Accommodations in tented camps.
Dates: May, June
Cost: Call

Good Grooming: Antelope in Kenya. Wild animals in Africa must maintain every ounce of their strength in order to escape predators, but parasites can severely deplete an animal's stamina. In this project, volunteers will help UREP researchers examine how Thomson's gazelle, impala, oryx, and Coke's hartebeest use grooming to reduce or remove parasites from their bodies. Project is based in Kenya's Laikipia region.
Dates: June, July
Cost: Call

Strangers in Paradise. More than half the land mass of St. John in the U.S. Virgin Islands has been set aside as a national park. Among the myriad tropical plants are the succulents, whose extraordinarily diverse members include forest orchids and cacti. Volunteers help researchers locate tropical flowering succulents and note environmental conditions where they occur, investigate the distribution of epiphytes, and conduct field experiments.
Date: July
Cost: $1,385

Mountain Marmots of the Himalayas. Wildlife officials are trying to collect information about the natural history and habitat of remote and beautiful Khunjerab National Park in Pakistan in order to develop sound management decisions. Volunteers help researchers collect baseline data on the area's vegetation and animal life, with a particular focus on the golden marmot to determine how they protect themselves from predators such as the snow leopard, golden eagle, wolf, and fox. Accommodations in tents.
Dates: June, August (two sessions)
Cost: $1,285

Thy Daily Bread: Children's Nutrition in Brazil. The production of sisal is central to survival in the State of

Bahia, Brazil. Not long ago, studies revealed that children not old enough to work in the sisal fields were being deprived of food. As a result, the government began a school-based nutrition program for children. This expedition will examine the general state of health and nutrition among these youngsters and their families today in order to determine the success of the government's intervention. Volunteers will conduct household surveys. Accommodations in farmhouses.

Dates: July, August (two sessions)
Cost: $1,495

service trips

If you want to help improve the environment in a very direct way and spend more time than money, a service trip may be for you. Hiking clubs, conservation organizations, and state and national government agencies organize these service-oriented vacations. Typical ones involve building trails, restoring habitats, and eradicating invasive non-native plants in state and national parks, forests, and wilderness areas. The cost is a small registration fee that helps cover administration costs and insurance. Sponsoring organizations typically provide food and shelter, and cooperating agencies usually supply tools and equipment. While the work is often hard and physically demanding, you stay in some of the most beautiful wilderness areas in the country and have time to explore, fish, or hike on your own.

Many of the service trips require participants to be in good physical condition. Always read the trip description thoroughly and consult the sponsoring organization before you enlist. The organization should supply you with a detailed equipment list. Make sure you follow it closely.

For most projects, you need to arrange and pay for your own transportation to and from the project site, though the sponsoring agency will usually arrange transportation from a staging area to the final location on projects where the site is extremely remote. Housing and meals are usually provided, but you need to check with the sponsoring organization to make sure.

◆ **Alaska State Parks**
P.O. Box 107001
Anchorage, AK 99510
(907) 762-2665

State park system needs volunteers to staff campgrounds, assist rangers, maintain trails, and provide visitor services for four weeks minimum.

Dates: May through September
Cost: Expenses to and from site; food stipend and
housing provided

◆ **American Hiking Society (AHS)**
Volunteer Vacations
P.O. Box 86
North Scituate, MA 02060
(617) 545-7019

Begun in 1979, the AHS Volunteer Vacations program
arranges trail building and maintenance projects for the
U.S. National Park Service and Forest Service from Alaska
to the U.S. Virgin Islands. Volunteers do hard manual
labor in rugged, remote wilderness locations.
Dates: Summer months
Cost: $30 registration fee plus transportation to
project site
Sample projects:

Admiralty Island National Monument. Volunteers
maintain cabins in Alaska. Work includes repairing
facilities and cutting firewood.
Hawaii Volcanoes National Park. Volunteers
participate in exotic plant control program that benefits
native plants. Work includes uprooting and spraying
introduced plants.

◆ **Appalachian Mountain Club (AMC)**
P.O. Box 298, Route 16
Gorham, NH 03581
(603) 466-2727

Established in 1876, AMC coordinates trail building
and maintenance projects in various national parks and
forests from Alaska to the U.S. Virgin Islands, with an
emphasis on trails in the northeast.
Dates: Summer months
Cost: $50 to $125 plus transportation to project site
Sample projects:

Chugach National Forest. Workers rebuild trails,
including brushing and tread construction.
Accommodations at base camp during week and at U.S.
Forest Service work center in Cordova on weekends.
Grand Teton National Park. Crew does a variety of
maintenance and restoration work on a canyon trail in the
central part of this Wyoming park.
Virgin Islands National Park. Crew does a variety

of trail maintenance and rehabilitation tasks on trails
throughout the park, located on the island of St. John.

◆ **Appalachian Trail Conference (ATC)**
   P.O. Box 807
   Harpers Ferry, WV 25425
   (304) 535-6331

   ATC is a nonprofit organization that coordinates
public and private efforts with the U.S. Forest Service to
maintain and protect the 2,100-mile-long Appalachian
Trail, America's first National Scenic Trail and one of the
longest marked footpaths in the world.
   Dates: June through August
   Cost: Transportation costs to project sites

◆ **Arizona State Parks**
   800 W. Washington St.
   Suite 415
   Phoenix, AZ 85007
   (602) 255-4174

   State needs volunteers to work as campground hosts,
interpretive guides, and visitor service hosts at parks
throughout Arizona, usually for stays of at least four
weeks.
   Dates: Year-round
   Cost: Transportation to campground plus
   living expenses

◆ **California Department of Parks and Recreation**
   P.O. Box 942896
   1416 9th St.
   Sacramento, CA 94296
   (916) 445-4624

   State needs volunteers to work as campground hosts
and interpretive guides at parks throughout California,
usually for stays of at least four weeks.
   Dates: Year-round
   Cost: Transportation to campground plus living
   expenses. Campsites are free.

◆ **Chincoteague National Wildlife Refuge**
   P.O. Box 62
   Chincoteague, VA 23336
   (804) 336-6122

The Assateague Island refuge needs volunteers to assist biologists in monitoring wildlife populations and collecting information on threatened and endangered species.
Dates: Year-round
Cost: Expenses

◆ **Colorado Trail Foundation**
548 Pine Song Trail
Golden, CO 80401
(303) 526-0809

Trail building and maintenance on a 470-mile trail that stretches from Denver to Durango.
Dates: Summer months
Cost: $25 registration fee

◆ **Connecticut State Office of Parks and Recreation**
165 Capitol Ave.
Hartford, CT 06106
(203) 566-2304

State needs campground hosts and interpretive guides at parks and forests throughout Connecticut, usually for stays of at least four weeks.
Dates: Memorial Day through Labor Day
Cost: Transportation to campground and living expenses

◆ **Council on International Educational Exchange (CIEE)**
205 E. 42nd St.
New York, NY 10017
(212) 661-1414

CIEE organizes work camps in Europe and the United States. Volunteers do conservation, construction, and renovation work at a variety of sites in a multicultural setting.
Dates: Summer
Cost: $100 application fee plus transportation costs to project site and incidental expenses

◆ **Florida Department of Natural Resources**
Division of Recreation and Parks
2900 Commonwealth Blvd.
Tallahassee, FL 32399
(904) 488-8243

State needs campground hosts, interpretive guides, and maintenance workers at parks throughout Florida, usually for six to twelve weeks.
Dates: Year-round
Cost: Transportation to campground and living expenses

◆　**Hawk Mountain Sanctuary**
R.D. 2, Box 191
Kempton, PA 19529
(215) 756-6961

This world-famous sanctuary needs volunteers to perform outdoor maintenance chores as well as office and library work.
Dates: January through April
Cost: Expenses

◆　**Illinois Department of Conservation–
Land Management**
600 N. Grand Ave.
Springfield, IL 62701
(217) 782-6752

State needs campground hosts, interpretive guides, and technicians at parks throughout Illinois, usually for a minimum of four weeks.
Dates: Year-round
Cost: Transportation to campground and living expenses

◆　**Indiana Division of State Parks**
616 State Office Building
Indianapolis, IN 46204
(317) 232-4124

State needs campground hosts, interpretive guides, and maintenance workers at parks throughout Indiana.
Dates: Year-round
Cost: Entrance fee to park and camping fees

◆　**Missouri Department of Natural Resources**
Division of Parks, Recreation,
and Historic Preservation
P.O. Box 176
Jefferson City, MO 65102
(314) 751-2479/1-800-334-6946

State needs campground hosts, interpretive guides, park aides, and trail maintenance workers at parks throughout Missouri.
Dates: May through September
Cost: Transportation to campground and living expenses

◆   **National Wildflower Research Center**
2600 FM 973 N
Austin, TX 78725
(512) 929-3600

Volunteers are needed from across the country to provide center with information on the state's native wildflowers.
Dates: Year-round
Cost: Free

◆   **Nevada Division of State Parks**
201 S. Fall St.
Room 119
Carson City, NV 89710
(702) 885-4384

State needs campground hosts, interpretive guides, and backcountry rangers at parks throughout Nevada.
Dates: Year-round
Cost: Transportation to park and living expenses

◆   **Sea Shepherd Conservation Society**
P.O. Box 7000
Redondo Beach, CA 90277
(213) 316-8309
Sea Shepherd is dedicated to the protection of marine mammals and seabirds by documenting whaling violations, holding sealing protests, and interfering with dolphin and whale slaughters. Volunteers work on ships and take part in operations.
Dates: Year-round
Cost: Transportation to project site

◆   **Sierra Club**
Service Trips
730 Polk St.
San Francisco, CA 94109
(415) 923-5630

The largest program of its kind, the Sierra Club organizes service trips to build and maintain trails, clean up and restore native vegetation, and improve trout habitat in national parks, monuments, forests, and wilderness areas throughout the country. Volunteers do hard manual labor in rugged, remote wilderness locations.

Dates: March through September

Cost: $110 to $255 in addition to transportation to project site

Sample projects:

Allagash Wilderness Waterway, Maine. Improve the Allagash Falls portage trail for 100-mile chain of lakes and rivers used by canoers.

Pine Lake Annual Women's Trip, Marble Mountain Wilderness, California. Build check dams and rehabilitate trail in Klamath National Forest.

Chesapeake Bay Archaeology, Maryland. Work at archaeological excavation at Saint Marys City.

South San Juan Wilderness Trout Habitat Project, Colorado. Improve trout stream habitat and maintain trail in Rio Grande Forest wilderness.

Tuolumne Meadows Revegetation Project, California. Restore heavily visited area in Yosemite National Park. Work involves planting sod plugs and native grasses, and installing boulders at illegal campsites to discourage use.

Santa Cruz Island Preserve Restoration, California. Help The Nature Conservancy, which protects the island, with maintenance, fence building, vegetation monitoring, and exotic plant removal.

◆ **Student Conservation Association, Inc.**
   P.O. Box 550
   Charlestown, NH 03603
   (603) 826-5206

Working like a job placement agency, the Student Conservation Association places students in volunteer positions with the National Park Service, U.S. Forest Service, Bureau of Land Management, and U.S. Fish and Wildlife Service at sites throughout the country. Jobs range from wildlife field surveys to park restoration to academic research, usually for twelve weeks. Special emphasis on placing people with physical disabilities.

Dates: Year-round

Cost: Free

◆ **Tahoe Rim Trail**
P.O. Box 10156
South Lake Tahoe, CA 95731
(916) 577-0676

Volunteers needed for building, construction, and maintenance of a 150-mile trail around Lake Tahoe in California.
Dates: May through October
Cost: Transportation to site and living expenses

◆ **Timpanogos Cave National Monument**
R.R. 3, Box 200
American Fork, UT 84003
(801) 756-5238

Spelunking enthusiasts needed to perform maintenance chores and provide visitor information services at Utah caves.
Dates: Summer
Cost: Free

◆ **U.S. Fish and Wildlife Service**

For North Dakota, South Dakota, Nebraska, Kansas, Montana, Colorado, Utah:
Region 6
P.O. Box 25486
Denver Federal Center
Denver, CO 80225
(303) 236-8152

For Alaska:
Region 7
1011 E. Tudor Road
Anchorage, AK 99503
(907) 786-3399

Volunteers needed to assist in fish and wildlife management at ecological field stations, wildlife management centers, and fish hatcheries.
Dates: Year-round
Cost: Transportation to site and living expenses

◆ **U.S. Forest Service**

For the Pacific Northwest:
P.O. Box 3623
Portland, OR 97208
(503) 326-3816

For Utah, Nevada, southern Idaho,
southwestern Wyoming:
324 25th St.
Ogden, UT 84401
(801) 625-5112

For North Dakota, South Dakota, Montana,
northern Idaho:
Federal Building
P.O. Box 7669
Missoula, MT 59807
(406) 329-3194

For Sequoia National Forest, California:
900 W. Grand Ave.
Porterville, CA 93257
(209) 784-1500

Volunteers needed for backcountry cleanup,
campground hosts, fire lookouts, trail maintenance
workers, and wilderness aides.
Dates: Year-round
Cost: Transportation to site and living expenses

◆ **U.S. National Park Service**

For Maryland, Delaware, Pennsylvania,
West Virginia, Virginia:
Mid-Atlantic Region
143 S. Third St.
Philadelphia, PA 19106
(215) 597-5374

For North Dakota, South Dakota, Montana,
Wyoming, Colorado, Utah:
Rocky Mountain Region
12795 W. Alameda Parkway
Box 25287
Denver, CO 80225
(303) 969-2630

National Park Service needs campground hosts,
visitor information aides, and researchers in archaeology
and natural sciences at parks.
Dates: Year-round
Cost: Transportation to park and living expenses.
Park pays some out-of-pocket expenses.

◆ Washington State Parks and
Recreation Commision
7150 Cleanwater Lane
Olympia, WA 98504
(206) 753-5759

State needs campground hosts, trail-building and
maintenance workers, and interpretive guides at parks
throughout Washington.
Dates: April through September
Cost: Transportation to site and living expenses

◆ The Wild Canid Survival and
Research Center and Wolf Sanctuary
P.O. Box 760
Eureka, MO 63025
(314) 938-5900

The center needs volunteers to help with a variety of
tasks, including fundraising and research assistance.
Naturalists are needed to staff the sanctuary.
Dates: Year-round
Cost: Expenses

◆ Wisconsin Department of Natural Resources
Bureau of Recreation and Parks
P.O. Box 7921
Madison, WI 53707
(608) 266-2152

State needs campground hosts, trail-building and
maintenance workers, and interpretive guides at parks
throughout Wisconsin.
Dates: Year-round
Cost: Transportation to site and living expenses

◆ Wyoming Recreation Commission
122 W. 25th St.
Cheyenne, WY 82002
(307) 777-6314

State needs campground hosts, trail-building and
maintenance workers, and interpretive guides at parks
throughout Wyoming.
Dates: Year-round
Cost: Transportation to site and living expenses

10

nature-study travel programs

Another way to experience the wild places of the world through a tour sponsored by a conservation group, natural history museum, or university field study program. Use the information in this chapter to:

• Pinpoint the environmental issue you'd most like to study.

• Decide where to donate to support your favorite conservation issue with well-spent travel dollars.

• Meet like-minded people who share your values and love of the natural world.

• Do your part to make the world safe for all living things.

nature-study travel programs

Visiting the wild places of the world on a tour sponsored by a conservation group, natural history museum, or university field study program can be one of the best learning experiences possible. Not only do scientists, naturalists, and regional experts typically lead these kinds of tours, but most programs usually include lectures, group discussions, and multimedia presentations as part of the package. On a tour such as this, you don't just read and hear about the natural world; you experience it firsthand in the company of experts.

Trips sponsored by universities and learning centers often offer college credit for traveling as an additional benefit. Nature-study travel programs also serve as a terrific way for environmentally minded travelers to donate to their favorite conservation causes. Most nonprofit conservation groups, natural history museums, and learning centers conduct travel programs primarily for fundraising purposes. Because tour sponsors typically limit participation to members only, you must first pay a membership fee before signing up—annual dues typically cost about $25. Many organizations frequently tack on an additional $100 to $250 contribution as part of the trip's cost to help fund conservation efforts at home and abroad. The fees are usually tax-deductible. Another benefit of traveling with a nature-study travel program is that you travel with people who share your values, interests, and love of the natural world.

This chapter lists the various types of institutions that offer nature-oriented travel programs. By no means does it include every organization. You should also contact conservation groups, museums, learning centers, and universities in your local area to determine whether or not they offer similar programs. Because of the dynamic nature of travel, you need to directly contact the group with which you are considering traveling to obtain an up-to-date schedule of trips, itineraries, costs, and departure dates. Don't forget to ask them what steps they take to ensure that their programs are environmentally responsible. If the trips are used as fundraising vehicles, ask them exactly which projects benefit.

Adirondack Mountain Club
P.O. Box 867
Lake Placid, NY 12946
(518) 523-3441

Established in 1922, the nonprofit Adirondack
Mountain Club sponsors a variety of field natural history
programs, including one- and two-day summer workshops
at the Adirondack Loj and John Brooks Lodge in New
York's 6-million-acre Adirondack Park.
Cost: Workshop fees range from $10 to $55

Appalachian Mountain Club (AMC)
P.O. Box 298
Gorham, NH 03581
(603) 466-2727

Established in 1876, AMC offers more than fifty
nature-study programs, workshops, and travel seminars
focusing on natural history and ecology to domestic and
international destinations. Subject matter includes plant
identification, birding, orienteering, climatology, geology,
and ecology. Trips are led by specialists and feature
lectures and group discussions. Appalachian workshops
are held at Pinkham Notch Camp in the heart of New
Hampshire's White Mountain National Forest.
Cost: Workshop fees range from $65 to $350.

Conservation International (CI)
1015 18th St., N.W.
Suite 1000
Washington, DC 20036
(202) 429-5660

Established in 1987, CI is a private nonprofit
organization dedicated to the protection and preservation
of natural ecosystems and the species that rely on these
habitats for their survival. It complements its efforts to
build local capacity for conservation in tropical countries
with a limited number of trips to the rainforest for
members and supporters. Destinations include El Triunfo
Biosphere Reserve and the Gulf of California, both in
Mexico.
Cost: $1,800 to $2,300

The Cousteau Society
Project Ocean Search
930 W. 21st St.
Norfolk, VA 23517
(804) 627-1144

Since 1973, the nonprofit conservation organization
founded by marine explorer Jacques Cousteau has been
conducting a series of two-week field study programs
designed to promote appreciation and understanding of
nature, specifically marine resources. Participants join a
Cousteau team on expeditions to remote islands
throughout the world. Locations range from Fiji to Santa
Cruz Island, California, and from Papua New Guinea to the
British Virgin Islands. Daily activities feature scuba diving
and island exploration. Topics include fish ecology,
marine mammals, coral reefs, and island culture.
Cost: Averages $150 a day

Federation of Ontario Naturalists (FON)
Canadian Nature Tours
355 Lesmill Road
Don Mills, ON M3B 2W8
Canada
(416) 444-8419

Established in 1976 and operated by FON, one of
Canada's largest conservation groups, Canadian Nature
Tours offers fifty tours a year to North American
destinations. Tours are led by experienced naturalists.
Profits from trips are used for conservation projects in
Canada.
Cost: Ranges from $320 to $4,050
(in Canadian dollars)

International Bicycle Fund
Bicycle Africa
4887 Columbia Drive South
Seattle, WA 98108
(206) 628-9314

Established in 1982, the nonprofit International
Bicycle Fund, which assists economic development
projects, sponsors six bicycle tours a year in Africa
focusing on natural history and culture. Trips are
accompanied by two leaders and limited to twelve
participants each.
Cost: Range from $895 to $2,225 (partly
tax-deductible)

Massachusetts Audubon Society
Wellfleet Bay Wildlife Sanctuary
P.O. Box 236
South Wellfleet, MA 02663
(508) 349-2615

The Massachusetts chapter of the National Audubon
Society sponsors one-week courses in the natural history
of Cape Cod held at the Wellfleet Bay Wildlife Sanctuary.
The program highlights the ongoing scientific research
being conducted at the sanctuary. Subject matter includes
coastal ecology, ornithology, marine life, and botany.
Outdoor field trips are combined with indoor discussions
and multimedia presentations.
Cost: $220 to $410 for enrollment, $105 for housing

National Audubon Society (NAS)
950 Third Ave.
New York, NY 10022
(212) 546-9140

Founded in 1905, NAS is one of the oldest and largest
conservation organizations in the country. It carries out a
balanced program of research, education, and action.
Audubon was the first conservation organization
sponsoring travel programs to write a "Travel Ethic."
Audubon offers approximately twenty-four trips a year to
domestic and international destinations. Tours are led by
Audubon senior staff members. Destinations include the
American Southwest, Antarctica, Central America, the
Seychelles, the Caribbean, and Baja California.
Cost: Varies

National Wildlife Federation (NWF)
Conservation Summits
1400 Sixteenth St., N.W.
Washington, DC 20036
(703) 790-4363

Organized in 1936, NWF is a nonprofit conservation
education organization dedicated to creating and
encouraging public awareness of the need for wise use
and proper management of natural resources. Its
Conservation Summits provide a unique opportunity to
experience some of our nation's most spectacular areas.
The program allows adults to design their own schedules,
choosing from approximately twenty different classes and
field trips at each location. Each class or field trip is led by
highly qualified naturalists who share their in-depth

knowledge of the topic. There is ample time for nature walks, wildflower viewing, and birding. NWF conducts separate programs for preschoolers, youths, and teens. Classes include junior naturalist programs, environmental ethics, urban nature studies, ecology, and citizen action. Summit locations include Estes Park, Colorado; Black Mountain, North Carolina; Big Sky, Montana (near Yellowstone National Park); and the Adirondacks, New York. Accommodations are in dormitories and lodges.

Cost: Program fees range from $70 for preschoolers to $200 for adults; accommodations are extra

Natural Resources Defense Council (NRDC)
40 W. 20th St.
New York, NY 10011
(212) 727-2700

Founded in 1970, NRDC is a nonprofit organization dedicated to protecting endangered natural resources and to improving the quality of the human environment. Its professional staff is made up of lawyers and scientists. Among its areas of concern are Alaska and domestic tropical forests. It offers trips for members to experience firsthand the natural resources of Hawaii and Alaska and to view the environmental threats those areas face.

Cost: Call for information

The Nature Conservancy
1815 N. Lynn St.
Arlington, VA 22209
(703) 841-5300

Organized in 1951, the nonprofit Nature Conservancy is committed to the preservation of biological diversity through the protection of natural lands and the life they harbor. It has built the largest private land reserve system in the United States, with many preserves near urban centers (see page 27). It also manages preserves in the Caribbean and Latin America. Many of the more than 1,100 nature sanctuaries are open to the public. The Nature Conservancy also conducts tours to domestic and international destinations, including Alaska, Hawaii, Mexico, Belize, Costa Rica, and Ecuador.

Cost: International tour programs range from $1,498 to $4,090

Oceanic Society Expeditions (OSE)
Fort Mason Center, Building E
San Francisco, CA 94123
1-800-326-7491

OSE is a nonprofit organization founded in 1972 to
create opportunities for individuals to learn about the
natural world by participating in educational ecotours. It
serves as the environmental travel arm for the merger of
the Oceanic Society and Friends of the Earth. All trip
proceeds go directly to helping the environment, from
supporting research projects to furthering conservation
efforts. Destinations include Alaska, British Columbia,
Hawaii, Baja California, Belize, Costa Rica, Ecuador, Peru,
Brazil, East Africa, and Australia.
Cost: Ranges from $895 to $4,490

Sierra Club
Outings Department
730 Polk St.
San Francisco, CA 94109
(415) 923-5630

The granddaddy of environmental organizations, the
Sierra Club was founded in 1892 by John Muir. Its charter
is to explore, enjoy, and protect the wild places of the
earth; to practice and promote the responsible use of the
earth's ecosystems and resources; and to educate and
enlist humanity to protect and restore the quality of the
natural and human environment. Its Outings Department
operates as a service to club members and offers several
hundred trips each year. Tours range from backpacking to
bicycling, from rafting to kayaking, from photography to
fishing. Destinations include Alaska, the Sierra Nevadas,
Hawaii, Mexico, the Soviet republics, Nepal, Europe, East
Africa, and China. Trips are led by volunteers, which helps
keep costs low.
Cost: Domestic backpack trips average $300,
international trips range from $1,200 to $3,200

Wildlife Conservation International (WCI)
The New York Zoological Society
c/o The Bronx Zoo
Bronx, NY 10460
(212) 220-5155

Established in 1895, WCI is the international
conservation program of the New York Zoological Society
and is dedicated to increasing public understanding of the

biology of endangered species and ecosystems. The organization operates a travel program for members, with trips to Alaska, Kenya, Patagonia, and Baja California.
Cost: Ranges from $2,000 to $4,000

World Wildlife Fund (WWF)
1250 24th St., N.W.
Washington, DC 20037
(202) 293-4800

Founded in 1961, WWF is the largest private U.S. organization working worldwide to protect endangered wildlife and habitats. It has helped protect some 180 national parks and nature reserves and works with local groups to take the lead in conservation projects. It conducts a comprehensive travel program for members. The trips are designed to provide opportunities to view wildlife in often spectacular natural settings. Trips often feature visits to research field stations and talks by experts. Destinations include Baja California, East Africa, Dominica, India, Costa Rica, the Galapagos Islands, Alaska, Australia, Argentina, and Southeast Asia.
Cost: $2,000 to $5,000

museums, zoos, and aquariums

American Museum of Natural History Discovery Tours
Central Park West at 79th St.
New York, NY 10024
(212) 769-5700/1-800-462-8687

New York's American Museum of Natural History offers more than twenty-five travel programs focusing on natural history to domestic and international destinations, including Alaska, Mexico, Costa Rica, Egypt, Great Britain, Scandinavia, the Soviet republics, and East Africa. Tours are led by specialists and feature lecture programs and group discussions. Trips are equally divided between land expeditions and luxury cruises.
Cost: Ranges from $2,095 to $6,390

Anita Purves Nature Center
1505 N. Broadway
Urbana, IL 61801
(217) 384-4062

The center offers field trips to adjacent Busey Woods to explore local wildlife and ecosystems.
Cost: Free to $20

Cable Natural History Museum
P.O. Box 416
Cable, WI 54821
(715) 798-3890

The museum leads field trips to various areas of the northern Great Lakes region to study natural history and wildlife.
Cost: $1 to $600

Cabrillo Marine Museum
3720 Stephen White Drive
San Pedro, CA 90731
(213) 548-7563

As its name implies, the museum is marine oriented. It offers one-day workshops focusing on Southern California ocean life, with field studies at nearby tidepools, mudflats, and sandy beaches. It also offers week-long day-camp programs for school-age children.
Cost: From $1 for tidepool walks to $70 for day camp

Cincinnati Zoo Travel Programs
2800 Atrium Two
221 E. Fourth St.
Cincinnati, OH 45202
(513) 621-4900/1-800-543-2120

The Cincinnati Zoo offers travel programs focusing on natural history and wildlife behavior to a variety of international destinations, including Antarctica, East Africa, Costa Rica, and the Galapagos Islands. Trips are led by professional zoologists and zookeepers.
Cost: Ranges from $2,100 to $8,000 (includes $100 to $250 tax-deductible contribution to zoo)

Dallas Museum of Natural History
P.O. Box 150433
Dallas, TX 75315
(214) 670-8458

Focusing on the natural history of Texas, this museum offers a variety of programs, including weekend

discovery centers and week-long day camps.
Cost: Free to $30

Denver Museum of Natural History
Public Programs Department
2001 Colorado Blvd.
Denver, CO 80205
(303) 370-6307

Begun in 1972, the domestic and international travel
program for the Denver Museum of Natural History offers
a variety of trips focusing on archaeology, anthropology,
ethnography, culture, geology, ecology, marine biology,
and ornithology. Approximately twenty tours are held
each year, with such destinations as the Grand Canyon,
the American Southwest, the Upper Amazon, Machu
Picchu, Central Asia, the Soviet republics, East Africa, and
Belize. Most tours are led by the museum's curatorial
staff.
Cost: Ranges from $150 to $7,500

Greenburgh Nature Center
Dromore Road
Scarsdale, NY 10583
(914) 723-3470

Besides live animal exhibits, this regional center
offers a variety of programs for all ages, focusing on
natural history, plant and animal identification, and
environmental education.
Cost: Varies

Hawaii Nature Center
2131 Makiki Heights Drive
Honolulu, HI 96822
(808) 973-0100

All ages are welcome on the center's varied programs
of nature discoveries and guided interpretive hikes.
Cost: Varies

High Desert Museum
59800 S. Highway 97
Bend, OR 97702
(503) 382-4754

Focusing on the natural history of the high desert of

the intermountain region, the museum offers field
excursions to regional areas.
Cost: Varies

Kokee Natural History Museum
P.O. Box 100
Kekaha, HI 96752
(808) 335-9975

A variety of programs is offered by this Hawaii
museum that features indoor classes as well as outdoor
field trips to various ecosystems and native habitats on the
Hawaiian archipelago.
Cost: Free to $250

Maryland Zoological Society
Druid Hill Park
Baltimore, MD 21217
(301) 467-4387

Established in 1980, the zoo's travel program offers
day and weekend trips to zoological attractions in the
United States and two- to three-week trips to such
locations as the Amazon and the Galapagos Islands.
Members of the zoo's curatorial staff accompany the trips.
Cost: $1,200 to $7,000

National Aquarium in Baltimore
501 E. Pratt St.
Baltimore, MD 21202
(301) 576-3870

The aquarium sponsors a variety of educational
programs and travel opportunities focusing on marine
sciences to both domestic and international destinations.
Trips range from a one-day excursion to Cape Henlopen
State Park to study horseshoe crabs, to an expedition to
Iceland to study and observe puffins.
Cost: $22 to $68 for day trips, $375 to $4,000 for
longer trips

**Natural History Museum of
Los Angeles County Travel Program**
900 Exposition Blvd.
Los Angeles, CA 90007
(213) 744-3350

Established in the mid-1960s, the museum's travel program offers more than fifteen trips a year focusing on archaeology, wildlife, native culture, and natural history to a variety of domestic and international destinations. Tours are led by museum curatorial staff and feature discussions and lectures. Itineraries range from a study of the Indian Market in Santa Fe, New Mexico, to a one-month cruise to Antarctica. Other destinations include Australia, East Africa, Indonesia, and South America.

Cost: Domestic tours start at $1,000, international trips range from $3,000 to $17,000

The New York Botanical Garden Travel Program
Bronx, NY 10458
(212) 220-8982

The garden's Travel Program features trips and tours to domestic and international destinations for people interested in horticulture, flora, and the natural world. Domestically, the garden offers day hikes and trips to nearby public and private gardens. Internationally, there are trips to the Amazon, Belize, the Galapagos Islands, Ecuador, and French Guiana. Tours feature visits to the garden's research facilities.

Cost: $29 to $56 for day trips, $1,500 to $3,000 for international tours

North Park Village Nature Center
5801 N. Pulaski
Chicago, IL 60646
(312) 583-3714

Field trip programs, natural history education, wildflower identification, and bird walks are some of the opportunities offered by this urban nature center dedicated to exposing city dwellers to the wild side of life.

Cost: Free

Potomac Overlook Regional Park and Nature Center
2845 Marcey Road
Arlington, VA 22207
(703) 528-5406

Paddle a canoe, explore the marsh, and discover the region's wildlife as part of the center's program.

Cost: Free to $5 for canoe trips

San Diego Natural History Museum
P.O. Box 1390
San Diego, CA 92112
(619) 232-3821

The museum sponsors a variety of trips along the
West Coast, including Baja California, with a natural
history emphasis. Trips are led by museum staff and
qualified naturalists.
Cost: $750 to $1,100

San Francisco Bay Bird Observatory
P.O. Box 247
Alviso, CA 95002
(408) 946-6548

Volunteer-led bird walks and natural history tours are
featured at this research center based on the marshes and
salt ponds of South San Francisco Bay. Camping tours are
also available.
Cost: $30 to $500

Smithsonian Study Tours and Seminars
The Smithsonian Institution
Department 0049
Washington, DC 20073
(202) 357-4700

Begun in 1970, the Study Tours and Seminars
program of the Smithsonian Institution offers nearly 200
programs throughout the world, many of them nature
oriented. Various itineraries include camping in Hawaii,
exploring Maine's rocky coast, touring California's
Channel Islands, and birding in Chesapeake Bay, as well
as wildlife safaris in Kenya and in Finland. Tours and
seminars are led by academicians and local experts.
Cost: $600 to $1,600 for domestic programs,
$2,800 to $5,200 for international expeditions

Tree Hill, Jacksonville Nature Center
7152 Lone Star Road
Jacksonville, FL 32211
(904) 724-4646

This preserve features two trails, a garden parcourse,
and a natural history museum. The emphasis is on natural
history, environmental education, and field studies.
Cost: Varies

Zoological Society of San Diego
Worldwide Tours Program
P.O. Box 551
San Diego, CA 92112
(619) 231-1515

This organization sponsors ten- to seventeen-day trips
with a natural history/wildlife focus to such destinations
as East Africa, Alaska, and Baja California. Trips feature
lectures and discussions.
    Cost: $2,900 to $4,600

universities, institutes, and learning centers

Adirondack Outdoor Education Center
Pilot Knob, NY 12844
(518) 656-9462

The center offers a variety of expeditional,
educational, and recreational programs on Lake George
lasting from one to five days.
    Cost: $20 per day

Audubon Naturalist Society of the
Central Atlantic States
8940 Jones Mill Road
Chevy Chase, MD 20815
(301) 652-5964

The society offers environmental educational field
trips to destinations in the Central Atlantic states.
    Cost: Varies

California Alumni Association
Travel Program
Alumni House
Berkeley, CA 94720
(510) 642-3717

The Alumni Association of the University of California
at Berkeley sponsors twenty travel programs a year to
domestic and international destinations, including the
American Southwest, Asia, Africa, the Soviet republics,
Antarctica, and New Zealand. Many of the programs focus
on the natural history of the region and include visits to
research sites. Trips are usually accompanied by a faculty
lecturer.
    Cost: Ranges from $1,745 to $7,650

Canyonlands EdVentures
Canyonlands Field Institute
P.O. Box 68
Moab, UT 84532
(801) 259-7750

Established in 1984, this educational nonprofit
organization conducts tours focusing on the natural
history, wildlife, ecology, and culture of the Colorado
Plateau. Trips include exploring the little-visited areas of
Arches and Canyonlands national parks, as well as tours of
the Hopi and Navajo reservations, photography
workshops, and wildlife ecology. Led by experienced
naturalists, biologists, ecologists, anthropologists, and
photographers.
    Cost: Ranges from $35 (one-day seminar) to
$685 (seven-day backcountry trip)

Carrie Murray Outdoor Education Campus
1901 Ridgetop Road
Baltimore, MD 21207
(301) 396-0808

This year-round education program offers
environmental adventure learning trips and summer
nature camps for people of all ages.
    Cost: Ranges from $15 to $800

Clemson University Alumni Association
Travel Program
Alumni Center
Clemson, SC 29634
(803) 656-2345

Clemson University sponsors a half dozen study tours
focusing on natural history and culture to a variety of
international destinations, including Dominica, Central
America, South America, Asia, Europe, Egypt, and the
Soviet republics. Faculty members accompany trips and
offer lectures and lead group discussions.
    Cost: $1,300 to $3,500

**Columbia University's Alumni
Travel/Study Program
The Alumni Federation of
Columbia University, Inc.**
Box 400
Columbia University
New York, NY 10027
(212) 854-3237

The Alumni Federation sponsors a variety of tours,
including some with a natural history focus, to a variety of
domestic and international locations, including Alaska,
Canada, Europe, and Japan. Trips feature informal lectures
by distinguished Columbia University faculty members.
    Cost: Ranges from $2,400 to $6,300 (includes $100 to
$250 tax-deductible contribution)

Cornell Adult University
626 Thurston Ave.
Ithaca, NY 14850
(607) 255-6260

The university-sponsored program offers on-campus
natural history workshops during the summer in addition
to about two dozen expeditions of varying lengths to a
variety of national and international destinations. All are
led by Cornell professors. Itineraries range from studying
insects in upstate New York to walking tours of New
Zealand.
    Cost: Varies

**Duke Travel
Duke University**
614 Chapel Drive
Durham, NC 27706
(919) 684-5114

Duke University sponsors a dozen trips a year to a
variety of international destinations. Faculty members
usually accompany the tours. Itineraries include
Antarctica, the British Virgin Islands, India, Southeast
Asia, South America, Europe, and the Soviet republics.
    Cost: $1,450 to $4,895

Elderhostel
80 Boylston St.
Suite 400
Boston, MA 02116
(617) 426-7788

Established in 1975, Elderhostel is an educational
program for older adults (participants must be at least
sixty years of age, or at least fifty if accompanied by a
spouse or companion who is at least sixty years old) who
want to expand their horizons and develop new interests
and enthusiasms. Participants enjoy inexpensive, short-
term academic programs at more than 1,500 educational
institutions in all fifty states, all ten Canadian provinces,
and more than forty countries around the world.
Elderhostel students live on the campus of the host
institution, thus making for an excellent way to live and
study abroad inexpensively. Among the huge assortment
of classes available are more than 120 environmental
programs, ranging from "How We Use Our Forests" to
"Desert Ecology" to "Environmental Theater." Programs
feature classes in the morning and course-related
excursions in the afternoon. There is time to explore the
area of your study on your own. Most programs are two to
four weeks in length.
Cost: Average of $2,000 for a two- to three-week stay

Environmental Traveling Companions (ETC)
Fort Mason Center
San Francisco, CA 94123
(415) 474-7662

ETC is a nonprofit organization that arranges outdoor
education and adventure trips for people with physical and
cultural disabilities. Trips include sea kayaking,
whitewater rafting, and hiking.
Cost: Call

Field Studies in Natural History
Office of Continuing Education
San Jose State University
One Washington Square
San Jose, CA 95192
(408) 924-2680

This nonprofit organization sponsors approximately
six trips a year to such areas as Redwood National Park,
Death Valley National Monument, and the Grand Canyon.

Trips, led by instructors of biology, botany, ecology, geology, natural history, and zoology, feature lectures, films, and discussions.
   Cost: $100 to $1,600

The Four Corners School of
Outdoor Education
East Route
Monticello, UT 84535
(801) 587-2859/1-800-525-4456

This nonprofit organization offers more than forty programs in the archaeology, biology, ethnography, geology, and natural history of the Colorado Plateau. Programs include hiking, boating, exploring seldom-visited areas, photography, and writing. Programs are co-sponsored by such groups as Earthwatch, Sierra Club, and the Utah Museum of Natural History. Field experts accompany every tour.
   Cost: Ranges from $275 to $1,395

The Glacier Institute
P.O. Box 1457A
Kalispell, MT 59903
(406) 752-5222/(406) 888-5215

This nonprofit organization sponsors natural science field courses at Glacier National Park. Subject matter includes wildlife, ecology, meteorology, natural history, and Native American culture. Programs range from one to five days and are led by regional experts.
   Cost: $90 to $200

Global Exchange
2141 Mission St., Suite 202
San Francisco, CA 94110
(415) 255-7296

Global Exchange Reality Tours are an exciting alternative to a commercial vacation. Trips are organized to countries throughout the Third World—from Brazil to India to Zimbabwe. Participants meet with farmers, religious leaders, women's groups, unions, government figures, and opposition leaders in order to learn firsthand about pressing issues. Tours include visits to controversial development projects, schools, and villages. Tours include "Behind the Rainforest Crisis in Brazil" and "Environmentalism in India." On the latter, participants visit three

controversial World Bank–funded power projects and
meet with resident activists who are working to reverse
the environmental impacts caused by their development.
Cost: Call

**Great Smoky Mountains
Institute at Tremont**
Route 1, Box 81
Townsend, TN 37882
(615) 448-6709

The institute offers a wide variety of programs
focusing on the natural resources of Great Smoky
Mountains National Park, including camps, school
programs, field trips, and workshops.
Cost: $16 to $25 per day

International Zoological Expeditions, Inc.
210 Washington St.
Sherborn, MA 01770
(508) 655-1461

This private company conducts natural history
expeditions to Belize. Many trips are cosponsored by
schools and colleges. Subject matter includes the area's
wildlife, coral reefs, and rainforests. Credit is available for
teachers and students.
Cost: $350 to $2,000

Leelanau Center for Education
One Old Homestead Road
Glen Arbor, MI 49636
(616) 334-3072

The center has been sponsoring outdoor natural
history workshops at the Sleeping Bear Dunes National
Lakeshore on Lake Michigan since 1982. Subjects include
environmental monitoring, field identification, ecology,
and wildlife behavior. Accommodations in dormitories or
rustic cabins.
Cost: $180 for enrollment, $175 to $290 for
room and board

**National Audubon Society
Expedition Institute**
Sharon, CT 06069
(203) 364-0522

The institute, in conjunction with Lesley College in Cambridge, Massachusetts, offers unique and exciting courses of study in environmental education for high school and college students. It combines classroom study with expedition courses. Students in the expedition program spend nine months on the road, camping, living, and learning in the outdoors. They travel throughout the United States and Canada observing and studying societal patterns of behavior and their impact on our fragile ecosystems. Expedition sites include downeast Maine, maritime Canada, southern Appalachia, the American Southwest, the Pacific Northwest, Yosemite National Park, Hopi Indian Reservation, Pine Ridge Reservation, and the Texas coast. High school and college credits are available.

Cost: $8,300 for full-year program, $4,890 for semester; tuition for credits from Lesley an additional $75 per credit

Olympic Field Seminars
Olympic Park Institute
HC 62 Box 9T
Port Angeles, WA 98362
(206) 928-3720

One of three campuses operated by the Yosemite Institute, the Olympic Park Institute's field seminar series offers programs on a variety of nature-oriented topics in Olympic National Park. Topics include wildlife, forest ecosystems, marine sciences, coastal studies, earth sciences, and botany. Accommodations are in cabins within the park.

Cost: $75 to $255

Pocono Environmental Education Center
R.D. 2, Box 1010
Dingmans Ferry, PA 18328
(717) 828-2319

Established in 1972, this nonprofit center sponsors one- and two-day nature study programs focusing on the wildlife and ecosystem of the Pocono Mountains. Programs feature field trips, day hikes, and evening discussions.

Cost: $45 to $100

Point Reyes Field Seminars
Point Reyes National Seashore Association
Bear Valley Road
Point Reyes Station, CA 94956
(415) 663-1200

Established in 1976, this program offers one- and two-
day seminars in natural history, environmental education,
and birding held at Point Reyes National Seashore in
California. The programs feature hiking, wildflower
identification, geology, tidepooling, birding, and
seismology. Seminars are led by scientists and natural
history experts. Some seminars earn college credit.
Cost: $20 to $75

Recursos de Santa Fe
826 Camino de Monte Rey
Santa Fe, NM 87501
(505) 982-9301

This nonprofit organization has been conducting a
variety of seminars and study tours in the American
Southwest, Baja California, and Costa Rica since 1984 as a
way to promote appreciation and understanding of the art,
archaeology, natural history, and native culture in those
areas. Trips range from two days to two weeks. Seminars
and tours are conducted by professional naturalists and
museum curators.
Cost: Seminars average $125 per day;
international trips start at $1,000

San Diego State University
Travel Study Programs
5630 Hardy Ave.
San Diego, CA 92182
(619) 594-2645

Through its College of Extended Studies, San Diego
State sponsors some twenty travel study programs a year,
many of them focusing on natural history themes, to
domestic and international destinations. Itineraries range
from an exploration of the unique flora and fauna of the
Galapagos Islands to a study of the natural history of
Hawaii. Tours feature lectures, seminars, and discussions.
All programs are accompanied by university faculty
members.
Cost: $1,700 to $3,400

San Jose State University
International Travel Programs
Office of Continuing Education
San Jose State University
San Jose, CA 95192
(408) 924-2680

Through its Continuing Education Department, San
Jose State sponsors some twenty-five travel-study
programs to a variety of international destinations,
including the Galapagos Islands, East Africa, Southeast
Asia, Nepal, Brazil, and the Soviet republics. All programs
are conducted by university faculty members.
Cost: $2,100 to $3,500

Sitka Center for Art and Ecology
P.O. Box 65
Otis, OR 97368
(503) 994-5485

This learning center for art and ecology on the central
Oregon coast offers one- and two-day natural science
workshops on such topics as old-growth forests, marine
ecosystems, and organic farming. Programs combine
walking tours with lectures and multimedia presentations.
Cost: $10 to $20 per day

University of California at Los Angeles
Field Study Program
UCLA Extension
P.O. Box 24901
Los Angeles, CA 90024
(213) 825-7093

Since 1972, UCLA Extension has designed more than
300 in-depth itineraries reaching into every corner of the
globe for its field study program focusing on natural
history and archaeology. The tours explore the land and
life of some of the most fascinating and spectacular areas
of the world, from the tropical habitats of Costa Rica to the
rainforests of Papua New Guinea, from Lake Atitlán in
Guatemala to the mountains of Morocco.
Cost: Call to request a current extension catalog

University of the Pacific
Office of Lifelong Learning
Stockton, CA 95211
(209) 946-2424

The university sponsors a variety of programs and study tours in the United States and abroad, many of them nature oriented. Topics include natural history, ecology, geology, and archaeology. Tours are led by university faculty members and experts.
Cost: Call

University of South Florida
Travel-Study Programs Division
of Special Programs/Travel-Study
LLL 012
University of South Florida
Tampa, FL 33620
(813) 974-3218

The university offers a variety of residential and study programs to various international destinations. All offer academic credit. Tours to Asia, Central America, South America, and Africa are regularly scheduled. Tours are led by university faculty.
Cost: $1,900 to $4,000

Wild Basin Wilderness Preserve
P.O. Box 13455
Austin, TX 78711
(512) 327-7622

The preserve offers a variety of field programs focusing on the natural history and natural resources of Wild Basin.
Cost: Most programs are free

Wilderness Southeast
711 Sandtown Road
Savannah, GA 31410
(912) 897-5108

This nonprofit school of the outdoors takes small groups into a variety of wilderness areas for close-up looks at their ecosystems.
Cost: $235 to $2,985

The Yellowstone Institute
P.O. Box 117
Yellowstone National Park, WY 82190
(307) 344-7381

The nonprofit Yellowstone Institute offers more than
eighty study programs and nature vacations. Topics
include the ecology, botany, geology, wildlife, and natural
history of the Yellowstone region. Programs also feature
horsepacking, fly fishing, hiking, photography, and llama
trekking. There are opportunities to join research field
trips with park scientists. Accommodations are at rustic
cabins.
   Cost: $20 to $400 for study programs; lodging is
$7 per day (no meals included)

The Yosemite Institute
P.O. Box 487
Yosemite, CA 95389
(209) 372-4441

The nonprofit Yosemite Institute offers study
programs and nature vacations focusing on the ecology,
botany, geology, wildlife, and natural history of the
Yosemite region. Programs feature hiking, climbing,
photography, and wildlife identification. Accommodations
are at rustic cabins.
   Cost: Call for information

11

tour operators & travel agencies

Here, for your convenience, is a list of commercial tour operators and travel agencies that specialize in nature tours.

Whether your primary interest is in rare birds or orchids, river rafting or mountain climbing, trekking through the tropics or gazing at glaciers, you will probably find an outfitter here that caters to your quest.

tour operators
& travel agencies

In countries around the world that are both biologically rich and in need of economic development, nature tourism promises to be a valuable tool in helping conservationists work with local people to protect environmentally important regions. While conservationists look to ecotourism as a means of creating economic incentives for local governments and local populations to protect nature, they also realize that developing sound ecotourism guidelines and practices poses an enormous challenge and reason for concern.

Standards for evaluating ecotourism companies as environmentally sound are still evolving. Environmental organizations, while supporting well-managed ecotourism, have to date been unable to develop standards by which to measure or assess the environmental travel companies discussed here.

Although no standard now exists for certifying a company as environmentally responsible, all companies listed below claim to be so. It is up to you to decide if they live up to their claims. Ask questions. Demand answers. (See "15 questions to ask a tour operator or travel agent," page 4.) If you have any doubts, try another operator.

tour operators

Above the Clouds Trekking
P.O. Box 398
Worcester, MA 01602
(508) 799-4499/1-800-233-4499

Established in 1981, Above the Clouds specializes in small group trekking tours of the Himalayas and other mountainous regions, with an emphasis on taking the traveler inside the minds and hearts of other cultures while experiencing the beauty of the planet.
Destinations: Himalayas, Andes, Alps, East Africa
Cost: $1,500 average

Adventure Source International (ASI)
5353 Manhattan Circle, Suite 103
Boulder, CO 80303
1-800-346-8666

ASI offers a range of nature programs and ecology tours that include such activities as trekking, biking, diving, and rafting.
Destinations: Belize, Costa Rica, Australia, New Zealand
Cost: $600 to $3,000

Amazonia Expeditions, Inc.
1824 N.W. 102nd Way
Gainesville, FL 32606
(904) 332-4051

Amazonia organizes small tours to the Amazon jungle with special attention to photography, bird-watching, insect and plant collecting, anthropology, and scientific research. Participants are encouraged to bring items such as clothing, medicine, and school supplies to donate to natives.
Destination: Peru
Cost: $1,700

Baja Expeditions Inc.
2625 Garnet Ave.
San Diego, CA 92109
(619) 581-3311/1-800-843-6967
Founded in 1974, Baja Expeditions is the largest and oldest outfitter of natural history and adventure travel in Baja California. Its whale-watching trips cruise the Pacific and the Gulf of California. It also offers sea kayaking and mountain biking trips.
Destinations: Baja California, Costa Rica
Cost: $100 to $120 per day

Biological Journeys
1876 Ocean Drive
McKinleyville, CA 95521
(707) 839-0178/1-800-548-7555
Biological Journeys takes travelers on close-up tours of Earth's great marine areas. Trips are led by professional naturalists and focus on natural history, whale watching, bird-watching, and marine sciences.
Destinations: Baja California, southeast Alaska, San Juan Islands, British Columbia, Galapagos, Tierra del Fuego, Australia, New Zealand
Cost: $1,195 to $3,295

Cheeseman's Ecology Safaris, Inc.
20800 Kittredge Road
Saratoga, CA 95070
(408) 867-1371

Doug and Gail Cheeseman lead small groups of non-smokers on natural history tours, focusing on ecology, wildlife behavior, and flora and fauna identification. Part of the trip's cost is donated to conservation projects within the host country. Company donates entire proceeds of its Costa Rica trip to a local conservation group to maintain Lomas Barbudal Biological Preserve.
Destinations: Central America, South America, East Africa, Seychelles, India, Papua New Guinea
Cost: $2,015 to $4,250

Ecotour Expeditions
60 Walden St.
P.O. Box 1066
Cambridge, MA 02238
(617) 876-5817/1-800-688-1822

This outfit stresses a thoughtful approach to natural history tours and uses scientists as guides. Its expeditions up the Amazon River and its tributaries feature exploratory itineraries. It alternates visits to particular sites to avoid impacting wildlife.
Destination: Brazil
Cost: $1,750 to $2,650

Forum Travel International, Inc.
91 Gregory Lane, Suite 21
Pleasant Hill, CA 94523
(510) 671-2900

Since 1965, Forum has created more than 1,200 ecotourism programs to destinations around the globe. It is the professional "travel arm" for many educational and scientific programs. Its trips stress environmental and social responsibility.
Destinations: Latin America, Europe, Africa, Asia, South Pacific, North America
Cost: Varies

Geostar Travel, Inc.
1240 Century Court, Suite C
Santa Rosa, CA 95403
(707) 579-2420/1-800-624-6633

Operated by biologists and longtime conservationists Barbara and John Hopper, Geostar, which was established in 1977, offers small group natural history tours to habitats of special concern throughout the world. Many of the trips are fundraising tours for conservation causes, colleges and universities, and organizations such as The Nature Conservancy, Audubon Society, and the Native Plant Society.

Destinations: Costa Rica, Ecuador, Belize, Honduras, Brazil, Australia, New Zealand, Africa, Malaysia, Alaska, Hawaii, Mexico
Cost: $1,995 to $3,195

Inca Floats
1311 63rd St.
Emeryville, CA 94608
(510) 420-1550

Since 1976, Inca Floats has been operating small-group natural history tours aboard chartered yachts to the Galapagos Islands, led by licensed Galapagos naturalist guides. Focus is on learning firsthand about the islands' unique ecosystem. Inca Floats also offers tours of Peru and Ecuador and guided treks along the Inca Trail.

Destinations: Galapagos, Ecuador, Peru
Cost: $1,895 to $3,995

InnerAsia Expeditions
2627 Lombard St.
San Francisco, CA 94123
(415) 922-0448/1-800-777-8183

Since 1981, InnerAsia has been offering distinctive journeys to some of Asia's most extraordinary destinations. Itineraries range from trekking to elephant-back wildlife safaris, and arrangements from luxury to exploratory expeditions. InnerAsia supports the work of Conservation International.

Destinations: Himalayas, India, Patagonia, Mongolia, the Soviet republics, Alaska, Turkey, Japan
Cost: $1,850 and up

International Expeditions, Inc.
One Environs Park
Helena, AL 35080
(205) 428-1700/1-800-633-4734

The company conducts ecologically oriented travel

programs to more than thirty remote destinations worldwide, designed to promote an appreciation of nature and native cultures. International Expeditions plans and implements travel programs for more than 100 universities, zoos, museums, conservation groups, and nature centers. It sponsors international workshops on rainforest ecology and encourages nonintrusive interaction between travelers and local inhabitants.

Destinations: Central America, South America, Asia, Africa, Australia, Papua New Guinea, Alaska, Hawaii
Cost: $1,498 to $5,998

Lemur Tours
2562 Noriega St., Suite 201
San Francisco, CA 94122
(415) 681-8222

Lemur Tours is dedicated to promoting ecotourism and cultural exchange in Madagascar. Its tours, led by professionally trained guides, feature guest lecturers including zoo directors and wildlife specialists. Many of the trips are in association with such groups as the Audubon Society, Wildlife Preservation Trust, Conservation International, and various zoos and museums.

Destination: Madagascar
Cost: $4,300 to $5,045

Mountain Travel–Sobek
6420 Fairmount Ave.
El Cerrito, CA 94530
800-227-2384

Mountain Travel–Sobek is a merger of two of the nation's largest nature/adventure travel operators. The outfitter, which combined tours and staff from the two old firms in 1991, offers about 125 programs. Mountain Travel has been conducting thoughtfully organized treks, outings, and expeditions to the far reaches of the globe in a low-impact form of environmentally sensitive travel. Its Mountain Travel Fund assists the specific environments in which its trips take place. Sobek has been conducting adventure trips to some of the most remote spots on Earth, specializing in first descents of wilderness rivers. Many trips include direct contributions to local conservation programs.

Destinations: Africa, Asia, Oceania, South America, Antarctica, Europe, Alaska
Cost: $2,200 average

Natural Habitat Wildlife Adventures
Route 517 North (Box 789)
McAfee, NJ 07428
(201) 209-4747/1-800-543-8917

This operator offers a select group of wildlife
programs that take animal enthusiasts and photographers
to see wildlife species in their own environment. The
company's goal is to protect wildlife by supporting local
economies that formerly depended on hunting.
Destinations: Churchill, Canada; Magdalen Islands;
Africa; Baja California
Cost: $1,295 to $4,995

Nature Expeditions International (NEI)
P.O. Box 11496
Eugene, OR 97440
(503) 484-6529/1-800-869-0639

Founded in the early 1970s, NEI mixes adventure and
discovery to create learning vacations. The trips provide
travelers with an opportunity to explore the world and
appreciate the interdependence of all life on Earth, as well
as highlight the urgent need for increased preservation of
natural areas and traditional societies.
Destinations: Africa, Asia, Oceania, South America,
Central America, North America
Cost: $1,490 to $4,890

Overseas Adventure Travel (OAT)
349 Broadway
Cambridge, MA 02139
(617) 876-0533/1-800-221-0814

Founded in 1979, OAT offers adventure travel trips to
more than fifty nations around the globe. It takes a
conservation-oriented approach to travel. Included in the
costs of some of its trips are donations to local
conservation programs. For example, it contributes to the
African Wildlife Foundation and the Rhino Ark Fund. In
Nepal, it is funding the Loboche Conservation Project.
Destinations: Africa, Asia, South America,
South Pacific
Cost: $150 a day average

Questers Worldwide Nature Tours
257 Park Avenue South
New York, NY 10010
(212) 673-3120

Questers conducts in-depth natural history tours to over thirty destinations worldwide. It emphasizes small groups and first-class arrangements.
Destinations: Alaska, Central America, South America, Africa, Australia
Cost: $1,800 to $4,725

R.E.I. Adventures
P.O. Box 88126
Seattle, WA 98138
(206) 395-7760/1-800-622-2236

This outdoor equipment co-op retailer conducts trips to out-of-the-way destinations focusing on active, human-powered participation. The trips are designed to maintain a minimum of impact on the people and places visited while providing a hands-on feeling of adventure travel.
Destinations: Soviet republics, China, Alaska, Himalayas, Alps, Brazil, Ecuador
Cost: $100 to $150 a day average

Salen Lindblad Cruising, Inc.
133 E. 55th St.
New York, NY 10022
(212) 751-2300/1-800-223-5688

Pioneers in expedition cruising, Salen Lindblad operates a variety of cruises to the far-flung reaches of the world aboard the *M.S. Frontier Spirit.* There is a special emphasis on natural history and onboard lectures and discussions. Passengers are asked to abide by a ecologically oriented traveler's creed.
Destinations: Antarctica, Australia, Oceania, Asia, Alaska, Northwest Passage, South America, Caribbean
Cost: $3,050 to $26,200

Society Expeditions
3131 Elliott Ave., Suite 700
Seattle, WA 98121
(206) 285-9400/1-800-426-7794

Society operates expedition-class cruises aboard the *Society Explorer, World Discover,* and *Society Adventurer* to exotic destinations on the seven seas. Special emphasis is on natural history, cross-cultural exchange, and exploration. Onboard lecturers and trained naturalists accompany each tour. Passengers are coached in environmentally responsible travel. The company has donated tour profits to local conservation and restoration projects in Papua New Guinea, Easter Island, and Antarctica and has joined forces with the World Wildlife Fund in funding preservation projects in Indonesia and Madagascar.

Destinations: Arctic, Antarctica, Oceania, Soviet republics, Far East, South America

Cost: $2,990 to $25,750

Trans Niugini Tours
P.O. Box 371
Mount Hagen, Papua New Guinea
52-1438

Trans Niugini conducts a variety of tours throughout Papua New Guinea, including jungle treks, river cruises, and visits to native villages. Special emphasis is on cross-cultural exchange, anthropology, and wildlife.

Destination: Papua New Guinea

Cost: $1,154 to $2,062

Victor Emanuel Nature Tours (VENT)
P.O. Box 33008
Austin, TX 78764
(512) 328-5221/1-800-328-VENT

Founded in 1974, VENT offers more than a hundred birding and natural history tours worldwide. Trips are led by some of the foremost birding experts in the world. The company is committed to conservation and has organized tours for The Nature Conservancy, National Audubon Society, and Conservation International.

Destinations: United States, Canada, Mexico, Central America, South America, Africa, Antarctica, Asia, Oceania, Europe

Cost: Up to $7,365

Voyagers International
P.O. Box 915
Ithaca, NY 14851
(607) 257-3091

Voyagers organizes worldwide ecotours for individuals and leading nonprofit nature and conservation organizations, museums, and zoos throughout the United States and Canada. The trips focus on the natural history and traditional cultures of an area and provide low-impact travel that is environmentally sound and culturally sensitive. It supports local conservation efforts such as the East African Wild Life Society, the African Wild Dog Project, and Darwin Research Station.

Destinations: Hawaii, Central America, Galapagos, Antarctica, East Africa, India, Oceania, Ireland
Cost: $2,200 and up

Wilderness Expeditions
310 Washington Ave., S.W.
Roanoke, VA 24016
(703) 342-5630/1-800-323-3241

This outfit conducts nature-oriented tours exploring the ecological and cultural diversity of Amazonia. Its Peruvian trips support a conservation program affiliated with the International Society for the Preservation of the Tropical Rainforest.

Destinations: Peru, Ecuador, Chile
Cost: $100 to $200 per day

Wilderness Travel
801 Allston Way
Berkeley, CA 94710
(510) 548-0420/1-800-247-6700

Established in 1977, Wilderness Travel offers more than eighty adventures to five different continents. The trips feature small groups and host country experts. The company actively promotes cultural preservation, conservation, and environmental protection by supporting a number of environmental and cultural projects and organizations, promoting minimum-impact camping and traveling, and encouraging cross-cultural ties.

Destinations: Asia, Africa, Europe, South America, Galapagos, Oceania
Cost: $1,000 to $5,590

Wildland Adventures
3516 N.E. 155th
Seattle, WA 98155
(206) 365-0686/1-800-345-4453

Established in 1976, Wildland Adventures offers small group tours to destinations worldwide with a special emphasis on increasing travelers' appreciation and understanding of the places and cultures they encounter. Each trip contributes to a conservation or community development project in host countries through the Earth Preservation Fund (EPF). Travelers can participate directly in ongoing EPF projects such as restoring monasteries in Ladakh, planting trees in Nepal, and cleaning up the Inca Trail. In Africa, Journeys contributes to the conservation efforts of the East African Wildlife Society and Wildlife Clubs of Kenya.

Destinations: Latin America, Alaska, Hawaii, Asia, Africa, Himalayas, Turkey
Cost: $990 to $2,890

travel agencies

North-South Travel
16140 N.E. 87th St.
Redmond, WA 98052
(206) 881-3117/1-800-852-8818

This agency promotes and develops tourism projects that benefit local people and the environment. All profits go to development projects in the Third World through a charitable trust.

Sanctuary Travel Services
3701 E. Tudor Road
Anchorage, AK 99507
(907) 561-1212/1-800-247-3149

The agency represents many Alaska-based outfitters and donates 20 percent of its commissions to nonprofit environmental organizations.

Schilling Travel Service
7222 Second Ave. South
Minnesota, MN 55402
(612) 332-1100/1-800-328-0302

Schilling provides socially and environmentally responsible travel services to individuals and small groups.

Travel Links
Co-op America
2100 M St., N.W., Suite 310
Washington, DC 20063
1-800-992-1903

The organization operates a socially responsible, full-service travel agency and arranges a variety of trips from ecotours to cultural and educational tours. A portion of the travel purchase is donated to the Economic Development Fund to directly help progressive organizations that are working for economic justice.

Working Assets Travel Service
230 California St.
San Francisco, CA 94111
1-800-332-3637

Operating like a full-service travel agency, Working Assets books travel arrangements and provides ticketing services. The agency donates 2 percent of the total cost to a pool of nonprofit organizations that includes conservation groups such as the African Wildlife Foundation, Conservation International, the Natural Resources Defense Council, the Rainforest Action Network, and the Trust for Public Land.

resources

On the following pages are the advocacy groups, directories, research papers, and scientific findings that can help you learn more about environmentally responsible travel, ecotourism, and ethical travel in developing countries, as well as focus on the issues that are of most interest to you.

resources

The following advocacy groups, directories, organizations, and publications can help you obtain additional information on specific issues dealing with environmentally responsible travel, ecotourism, and ethical travel in developing countries.

environmentally responsible travel organizations

The Adventure Travel Society
7500 E. Arapahoe Road, Suite 355
Englewood, CO 80112
(303) 770-3801

An association that promotes adventure travel, the society sponsors the World Congress on Adventure Travel and Ecotourism.

American Society of Travel Agents (ASTA)
P.O. Box 23992
Washington, DC 20026
(703) 739-2782

This society of travel agents has issued a set of environmental guidelines and asks its members to subscribe to them. ASTA has also undertaken studies and seminars to explore how travel can be more environmentally responsible. Members are being educated about the environment.

The Ecotourism Society
801 Devon Place
Alexandria, VA 22314
(703) 549-8979

The Ecotourism Society is made up of tour operators, conservation groups, and other organizations that practice tourism that benefits developing countries and protects the environment. Members adhere to a code of environmental travel ethics, support conservation groups and local conservation projects, and promote environmental understanding and appreciation.

The Ladakh Project
21 Victoria Square
Clifton, Bristol BS8 4ES
England

The Ladakh Project is a nonprofit organization specifically aimed at promoting environmental education and development of traditional Buddhist culture and environmental integrity in an area of the Himalaya Mountains known as Little Tibet. Associated with the local Ladakh Ecological Development Group (LEDEG), the project distributes guidelines for tourists and coordinates a program to develop traditional-style crafts.
(See page 93.)

Talamanca Association for Ecotourism and Conservation (ATEC)
Puerto Viejo de Talamanca
Limon, Costa Rica

This nonprofit group promotes the development of socially responsible ecological tourism in the Talamanca region of Costa Rica by educating the indigenous and Afro-Caribbean peoples of Talamanca as well as tourists about the ecology of the region. In addition, ATEC trains residents to serve as nature guides and provides technical and financial assistance to Talamanca residents in developing and managing ecologically appropriate tourism facilities and services.

Wildlife Tourism Impact Project (WTIP)
524 San Anselmo Ave., Suite 103
San Anselmo, CA 94960
(415) 453-4933

This nonprofit organization encourages environmentally responsible safari tourism by providing practical means of action for tourists, travel agents, and tour operators to participate in the protection of the wildlife, habitat, and culture of their destination. WTIP communicates information among the travel industry, wildlife organizations, and academic institutions, sharing the expertise of different experiences and approaches.

socially responsible travel organizations

**The North American Coordinating Center
for Responsible Tourism**
2 Kensington Road
San Anselmo, CA 94960
(415) 258-6594

This worthy organization is active in many areas of
socially responsible tourism. It serves as a clearinghouse
for information, a network for international groups, and a
watchdog on the tourism industry. It publishes a
quarterly newsletter on responsible traveling. ($10/year)

Ecumenical Coalition on Third World Tourism
P.O. Box 9-25
Bangkhen, Bangkok 0900
Thailand

This international organization serves as an
information clearinghouse and network for socially
responsible tourism groups in Third World countries. It
has issued a widely adopted code of travel ethics. It
investigates and publicizes unethical tourism practices.
Publishes an insightful newsletter. ($8/year)

home exchange organizations

Home exchange provides an environmentally
intelligent way to travel abroad without fueling
unnecessary development, such as hotel and resort
construction. By staying in existing homes, you can
experience living as a resident in a foreign land. Here are
two organizations that specialize in such exchanges:

Green Theme Home Exchange
Little Rylands Farm
Redmoor, Bodmin
Cornwall, PL30 5AR
England
0208-873123

The Invented City
41 Sutter St., Suite 1090
San Francisco, CA 94104
(415) 673-0347 (International)
1-800-788-CITY (U.S.)

directories

Alternative Tourism: Third World Travel Directory
edited by Betty Stott
Center for Responsible Tourism (CRT)
2 Kensington Road
San Anselmo, CA 94960
(415) 258-6594

This is a helpful guide to Third World destinations,
agencies, and organizations who plan Third World travel,
and responsible tourism developments. ($6)

Directory of Alternative Travel Resources
by Dianne G. Brause
One World Family Travel Network
81868 Lost Valley Lane
Dexter, OR 97431

This unique catalog lists 250 alternative and socially
responsible travel opportunities. ($7)

Directory of Low-Cost Vacations with a Difference
by J. Crawford
Pilot Industries
103 Cooper St.
Babylon, NY 11702

Among the low-cost or free alternative vacation
opportunities listed here are volunteer work programs and
farm stays. ($5.95)

Great Expeditions: The Magazine of
Off-the-Beaten Path Travel
P.O. Box 8000-711
Abbotsford, BC V26 6H1
Canada

A wealth of information on alternative destinations
can be found in each issue. ($18/year, 5 issues)

Helping Out in the Outdoors
American Hiking Society (AHS)
1015 31st St., N.W., 4th Floor
Washington, DC 20007

AHS publishes a directory of volunteer work projects

in America's public lands, national forests, and parks. ($3)

The International Directory of Volunteer Work
by David Woodworth
Vacation Work Publications
9 Park End St.
Oxford OXI 1HJ
England

This directory lists international opportunities for
volunteer vacations. (Write for price.)

Learning Vacations
by Gerson G. Eisenberg
Peterson's Guides
166 Bunn Drive
P.O. Box 2123
Princeton, NJ 08543

This guide to educational travel provides names and
addresses of organizations that sponsor seminars,
workshops, classes, and travel programs on a wide range
of subjects, from the environment to art, music, and
writing. ($11.70)

Specialty Travel Index
edited by Andy Alpine and C. Steen Hansen
Alpine Hansen Publishers
305 San Anselmo Ave.
San Anselmo, CA 94960
(415) 459-4900

This semiannual index lists resources for specialty
travel. ($15)

Traveling Healthy
108-48 70th Road
Forest Hills, NY 11375

Informative, bimonthly eight-page newsletter with
practical articles on health updates, travel tips, political
briefs, and feature stories. ($24/year)

Voluntary Service Bulletin
Volunteers in Mission
475 Riverside Drive, Suite 1126
New York, NY 10115

This United Presbyterian Church–sponsored directory lists volunteer opportunities in a variety of areas. ($5.50)

Volunteer Vacations
by Bill McMillon
Chicago Review Press
814 N. Franklin St.
Chicago, IL 60610

This directory lists 500 opportunities for people willing to volunteer their time to help others and the environment. ($11.95)

books, periodicals, and guides

Antarctica Visitor Guidelines/
Antarctica Tour Operator Guidelines
Society Expeditions, Inc.
3131 Elliott Ave., Suite 700
Seattle, WA 98121
(206) 285-9400

This joint publication by Society Expeditions, Ocean Cruise Lines, Salen Lindblad, Mountain Travel, and Travel Dynamics is an effort to formalize guidelines for visitors and tour operators traveling to Antarctica. (Free)

The Challenge of Tourism
edited by Alison O'Grady
Ecumenical Coalition on Third World Tourism
Center for Responsible Tourism (CRT)
2 Kensington Road
San Anselmo, CA 94960
(415) 258-6594

This critical look at tourism gives the origins of tourism—its economic, political, social, cultural, and environmental impacts. It also chronicles initiatives to create just and sustainable tourism. ($15)

Economics of Protected Areas:
A New Look at Benefits and Costs
by John Dixon and Paul Sherman
Island Press
Box 7
Covelo, CA 95428
1-800-828-1302
(Cloth $34.95, paper $19.95)

Ecotourism: The Light at the End of the Terminal
by Christian Kallen
E, The Environmental Magazine
(July/August 1990)
Adventurer and author Kallen examines ecotourism.

Ecotourism: The Potentials and Pitfalls
by Elizabeth Boo
World Wildlife Fund (WWF)
P.O. Box 4866
Hampden Post Office
Baltimore, MD 21211

This publication of WWF's investigation of the current status of ecotourism includes an evaluation of its economic and environmental impacts. It focuses on Latin America and the Caribbean. ($22.50)

Ecotourism: The Uneasy Alliance
by Karen Ziffer
Conservation International (CI)
1015 18th St., N.W.
Washington, DC 20036
(202) 429-5660

CI's Ziffer provides insights and analysis into the growing ecotourism movement. ($3)

"Ecotourism! Wild Hopes"
by Edward Warner
Environmental Action
September/October 1989

This article is a good introduction to the concept of ecotourism and analyzes its merits and possibilities.

The Educated Traveler
P.O. Box 220822
Chantilly, VA 22022
(703) 471-1063

A comprehensive newsletter designed as a resource for educated travelers. Contributors include professional and recreational travelers. It focuses on international specialty travel, including nature travel, ecotourism, learning vacations, and theme tours. ($75 annual subscription, 10 issues)

How to Plan a Conservation Education Program
by David and Diane Wood
World Resources Institute
P.O. Box 4852
Hampden Station
Baltimore, MD 21211
(301) 338-6963

A step-by-step guide to planning effective conservation education programs.

The Lonely Planet Guides
P.O. Box 2001A
Berkeley, CA 94702

The Lonely Planet guidebooks on Third World countries include two series, the comprehensive "Travel Survival Kit" and the economical "On a Shoestring." They provide hands-on information about specific countries or regions, with a focus on highlighting off-the-beaten-track destinations and attractions. Humorous yet authoritative, they are valuable traveling companions to the less-visited corners of the globe. Information is updated regularly through the release of new editions.

"The New Ethic in Adventure Travel"
by Kurt Kutay
Buzzworm: The Environmental Journal
Summer 1989
Commercial tour operator and naturalist Kurt Kutay provides an insightful report on the new ethics of socially and environmentally responsible travel.

New World of Travel
by Arthur Frommer
Prentice Hall, a Division of Simon & Schuster
15 Columbus Circle
New York, NY 10023

The man who invented *Europe on $5 a Day* has a revisionist outlook on travel, and in this comprehensive guide describes a bold new way to travel and lists many different options and opportunities. ($16.95)

Rainforests: A Guide to Research and Tourist Facilities
by James L. Castner
Feline Press
P.O. Box 7219
Gainesville, FL 32605

This comprehensive guide tells readers interested in Latin American rainforests where to find research facilities, accommodations, scientific organizations, funding sources, and research opportunities for countries south of the border. ($23.45)

*Soft Paths: How to Enjoy the Wilderness
Without Harming It*
by Bruce Hampton
National Outdoor Leadership School (NOLS)
P.O. Box AA
Lander, WY 82520

NOLS has put together a useful book on the basics of traveling in the wilderness using minimum-impact camping techniques that help protect the natural resources while enhancing your own appreciation of the environment. ($11.95)

Tourism: An Ecumenical Concern
edited by Koson Srisang
**Ecumenical Coalition on Third World Tourism
Center for Responsible Tourism (CRT)**
2 Kensington Road
San Anselmo, CA 94960
(415) 258-6594

This book is for people who want to understand in lay terms the general social critique of mass tourism in the Third World. ($9)

*Tourism and Ecology: The Impact of Travel
on a Fragile Earth*
**Ecumenical Coalition on Third World Tourism
Center for Responsible Tourism (CRT)**
2 Kensington Road
San Anselmo, CA 94960
(415) 258-6594

This is the report of a 1989 conference containing
reports, models, recommendations, and resources on
ecotourism. ($5)

*The Tourist Trap: Who's Getting Caught
Tourism and Development:
Breaking Out of the Tourist Trap*
Cultural Survival Quarterly
11 Divinity Ave.
Cambridge, MA 02138

This series analyzes mass tourism, gives case
examples of the problems it has created, and discusses
the merits of sustainable tourism. ($3 each)

index

about the author

Dwight Holing is the author of *California Wild Lands: A Guide to the Nature Conservancy Preserves* as well as books on coral reefs, rainforests, and offshore oil drilling. His articles on the environment and nature travel have appeared in numerous publications, including *Audubon, Discover, Islands, Los Angeles Times, Omni, Sierra,* and *Travel & Leisure.* He lives in Oakland, California with his wife and two children.

about conservation international

Conservation International (CI) is a private, nonprofit organization dedicated to balancing human needs with the urgent need for preserving critical ecosystems, particularly the world's rainforests, and the species that rely on these habitats for survival.

Nearly 90 percent of the forests of the tropics face imminent destruction by the year 2000 unless we act quickly. Known for its innovative approach to conservation, CI has pioneered strategies such as the Rapid Assessment Program to identify ecosystem "hot spots" in immediate need of protection.

With conservation programs in more than twenty-four countries, CI is a leader in conservation-based development and is helping to shape responsible conservation strategies worldwide. Conservation International:

- created the first comprehensive operational plan to save tropical rainforests: The Rain Forest Initiative;

- assembled the first Rapid Assessment Program (RAP), a group of world-renowned field biologists charged with establishing a new approach to quick biological assessment;

- continues to help launch and manage some of the most important biosphere reserves in rainforest countries;

- launched its Sorcerer's Apprentice Program, a program designed to record ethnobotanical knowledge for future generations of indigenous communities;

- sponsored the scientific expedition that rediscovered the hairy-eared dwarf lemur in Madagascar, not seen in the wild since 1964.

conservation international membership form

YES, I want to join Conservation International and support its efforts to save endangered rainforest and other ecosystems worldwide and the millions of plants and animals that rely on these habitats for survival.

I've enclosed a tax-deductible contribution of:

☐ $15 Student/Senior   ☐ $25 Friend

☐ $30 Family   ☐ $100 Contributor

☐ $250 Sustainer   ☐ $500 Supporter

☐ $1,000 Patron   ☐ Other $_____

Name _____

Address _____

City _____

State _____ Zip _____

Note: A gift of $15 or more entitles you to 12 months of membership, which includes a one-year subscription to CI's quarterly newsletter, TROPICUS, updates on CI's activities, special member-only travel opportunities, access to special publications and CI products with an environmental theme.

Please send your tax-deductible gift along with this form to Conservation International today.

Conservation International
Department MKTM, Suite 1000
1015 18th Street, N.W.
Washington, DC 20036

CONSERVATION
INTERNATIONAL